Chinese for Living in China

真实生活汉语

吴德安 （De-an Wu Swihart）
魏久安 （Julian K. Wheatley）
刘宪民 （Xianmin Liu） 编著
牧之筠 （Judy Zhijun Mu）
梁新欣 （Hsin-hsin Liang）

石安妮 （Anne Swihart） 插图

配有录音光盘

北京大学出版社
PEKING UNIVERSITY PRESS

图书在版编目(CIP)数据

真实生活汉语. 1/吴德安等编著. —北京：北京大学出版社, 2014.7
ISBN 978-7-301-24496-8

Ⅰ. ①真… Ⅱ. ①吴… Ⅲ. ①汉语－对外汉语教学－教材 Ⅳ. ①H195.4

中国版本图书馆CIP数据核字 (2014) 第 158922 号

封面图片由 http://www.123rf.com 提供

Copyright: <a href='http://www.123rf.com/profile_boggy22'>boggy22 / 123RF Stock Photo</a> = 25155450 TIFF

书中部分照片由吴德安（De-an Wu Swihart）拍摄

书　　名：真实生活汉语 1

著作责任者：吴德安（De-an Wu Swihart）　魏久安（Julian K. Wheatley）
　　　　　　刘宪民（Xianmin Liu）　牧之筠（Judy Zhijun Mu）
　　　　　　梁新欣（Hsin-hsin Liang）　编著

插 图 绘 制：石安妮（Anne Swihart）

责 任 编 辑：周　鹂

标 准 书 号：ISBN 978-7-301-24496-8 / H · 3550

出 版 发 行：北京大学出版社

地　　址：北京市海淀区成府路 205 号　100871

网　　址：http://www.pup.cn　新浪官方微博：@北京大学出版社

电 子 信 箱：zpup@pup.cn

电　　话：邮购部　62752015　发行部　62750672　编辑部　62752028　出版部　62754962

印 刷 者：北京大学印刷厂

经 销 者：新华书店

889 毫米 × 1194 毫米　16开本　17.5 印张　459 千字

2014 年 7 月第 1 版　2014 年 7 月第 1 次印刷

定　　价：115.00 元 （配有录音光盘）

Contents 目录

Preface
前言
Qiányán i

Abbreviations
缩略语
Suōlüèyǔ viii

Getting Started
热身课
Rèshēn Kè 1

Lesson One *Pinyin* and Standard Pronunciation
第一课 拼音和标准发音 6
Dì-yī Kè Pīnyīn Hé Biāozhǔn Fāyīn

In this lesson you will learn how to do the following
- Pronounce Chinese with the aid of *Pinyin*, the standard Chinese system for transcribing pronunciation
- Distinguish the basic features of the *Pinyin* syllable, including
  - the 21 initial sounds
  - the 38 rhymes
  - the 4 tones and the neutral tone
- Learn *Pinyin* spelling rules, including
  - the rules for tonal shifts
  - where syllable division needs to be indicated

Culture Notes
- Chinese phonetic systems
- The major dialects of Chinese

Lesson Two Chinese Characters
第二课 汉字 28
Dì-èr Kè Hànzì

This lesson deals with the following topics
- Chinese characters
- How characters evolved
- The simplified and traditional character sets
- Types of strokes used to compose characters
- The order of strokes
- The structure of characters
- Radicals and phonetic elements

This lesson also provides practice in
- Identifying types of strokes, stroke order, and character structure
- Writing characters

Culture Notes
- Names of some common radicals

Lesson Three How Do You Do?
第三课 你好 43
Dì-sān Kè Nǐ Hǎo

In this lesson you will learn how to do the following
- Greet people
- Introduce yourself
- Pose questions
- Invite people to do things with you

Grammar
- "好 hǎo" (good, well)
- "姓, xìng" (to be surnamed); "叫 jiào" (to call, to be called)
- "是 shì" (to be, to be the case)
- "也 yě" (also, too)
- "吗 ma" (question particle for yes-no questions)
- "呢 ne" (question particle for follow-up questions)
- "什么 shénme" (question word for "what" questions)
- "好吗 hǎo ma" (tag question: "OK?")

Culture Notes
- Greetings
- Conventional greetings in daily life

Lesson Four Counting
第四课 计算 60
Dì-sì Kè Jìsuàn

In this lesson you will learn how to do the following
- Count in Chinese
- Buy fruit

Grammar
- Numbers
- Verbs in series
- Measure words
- "二 èr" and "两 liǎng" (two)
- The adverb "还 hái" (still, yet, in addition, also, too)
- The question word "多少 duōshao" (how much, how many)
- When "零 líng" (zero) and "一 yī" (one) need to be expressed

Culture Notes
- Formal written numbers
- Chinese hand numbers
- Lucky and unlucky numbers
- Using an abacus

Lesson Five At a Restaurant
第五课 在餐馆 84
Dì-wǔ Kè Zài Cānguǎn

In this lesson you will learn how to do the following
- Request a particular seat in a restaurant
- Order drinks
- Order dishes for a meal
- Ask for, and pay the bill

Grammar
- Auxiliary verbs: "能 néng" (can, be able to), "可以 kěyǐ" (can, may) and "要 yào" (want to, would like to, need to, will)
- "(一)点儿 (yì) diǎnr" (a little, a bit, a small amount)
- Sentences with subjects omitted
- Verb-not-verb questions, e.g.: "要不要 yào bu yào" "喝不喝 hē bu hē"
- The particle "了 le"
- Prices and units of money

Culture Notes
- Addressing strangers
- Types of restaurants
- "小费 xiǎofèi" (tipping)
- "食堂 shítáng" (cafeterias)
- Foreign currency exchange

Lesson Six Asking for Directions
第六课 问 路 108
Dì-liù Kè Wèn Lù

In this lesson you will learn how to do the following
- Ask how to get to a certain place
- Give simple directions
- Explain where something is located

Grammar
- "有 yǒu" (there is, there are) expressing existence
- Location phrases
- The interrogative "怎么 zěnme" (how)
- "往 wǎng" (towards) indicating direction
- The particle "的 de" in location phrases
- The copula verb "是 shì"
- "在 zài" (to be at; at, on, in) expressing location
- "从 cóng" (from) indicating place of origin

Culture Notes
- City districts
- Street names and directions

Lesson Seven At a Hotel
第七课 在宾馆 133
Dì-qī Kè Zài Bīnguǎn

In this lesson you will learn how to do the following
- Ask about hotel reservations
- Explain what sort of room you would like
- Request that someone clean the room and change the linen
- Ask someone to fix some things that are not working in your room

Grammar
- Question words
- The "是 shì……的 de" construction, for emphasizing attendant circumstance (how, when, where, etc.)
- More on the particle "的 de"
- "给 gěi" as a main verb
- Duration phrases
- "好 hǎo" as a verb complement
- "……的时候 de shíhou" (when, during, while)
- Pivotal constructions

Culture Notes
- Types of hotels
- Taking care of valuables
- Arranging for an Internet connection and making long-distance telephone calls
- Room inspection at checkout

Lesson Eight Making Phone Calls
第八课 打电话 164
Dì-bā Kè Dǎ Diànhuà

In this lesson you will learn how to do the following
- Make inquiries about domestic and international phone calls
- Ask how to make inexpensive calls from your hotel room
- Find out how to buy and use phone-cards

Grammar
- Sentence pattern "先 xiān……再 zài……" (first…then…)
- "来 lái" (to come) and "去 qù" (to go) used as directional complements
- "太 tài……了 le" (too…, excessively…)
- Conditional sentences: "如果 rúguǒ……就 jiù……" (if… [then]…)
- Adverbs "都 dōu" (all) and "也 yě" (also)
- Verb reduplication

Culture Notes
- Telephone cards
- Busy signals
- Public phones
- Cheap times for long-distance calls
- Time zones in China
- Time differences between Beijing (or China) and North America

Lesson Nine What Time Is It Now?
第九课 现在几点 187
Dì-jiǔ Kè Xiànzài Jǐ Diǎn

In this lesson you will learn how to do the following
- Give an account of your daily schedule
- Make appointments to meet people
- Explain when activities or events occur

Grammar
- Time phrases and their position in the sentence
- Auxiliary verbs: "要 yào" (want to, have to, will, be going to), "会 huì" (be good at, likely, will), "想 xiǎng" (want, feel like doing something)
- Temporal clauses with "以前 yǐqián" (before) and "以后 yǐhòu" (after)
- Setences with "就 jiù…… 了 le"
- Verbs with generic objects (VOs)
- The preposition "跟 gēn " (with)

Culture Notes
- 12-hour and 24-hour time systems
- Working hours in China
- A typical daily schedule for a secondary school in China

Lesson Ten My Birthday
第十课 过生日 213
Dì-shí Kè Guò Shēngri

In this lesson you will learn how to do the following
- Make use of units of dates: week, month and year
- Ask about birthdays and decide how to celebrate them
- Ask about age and respond to questions about age

Grammar
- Units of time
- Dates
- The verb "喜欢 xǐhuan" (to be fond of, to like to)

Culture Notes
- Chinese calendars
- The 10 Heavenly Stems and 12 Earthly Branches
- Traditional Chinese festivals

Vocabulary
词汇表 235
Cíhuì Biǎo

Listening Scripts
录音文本 251
Lùyīn Wénběn

前 言 Qiányán

《真实生活汉语》全套共4册，每册10课，是适合欧美外国学生使用的初级到中级的汉语教材。本套教材也适用于准备去中国学习、工作、旅行，希望尽快掌握一些在中国生活所需中文的外国人；或已经生活在中国且需要开始或继续学会生活所需中文的外国人。

一、本书缘起

这套《真实生活汉语》系列教材是在《外国人实用生活汉语》（上、下）(北京大学出版社，2004年) 的基础上重新编写的。 那套教材是为参加CTLC（组织英语国家大学毕业生去中国教英语的美国教育组织）与北京大学外国语学院合作的暑期外教强化培训（1997年开始）的外教编写的。这些外教在培训后去深圳的公立中小学担任英语老师，在中国至少住一年；他们是英语为母语的外国人，有的学过中文，有的没有学过，有不同的学习需求，《外国人实用生活汉语》的编写反映了他们的需要，是一套直接与他们在中国的日常生活紧密相关的汉语课本，所以很受他们的欢迎。至今为止，已有1000多名学生使用过那套教材。

经过10年的积累，这套全新的《真实生活汉语》扩充至4册，课文内容根据10年后的生活用语重新编写，增加一倍，足够老师和学生使用两年。一般的汉语教材在第二年时会从对话课文改为阅读课文，更强调汉字读写，本书则继续以对话交流为主。这套新教材已经在北京大学暑期强化中文课和深圳大学对外汉语课上试用了3年，反映良好。

基于上千学生的使用经验，我们希望《真实生活汉语》系列将为在中国生活的外国人继续提供有益的帮助。

二、编写理念

1.口语交流 —— 培养学生听和说的能力

外国人在中国生活的关键是能与中国人进行口头交流，本书在设计上首要注重的是外国人在中国生活的会话需要，也就是注重培养学生听和说的实践能力。要培养这一能力，就需要精选生活在中国的外国人会遇到的典型情景会话。在中国的外国人都希望在课堂学到的汉语可以马上用到现实生活中去，这套书可以说满足了他们的需要。书中每课都与他们的现实生活有直接关系：换钱，买东西，理发，上饭馆，打的，看病，住宾馆，在学校上课或教书，在公司上班，租房，坐火车、飞机、地铁，安排在中国的旅游，文化参观，等等。本书作者根据多年对外国人在中国生活的调查，按照来华外国人的需要进行了精心选择，把他们最迫切需要的话题及用语都收入此书。因此《真实生活汉语》不但对话内容具有很强的真实性和实用性，而且对话语言简洁、生动、自然，非常适合学习者到中国后的生活需求。这些特点能极大地提高学生学习汉语的兴趣，增强他们的学习动力，使他们学得更快更好。教学实践表明，本教材受到了已经在华或准备来华学习汉语的外国人的喜爱。

2.汉字学习——培养学生读和写的能力

怎样解决英语为母语的外国人学习汉字困难的问题？本书采取了一些教学策略。

首先，为了不让汉语学习变成“老牛拉着汽车走”，要想办法不让缓慢的汉字读写速度拖住他们快速学会汉语会话的步伐。《真实生活汉语》是为英语为母语（不包括母语用汉字的日本、韩国学生），而且没有汉语学习经验的人设计的。所以最开始是拼音会话，比如第一册中每课的语音中大量运用拼音练习词汇发音和对话；再逐渐进入到汉字加拼音，让他们先学会说话；最后逐渐进入汉字学习。对于母语为拼音文字的人来说，有这样一个从拼音到汉字的渐进过程会比较容易接受，而且可以帮助他们准确发音。本系列4册课本都是拼音与汉字同时出现，就是为了减轻英语为母语的学生在学汉语时读写汉字的负担。学生需要较长时间才能把汉字的形状和声音联系起来并记住；按他们母语的习惯，记住了每个汉字的声音才能帮助他们阅读中文。我们认为这个过程大约需要两年的时间。

其次，汉字的读写不是要学生们死记硬背，而是强调让他们学会如何在生活实践中使用这些学过的汉字。本书所有汉字下面都附有拼音，学生可以把拼音用作拐杖。比如学习对话时，老师可以让学生盖住课文的拼音部分，利用已经熟悉了的对话内容，只看汉字来试着复述课文内容。当然，老师应该为学生分析每个汉字的结构和细节，这样可以帮助他们认出和记住一些字的相同偏旁部首，也可以要求学生们手写汉字帮助记忆。老师还应尽量将已经学过的汉字搭配成新词组，以帮助学生加深对汉字的理解并扩大词汇量。

本书采用的是在中国大陆普遍使用的标准简体字，但是在每课的词汇表中，如果出现的简体汉字同时有繁体字写法，就把繁体字并列在旁边。学生应该了解哪些汉字是有繁简两种字形的，并能辨认两种字形，因为在中国香港、中国台湾和海外的中国城都还使用繁体字。每课词汇表以外的其他部分则仅使用简体字。本书没有全书采用繁简字体对照是因为：其一是两种字形并用占用的空间太大，影响可读性；其二，也是最主要的原因，本书的主要目的是训练学生适应在中国大陆的生活，而中国大陆很少看到繁体字。由于本书强调培养学生的阅读能力，如果是已经学过繁体字的学生，应该能迅速适应用简体字阅读，并逐渐学会用简体字写作。

三、教材结构形式

1.课文：本书每课的课文几乎都是对话（第4课“计算”除外）。比如：在饭馆里顾客和服务员之间的交谈；中国学校里外教和中国老师之间的交谈；外国人在超市向服务员询问并付款；外国病人在中国医院和大夫谈病情；外国旅行者在机场寻找丢失的行李或购买火车票、飞机票， 等等。

2.生词：每课的新词在词汇表中列出，包括汉字、拼音、词性及英文翻译，并提供繁体字以便对照。

3.用译文复述课文：每课的课文后面有英文译文，但那不是单纯地给课文提供翻译，而是希望学生借助英文暗示的会话情景，用中文复述本课的对话内容。

4.语法点：每课都详细讲解本课对话中出现的重要语法点，以便学生充分理解中文的句子结构。同时为学生设计句型练习，帮助他们利用句型自己生成新句子。

5.练习：每课设计了丰富的练习和课堂活动帮助学生进一步掌握本课所学内容。练习包括：句式操练、发音训练、听力训练、交际活动、角色扮演，以及各种复习等。

6.中国日常生活文化：每课介绍三四个与课文内容相关的，在中国生活必须了解的中国文化常识，比如：怎样在医院挂号，如何寻找丢失的行李，如何存取款等。

7.拼音卡片：第1册书后附有拼音卡片，由石安妮（Anne Swihart）设计。每张卡片正面是拼音字母，背面讲如何发音——用英文的近似发音进行说明，并带有插图提示。比如：一般解释 “b” 的读法用 “菠菜”提示，但从英语为母语的外国人角度看，英文的“菠菜”是 “spinach”，发音跟“b” 没有关系。本书的拼音卡则用 “similar to boh in boy”，插图提示是一个男孩（boy），这样就更容易被学生接受。学生可以把所有卡片剪切下来使用。

对老师来说，把每课的内容材料转化为课堂活动的过程是一个挑战。课堂活动的重点应放在与口语交流相关的练习活动上，以提高学生在实际生活中与中国人交流的能力，满足学生的需要。本书第1册在正式上课前有个“热身课”，希望告诉老师和学生，从第一天上汉语课开始，就要掌握正确的学习方法，要每堂课前练习一下。尤其是零起点的学生，还没有任何汉语学习的经验，或者在课前没有做任何准备的情况下，这种热身准备活动会很有用。

四、作者简介

吴德安 (De-an Wu Swihart) 博士：毕业于北京大学中文系，在普林斯顿大学获得博士学位。在美国和加拿大教授汉语、中国文学和文化20多年，任教学校包括明德大学和麦基尔大学暑期学校、罗德大学、孟菲斯大学等。曾经任CTLC与北京大学外语学院合作的暑期外教强化培训项目主任15年。现为美国大学中国教学中心主任。出版过意大利文和德文两本中文教材，还是其他两套汉语系列课本的主要作者，也出版过3本中英文诗歌小说。主要负责《真实生活汉语》系列教材的总体设计及初稿编写。

魏久安 (Julian K. Wheatley) 博士：曾在康奈尔大学任教11年，在麻省理工大学任教9年，还曾在新加坡南洋理工大学国立教育学院和香港教育学院任教。目前是美国杜兰大学副教授，也是美国大学中国教学中心的负责人之一。

专门研究大陆东南亚及中国的语言和语言学（特别是缅甸语和汉语）。是《真实生活汉语》1–4册的作者之一。

梁新欣 (Hsin-hsin Liang) 博士：美国密执安大学语言学博士。曾任教于美国威斯康辛大学、密执安大学、康奈尔大学、明德大学中文暑校，以及美国各大学联合汉语中心（ACC）。现为美国弗吉尼亚大学东亚语言文学及文化系副教授、现代中国语言项目主任，同时也是"弗大在上海"暑期中文项目主任。是《真实生活汉语》系列教材第3、4册的第二作者，以及第1、2册作者之一。

刘宪民 (Xianmin Liu) 博士：美国明尼苏达大学汉语语言学博士。在美执教20余年。目前任教于美国范德堡大学，是该校汉语语言教学项目主任及范德堡大学在中国的暑期项目主任。在此之前，曾任教于明尼苏达大学、俄勒冈大学、俄亥俄大学及哈佛大学。曾多次担任美国CET留华暑期项目教学主任。主要研究方向为汉语句法、语义、语用学及汉语教学语法。曾合著其他对外汉语教材。是《真实生活汉语》第1册第三作者和第2册第二作者。

李金玉 (Jinyu Li)：毕业于南京大学和澳大利亚国立大学，在美国莱斯大学获得硕士学位。在美国从事大学汉语教学20多年，在任教于哈佛大学的十几年间曾任多门中文课主任教师。现为塔芙茨大学中文部高级讲师。主要研究方向为中英文句法特点的比较、文化与语言、词汇教学。是《真实生活汉语》第3、4册作者之一。

牧之筠 (Judy Zhijun Mu) 博士：美国伊利诺伊大学语言教育学博士。曾在美国明德暑期学校和普林斯顿大学任教，担任杜克大学在华项目主任多年。教学范围包括：初级到高级汉语、华裔班、法律汉语和商务汉语、汉语教学法等。1995年至今，任教于圣路易斯的华盛顿大学，同时担任华盛顿大学在复旦大学的留学项目主任。是《真实生活汉语》第1、2册作者之一。

五、鸣谢

衷心感谢帮助《真实生活汉语》成功出版的同事及朋友们，他们是：布朗大学的胡龙华老师，北京大学英语系的马乃强博士、于莹教授、陈冰老师，中国人民大学的陆姚老师，重庆大学的范红娟老师，深圳大学的朱庆红教授、贾陆依教授。他们曾为此书的编写提供过建议和修改意见，并且协助收集学生对此书的意见。此外，石安妮 (Anne Swihart) 女士设计了第1册的插图。我们在此向他们表示诚挚的感谢。

同时也要衷心感谢北京大学出版社，特别是我们的责任编辑周鹂，她细心阅读全书初稿并提出了非常宝贵的意见，为本系列教材的出版做出了很大贡献；汉语编辑室的王飙主任也对此书提供了很多宝贵建议和大力支持，在此一并表示感谢。

主笔：吴德安(De-an Wu Swihart)
参与作者：魏久安 (Julian K. Wheatley)
梁新欣 (Hsin-hsin Liang)
李金玉 (Jinyu Li)
刘宪民 (Xianmin Liu)
牧之筠 (Judy Zhijun Mu)

Preface

Chinese for Living in China is a textbook series in four volumes, each with ten lessons, which serves as a foundation for beginning and intermediate levels of language instruction and learning. It is designed for people studying Chinese with the intention of going to China to work or to continue their studies; and for people already in China, starting or continuing to learn the language there.

Conversational skills

Chinese for Living in China is designed for speakers of English who have no prior knowledge of Chinese. Since the key ingredient for living successfully in China is being able to talk to people – to communicate orally, *Chinese for Living in China* is organized first by conversational needs (listening and speaking). Initial conversational instruction proceeds incrementally, with *Pinyin* transcription providing access to language material and to correct pronunciation.

Lessons cover topics that are typically encountered by foreigners living in China: buying things, eating out, taking or teaching classes, mobile phones, banks, changing money, transportation, hotels and airports, doctor's visits, finding a place to stay, working in an office, making travel arrangements, finding employment, and so on. Many of these topics have immediate application in the daily lives of foreigners living in China and, as such, provide a powerful learning incentive which speeds up the process of mastery. The topics have been selected on the basis of the authors' own experiences, living, traveling, and working in China and observing the needs of their students.

Reading skills

The ability to communicate in Chinese can, with proper practice, proceed quite quickly. This provides learners with a sense of accomplishment. Learning the literary skills of reading and writing in characters, on the other hand, is much more challenging. It simply takes a long time to learn to reliably associate characters with sound. (Learners are doubly handicapped by not being able to utilize the sound hints found in the phonetic components of many characters which prove so useful to native speakers.)

Chinese for Living in China deals with the character problem in this way: In the first place, it does not let character recognition dictate the pace of spoken language learning. The dialogues that begin each lesson are natural, cover the topic sufficiently, and introduce new material at a rate that can be absorbed and utilized in conversation. In the second place, *Chinese for Living in China* emphasizes recognition of characters in context. Almost all Chinese material in the series is introduced in both characters and *Pinyin*. In the case of the narratives and dialogues, *Pinyin* is written below the character lines as continuous script. As learners become more familiar with the language through speaking practice in and out of class, they can cover the *Pinyin* lines and try to read the characters, using their familiarity with the text as a crutch, and checking the *Pinyin* as much as necessary. Naturally, a lot of attention will still need to be paid to hand-writing and character analysis to ensure proper attention to character detail. But as much as possible, characters will be learned by reading familiar material, where the focus can be on finding ways to associate characters with known words.

For character reading, *Chinese for Living in China* uses the simplified set of characters that is standard on the Mainland (as well as in Singapore). In vocabulary lists, whenever two forms exist, traditional characters are given alongside simplified ones. But elsewhere, only the simplified set is used. There are several reasons for the limited use of the traditional set. One is space and readability; having two versions of character material takes up excessive space and can be confusing. The main reason, however, is that the series is specifically geared to life on the Mainland where the traditional characters are rarely seen. In any case, given the emphasis on reading over writing in *Chinese for Living in China*, even those students who have started their study with traditional characters should be able to quickly adapt to reading the simplified, even if they cannot write them.

Organization

1. The dialogues: Except for lesson 4 which deals with numbers, lessons begin with a dialogue that illustrates the lesson's subject matter: a conversation between a customer ordering a meal and a waiter, for example; or one between two teachers (one foreign, one Chinese) and a supermarket worker about finding items and about check-out procedures; or a conversation between a foreign patient and a Chinese doctor in China; or a foreigner looking for lost luggage at an airport or buying train tickets; and so on.

2. Vocabulary: Individual words for each lesson are listed with characters, *Pinyin*, part-of-speech and English equivalents. For those cases in which the traditional form of the character differs from the simplified, the two are placed together in the vocabulary lists.

3. Re-enacting the dialogue: Along with the Chinese version of the texts, a fluid English translation is provided so that learners can cue the Chinese and, as a first step, practice producing Chinese, not just reading it.

4. Grammatical points: Important grammatical topics introduced in the course of the dialogues are discussed and further illustrated individually to help learners understand Chinese sentence structure and start to produce novel sentences themselves.

5. Exercises: Each lesson provides exercises and activities designed to help learners internalize new material. These include practice with sentence patterns, pronunciation drills, listening practice, and a host of communicative activities involving role play and group work.

6. Chinese everyday culture: Each lesson ends with three or four cultural notes relevant to the dialogues. These provide information crucial to everyday life in China: how to check in at a hospital, for example, how to find lost luggage, or how to deposit and withdraw money, etc.

7. *Pinyin* cards: At the back of the book there are ten pages of *Pinyin* cards, designed by Anne Swihart. On one side of each card is a letter – given in upper and lower case. On the other side is a picture of an object whose name in English begins with that letter. "Ff" is matched to the number "four" (Ff=f); "Qq", is matched to a wedge of "cheese" (Qq=ch). Along with the illustration is a hint (with color coding) that explains in terms of English spelling how the letter (on the front) is pronounced in *Pinyin*. So for "Qq", along with the picture of "cheese" is the hint "similar to chee in cheese"; with "Ff" and the picture of "4" is the hint "similar to foeh in four". The cards can be cut out and joined together to make *Pinyin* syllables (words) for self-testing.

For teachers, the process of transforming textbook material into classroom activities that serve the learner's needs is facilitated by the focus on the spoken language and the provision of communicatively relevant activities in each lesson. Volume 1 also contains an initial lesson ("Getting started") which includes classroom activities that ensure that the right pedagogical tone is established from the first day (when students are assumed to have no prior knowledge of the language and arrive without prior preparation).

Origins

Chinese for Living in China is based on an earlier two-volume series that was also published by the Peking University Press. It was called *Practical Chinese for English Speakers*, written by De-an Wu Swihart and Cong Meng, and edited by William H. O'Donnell. That series was written for overseas teachers participating in the Center for Teaching and Learning in China (CTLC). Since 1997, CTLC has been recruiting English teachers from English speaking countries to teach for at least a year in the Shenzhen school system. In collaboration with the Peking University School of Foreign Languages, CTLC has provided these teachers with an initial period of intensive training in the teaching of English in China, as well as intensive instruction in Mandarin. Practical Chinese for English Speakers was written to respond to the need for a textbook that would allow these teachers to make use of Chinese in their everyday lives.

The new *Chinese for Living in China* series has been completely revamped, with all content – including dialogues – rewritten to reflect changes in language usage and in society since the earlier volumes were written. The new series, with four volumes rather than the earlier two, doubles the amount of material and allows teachers and learners to use one series over the equivalent of two years of non-intensive language study. One of the unique features of the new series is that, while many texts shift from a conversational approach to a focus on reading and character recognition at the intermediate level, *Chinese for Living in China* retains the conversational format through all four volumes. Initial drafts of the new series have been tried and tested to good effect by over 1000 students over the last three years in CLTC's intensive language course at Peking University, and in the regular Chinese courses for foreigners at Shenzhen University. It is our hope that the series will continue to serve the many new learners who have plans to study, travel or work in China.

The authors

Dr. De-an Wu Swihart graduated from the Chinese Department at Peking University and received her Ph.D. from Princeton University. She has taught courses in Chinese language, literature and culture for over 20 years at a variety of institutions in the United States and Canada, including the University of Memphis, Rhodes College, Middlebury College Summer School, and McGill University Summer School. She has been director of the Summer Intensive Foreign Teachers' Training Program at Peking University, School of Foreign Languages for 15 years. She has been co-director of the Center for Teaching & Learning in China since 1997. She has published two Chinese textbooks in Italian and German and has been the main author of two other Chinese textbook series. She is also the author of three books on English and Chinese poetry and fiction. Dr. Swihart designed the *Chinese for Living in China* series and was responsible for initial drafts of all four volumes.

Dr. Julian K. Wheatley taught for eleven years at Cornell University and for nine years at MIT. More recently, he has been a guest teacher at the Singapore National Institute of Education, at the Hong Kong Institute of Education and at Tulane University. He is currently a one of the directors of the CTLC program. His research and publications involve the languages and linguistics of mainland Southeast Asia and China (particularly Burmese and Chinese). He is co-author of all four volumes of *Chinese for Living in China*.

Dr. Hsin-hsin Liang received her doctorate in linguistics from the University of Michigan. She has taught at a number of institutions, including the University of Wisconsin, the University of Michigan, Cornell University, Middlebury Summer Program, and the Language Center of the Associated Colleges in China (ACC). She is currently associate professor of Chinese in the Department of East Asian Languages, Literatures and Cultures at the University of Virginia, where she is director of the modern Chinese language program and field director of the UVA-in-Shanghai Chinese language program. She is second author of volumes 3 and 4 of *Chinese for Living in China*, as well as one of the co-authors of volumes 1 and 2.

Dr. Xianmin Liu received her Ph.D. in Chinese linguistics from the University of Minnesota. She has taught for over twenty years in the U.S. She is currently teaching at Vanderbilt University, where is the coordinator of the Chinese language program and director of the Vanderbilt Summer-in-China Program. Before joining the Vanderbilt faculty, she also taught at Minnesota, Oregon, Ohio and Harvard Universities. She has also served a number of times as the academic director for CET summer immersion programs in China. Her research interests include Chinese grammar, semantics and pragmatics, as well as Chinese language pedagogy. She has co-authored several Chinese textbooks for English speakers. She is third author for volume 1 of *Chinese for Living in China*, and second author for volume 2.

Jinyu Li received B.A. degrees from Nanjing University and from Australian National University, and an M.A. from Rice University. She has been involved with Chinese language teaching in the U.S. for almost 30 years. Before taking up her current position as senior lecturer at Tufts University, she was a preceptor at Harvard University, where she taught a variety of courses in the Chinese program. Her main areas of interest are Chinese-English comparative grammar, culture and language, and the teaching of vocabulary. She is one of the authors of volumes 3 and 4 of *Chinese for Living in China*.

Dr. Judy Mu received her Ph.D. in linguistics from the University of Illinois at Urbana-Champaign. She has taught Chinese at the Middlebury Summer Program and at Princeton University. She was director for Duke University in Beijing for many years. She has taught elementary to advanced levels of Chinese, Chinese for heritage speakers, courses in legal and business Chinese, and Chinese language pedagogy. From 1999, she has been teaching at Washington University in St. Louis. She also serves as field director for Washington University's study center in Shanghai. She is one of the authors for volumes 1 and 2 of *Chinese for Living in China*.

Acknowledgments

The authors wish to express sincere thanks to colleagues and friends who have made the publication of *Real Life Chinese* possible, and who provided valuable advice and suggestions for improvement, as well as helping to collect student feedback on draft versions of this book. They are: Hu Lung-hua from Brown University; Dr. Ma Naiqiang, Professor Yu Ying and Senior Lecturer Chen Bin all from the English Department at Peking University; Lu Yao from Renmin University of China

and Fan Hongjuan from Chongqing University; Professors Zhu Qinghong and Jia Luyi from Shenzhen University. In addition, artist Anne Swihart designed the illustrations for the first volume of the series. We are deeply grateful for the help and support these people have provided towards making *Chinese for Living in China* a success.

The authors would also like to thank the people at Peking University Press, particularly our editor, Zhou Li whose careful reading and comments on initial drafts of the manuscript were invaluable. We also deeply appreciate the strong support and useful suggestions provided by chief-editor Wang Biao.

Editor in chief: De-an Wu Swihart
Participating authors: Julian K. Wheatley
Hsin-hsin Liang
Jinyu Li
Xianmin Liu
Judy Zhijun Mu

Abbreviations 缩略语 Suōlüèyǔ

Abbreviation	English	*Pinyin*	Chinese
Adj	Adjective	xíngróngcí	形容词
Adv	Adverb	fùcí	副词
Attr	Attributive	dìngyǔ	定语*
Aux	Auxiliary	zhùdòngcí	助动词
BF	Bound Form	zǔhé xíngshì	组合形式
Conj	Conjunction	liáncí	连词
Det	Determiner	xiàndìngcí	限定词
DirC	Directional Complement	qūxiàng bǔyǔ	趋向补语
Exp	Expression	xíguàn yòngyǔ	习惯用语
Intj	Interjection	tàncí	叹词
IntPron	Interrogative Pronoun	yíwèn dàicí	疑问代词
Meas	Measure Word	liàngcí	量词
N	Noun	míngcí	名词
Num	Numeral	shùcí	数词
Part	Particle	zhùcí	助词
Pot	Potential Form	kěnéng bǔyǔ	可能补语
Pref	Prefix	qiánzhuì	前缀
Prep	Preposition	jiècí	介词
Pron	Pronoun	dàicí	代词
PropN	Proper Noun	zhuānyǒu míngcí	专有名词
PW	Position Word	fāngwèicí	方位词
RC	Resultative Complement	jiéguǒ bǔyǔ	结果补语
Q	Quantifier	shùliàngcí	数量词
Suf	Suffix	hòuzhuì	后缀
V	Verb	dòngcí	动词
VO	Verb-object	dòngbīn jiégòu	动宾结构

* 本书的"定语"就是一般所说的"非谓形容词"。

The "Attributive" in this book means what is generally called "non-predictive adjective".

Getting Started

热身课

Rèshēn Kè

Getting started with a new language requires simultaneously introducing new sounds, new ways of writing those sounds and new ways of expressing meaning. The process involves imitation, repetition, and feedback. So for at least the first dozen classes, you can expect to begin every class with the following set of activities designed to introduce you to the language and give you some simple Chinese material that you can try out right away. As you proceed, additional material will be incorporated from Lesson 1 (about the sounds of Chinese and the way the sounds are represented in writing), Lesson 2 (about the character writing system), and Lesson 3 and beyond (where the focus is on conversation).

You will probably be reading this after your first class. That is fine. Even though the Chinese is represented with Roman letters that look accessible (using the official "*Pinyin*" system of transcription), the values of the letters are often not obvious, so you have to wait until you learn the system before you can read it out accurately. However, even now, it does serve as a useful way of recording what is being covered.

Ideally, the activities in this lesson – even on the very first day of class – can be conducted entirely in Chinese, with gesture and modeling providing the necessary guidance. Students – or learners – can assume that most questions will be answered as the first few classes proceed. If not, they can at least be postponed. Incidentally, your teacher may invite you to stand up or even walk around while you are doing these activities. In any case, you won't need to write – this lesson will constitute your notes.

1. Counting and counting off (This topic will be introduced fully in Lesson 4.)

Begin with the numbers 1 to 10. Imitate your teacher and learn the basic numbers in sets of 5. Notice that in the written representations, each vowel (each main vowel as it turns out) has a tone mark above it. Chinese has four tones, which can be called (high) level (ā), rising (á), low (ǎ) and falling (à) – or first, second, third, and fourth. (There are also toneless syllables.) Start by imitating the sequence 1-5 (by listening). Then try counting off in fives on your own. When your teacher signals a problem, try to self-correct.

yī	èr	sān	sì	wǔ	liù	qī	bā	jiǔ	shí
1	2	3	4	5	6	7	8	9	10

Now you can start class everyday (after greeting your teacher – see below) with a count off: 1, 2, 3, etc. You may need some teens (11-20) to cover everyone, so here they are. They are formed with "10 shí" plus the unit numbers. 20 is "two-tens". The numbers are completely regular so you can easily figure out how to continue the count.

shíyī	shí'èr	shísān	shísì	shíwǔ	shíliù	shíqī	shíbā	shíjiǔ	èrshí
11	12	13	14	15	16	17	18	19	20

At the end of the daily count off, teachers will ask you (individually, or as a group) how many students you are. And you answer by rote, as shown. Note: The English below each line of Chinese in this section is a word-for-word gloss of the Chinese, not a full translation.

A: Bānshang yígòng yǒu duōshao xuésheng?
In class altogether have how-many students?

B: Bānshang yígòng yǒu [ ] ge.
In class altogether have [number] of-them.

The (toneless) "ge" may puzzle you. For now, just know that it is needed.

2. Tones

Almost every syllable in Chinese has a tone. So you need to deal with tones from the very start. Having a concept of what a tone is like will help you to produce it.

Tone concepts. Listen as your teacher (or other Chinese speaker) pronounces the five examples, then try to produce them yourself using the tone concepts ("sung out", etc.):

(1) (high) level	sung out	gāo zhāng duō dōu chī
(2) rising	questioning?	wáng chén máng hái qián
(3) low	mostly low	mǎi wǔ jiǔ shuǐ lǎo
(4) falling	determined!	jiàn xiè wàng bù duì

Tone combinations. Tones are easier to hear in combinations than on individual syllables. With four tones, there should be 16 combinations in all; in fact, there are only 15, because combinations of two low tones are regularly realized as rising plus low: "hěn hǎo" is pronounced "hén hǎo".

Of the 15 sets, 6 are presented below. Again, begin by imitation, then try them on your own, reading down at first, then across. (For reference, meanings are presented in small print. The goal now is to learn to pronounce the tones, not to learn the words or phrases.)

(1)	(2)	(3)
lǎoshī (teacher)	Zhōngguó (China)	zàijiàn (goodbye)
jǐnzhāng (anxious)	Zhōngwén (Chinese language)	kàn bào (to read newspapers)
Běijīng (Beijing)	Yīngwén (English)	shàngkè (to attend class)

(4)	(5)	(6)
bú rè (not hot)	hěn máng (quite busy)	càidān (menu)
bú lèi (not tired)	hěn nán (quite difficult)	shàngbān (to go to work)
bú duì (not right)	Měiguó (America)	dàngāo (cake)

3. Greetings (Greetings will be more fully dealt with in Lesson 3.)

Now you are beginning to get a feel for tones, it is time to greet your teacher (or, for practice, a series of teachers). When your teacher signals the beginning of class, you can greet him or her in chorus; or you can greet teachers on your own outside class.

Teachers are addressed with surname and title ("lǎoshī", teacher), in that order: Zhōu lǎoshī. Start with your own teacher, then greet other teachers in imaginary encounters, paying especial attention to tone.

Chinese Surnames
Zhōu
Wáng
Lǐ
Zhào
Zhāng
Chén
Kǒng
Xiè

Choral greeting with teacher response:

A: Zhāng lǎoshī(, nín) hǎo.
Surname teacher, (you-polite) be-well.

B: Dàjiā hǎo.
You-all be-well.

Individual greeting with teacher response:

A: Zhāng lǎoshī(, nín) hǎo.

B: Nǐ hǎo.

4. Purchases (This subject will be more fully developed in Lessons 4 and 5.)

Outside of the classroom, your first interactions (other than greetings) are likely to involve purchases, especially of food and drink. So here is a very short conversation (based on actual observation of buying coffee at a shop near Peking University).

You, as the purchaser, have the simpler part . You initiate by requesting coffee (kāfēi) or tea (chá)[1], making it clear that you want just one cup: kāfēi, yì bēi. The vendor then gives you a series of options, using "háishi" (or). (The translations provided are literal, word-for-word.)

A: Kāfēi, yì bēi.
Coffee, 1 cup.

B: Rè de háishi bīng de?
Hot one or iced one?

A: Rè de.
Hot one.

B: Hǎo, rè de. Dà bēi háishi xiǎo bēi?
OK, hot one. Big cup or small cup?

A: Xiǎo bēi.
Small cup.

B: Hǎo, xiǎo bēi. Yào dàizǒu háishi zài zhèr hē?
OK, small cup. Want take-away or at here drink?

A: Dàizǒu.
Take-away.

B: Hǎo, dàizǒu. ……Zàijiàn, màn zǒu.
OK, take-away …Again-see, slowly go (= take it easy).

A: Xièxie. Zàijiàn.
Thanks. Again-see (= goodbye).

By the way, if at some point, you need to indicate a mistake or show your confusion, you can say "duìbuqǐ" (sorry); your teacher (or other) will reassure you with "méi guānxi" (no problem, it's all right):

A: Duìbuqǐ, lǎoshī.
Sorry, teacher.

B: Méi guānxi.
Not-have problem.

---

[1] "Kāfēi" has obviously been borrowed into Chinese from English; "chá", on the other hand, has been borrowed from Chinese into many languages as "cha", "chai" and even "tea", the last being based on a dialect pronunciation of "chá".

5. Prices

Purchases also involve prices, and at the same time you are getting familiar with the numbers, you can start to learn how to express prices. The unit of currency in China proper (not Hong Kong or Macau) is the "yuán" (abbreviated ¥ or RMB = rénmínbì, People's currency). In spoken language "yuán" are usually expressed in terms of "kuài" (valued at roughly 1/6 of a dollar). "Máo" are "1/10 of a kuài". One important note: With measures like "kuài", "two" is expressed not with "èr", but with "liǎng": "liǎng kuài" (¥ 2.00). (But note: "sān kuài èr", ¥ 3.20; without a following measure, "2" remains "èr".)

Once again, start by rote recitation, then produce on your own (and you will get feedback from your teacher):

yí kuài	liǎng kuài	sān kuài	sì kuài	wǔ kuài
liù kuài	qī kuài	bā kuài	jiǔ kuài	shí kuài

A purchase typically involves a question about price and a response. The question can be posed with "duōshao" (how much) plus "qián" (money); or by "jǐ kuài" (how many *kuai*) plus "qián" (money).

A: Duōshao qián? / Jǐ kuài qián?
How-much money? / How-many *kuai* money?

B: Sān kuài èr.
¥ 3.20.

Other practice values: ¥ 1.60 / ¥ 4.80 / ¥ 2.90 / ¥ 1.30 / ¥ 2.80 / ¥ 0.50 / ¥ 7.10

6. Numbers of things

Instead of "kuài" (and "máo"), if you let the measure be "ge" (item), then you can also indicate how many items you want to purchase. In English, you can state just a number. But in Chinese, you usually have to state a number plus the equivalent of "of them", which is most commonly (but not always, as you will later learn) "ge":

yí ge   liǎng ge   sān ge   sì ge   wǔ ge   liù ge   qī ge   bā ge   jiǔ ge   shí ge

In a typical interchange, the vendor will ask you "how many do you want", using the verb "yào" (to want, to need) and "jǐ ge" (how many of them) (rather than "duōshao", which is also sometimes possible), and you respond with a number plus "ge":

A: Yào jǐ ge?
Want how-many of-them?

B: Yào liǎng ge.
Want 2 of-them.

Finally, the vendor may also ask you "which one you want", using "nǎ" (also pronounced "něi"): "Yào nǎge?" You can respond by pointing and saying either "zhège" (this one) or "nàge" (that one). (Some people say "zhèi" rather than "zhè", and "nèi" rather than "nà" – so be prepared for some variation.) This interchange also gives you a chance to practice the difference between low toned "nǎ / něi" in the questions ("which") and falling toned "nà / nèi" in the answers ("that"): Nǎge? / Nàge!

A: Yào nǎge?
Want which-one?

B: Yào nàge.
Want that one.

7. Initial sounds and symbols

Now that you have some exposure to the sounds of Chinese and the way sounds are represented, it is useful to summarize one part of the *Pinyin* system of transcription. On the left, below, is the traditional table of initial sounds. All can be recited on level tone. They are matched with a vowel to make them sayable. (The vowel differs from row to row because in Mandarin, not all vowels occur with all initials.) The traditional table has been expanded with the material on the right, which gives the initials with additional rhymes. As before, begin by mimicking, then repeat on your own. Within a few days, you should be able to repeat the left hand table by heart ("bo, po, mo, fo", etc.)

bo	po	mo	fo				
de	te	ne	le	duō	tuō	dōu	tōu
zi	ci	si		zài	cài		
zhi	chi	shi	ri	zhàn	chàn		
ji	qi	xi		jiàn	qiàn		
ge	ke	he		guò	kuò	gǒu	kǒu

Note that letter "i" has two entirely different values, one for the "zi" and "zhi" lines, another for the "ji" line. Learn this distinction, and you are well on your way to mastering *Pinyin*. It will take a few days, but eventually, you should be able to correctly pronounce a string of syllables such as the following (all potential words):

zī jī xī chī jī zhī cī chī xī shī sī xī

8. Daily ritual

This should be enough to get you started. By repeating the material in this lesson everyday, and getting feedback from your teachers, you should gain complete mastery of it (meaning near automatic response, with good pronunciation) within a few weeks. As you go along, other material and exercises from the first lessons will be added. But this initial material should serve as a kind of ritual beginning to your classes all the way through the first volume of *Chinese for Living in China*. By which time, people will be praising your Chinese; of course, you will respond modestly, as indicated:

A: Nǐ shuō de hěn hǎo.
You speak (de) very well.

B: Nǎli, nǎli, shuō de bù hǎo.
Where, where, speak (de) not well.

Lesson One *Pinyin* and Standard Pronunciation

第一课 拼音和标准发音

Dì-yī Kè Pīnyīn Hé Biāozhǔn Fāyīn

In this lesson you will learn how to do the following

- Pronounce Chinese with the aid of *Pinyin*, the standard Chinese system for transcribing pronunciation
- Distinguish the basic features of the *Pinyin* syllable, including
  - the 21 initial sounds
  - the 38 rhymes
  - the 4 tones and the neutral tone
- Learn *Pinyin* spelling rules, including
  - the rules for tonal shifts
  - where syllable division needs to be indicated

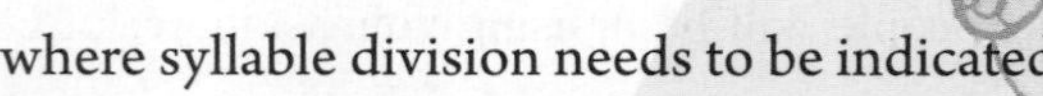

Culture Notes

- Chinese phonetic systems
- The major dialects of Chinese

Standard Chinese Pronunciation

On the Mainland, Standard Chinese (also called Mandarin in English) is called "普通话 pǔtōnghuà", literally "Common Speech". In Taiwan, it is called "国语 guóyǔ" (National Language). Today, 75% of people in China are said to be able to communicate in "普通话 pǔtōnghuà". But for thousands of years, the people of China spoke only regional or local dialects of Chinese, and speech remained extremely diverse until modern times.

Writing can be traced at least to the oracle bone inscriptions of the late Shang Dynasty (approximately 14th – 11th centuries BCE). The form of many modern characters can also be traced back to that time. By the early Han dynasty (first centuries BCE), a standard written language, now referred to as Classical Chinese, had developed, and with minor modifications, it remained the standard language for official and formal written communication until modern times.

Speech almost always differs from writing if only for the reason that speech is interpersonal and fleeting, while writing is, typically, remote and persistant. In the Chinese case, however, as the spoken language evolved, the written language remained more or less as it was two thousand years ago when the classical written style developed, so that ultimately, the written and spoken norms became almost like different languages (comparable to Latin and its descendents, such as Italian). The development of more colloquially based written styles in the 20th century brought the written language closer to the spoken, but writing styles continued to be influenced by Classical Chinese and still remain distinct from the spoken language.

Currently, at least a hundred regional dialects can be distinguished in China. At the extremes, they differ as much as, say, Portuguese and Spanish, or Spanish and Italian. Dialects vary in lexicon (words) and in grammar; but most noticeably, they vary in pronunciation. Linguists generally classify Chinese dialects into seven regional groupings, called "方言 fāngyán" (regional speech) in Chinese, with the greatest variety in the southern provinces of Guangdong, Fujian and neighboring areas.

Attempts to standardize spoken Chinese can be traced back to the 18th century. Since that time, the name applied to the standard language has changed, as well as the system for transcribing pronunciation. The more important phases in this development are listed below.

1. 官话 guānhuà

Standard Chinese has its roots in "官话 guānhuà" (official speech), that is, the speech of "Mandarins", who may have come from different parts of the country, speaking their own regional flavors of Chinese, but who made an effort to approximate the pronunciation of the capital, Beijing, to communicate with each other. By the middle of the 18th century, during the Qing dynasty, recognition of the need for a standard spoken idiom resulted in attempts to broaden the use of "官话 guānhuà" as a standard. However, a phonetically based system for writing it down was not available. Works of reference, such as the renowned *K'ang-hsi* (康熙 Kāngxī) *Dictionary* (named for the Qing Emperor in whose reign it was compiled), used the "反切 fǎnqiè" system, which indicated the pronunciation of a Chinese character in terms of two other, more familiar characters, the first having the same initial consonant as the given character and the second having the same rhyme. The pronunciation of "同 tóng", for example, would be given as "徒红切 tú hóng qiè", i.e. the initial consonant of "徒 tú" "cut and matched to" the rhyme of "红 hóng": t + óng = tóng.

2. The Old National Phonetic System: 老国音 lǎo guóyīn

In 1913, the National Bureau of Education of the Republic of China held a conference on standardization. Representatives from each province agreed to a National Pronunciation, or "国音 guóyīn", which was based by and large on the language of Beijing, but gave some consideration to southern usage as well. (For example, "国音 guóyīn" recognized a fifth tone, the "entering tone", that was distinguished in southern dialects, such as Cantonese, but not in northern speech.) To represent "国音 guóyīn", the conference created the National Phonetic Alphabet "注音字母 zhùyīn zìmǔ", which made use of symbols based on archaic characters. It was officially published in 1918.

3. The National Romanization: 国语罗马字 guóyǔ luómǎzì

Because the Old National Phonetic System was not, in fact, based on any particular dialect or speech community, it proved difficult to promote. So around the time of the May 4th Movement in 1919, proposals for using the actual speech of Beijing as the model, and developing a system of transcription based on Roman letters were considered. One of these systems, developed by the linguist Yuen Ren Chao, is still in use. Chao's system indicates tone by changing the spelling rather than by writing accents above the vowel. (The spellings, "Shaanxi" versus "Shanxi" seen on maps for the adjacent provinces of "陕西 Shǎnxī" and "山西 Shānxī" – whose names differ only in tone – is a vestige of the old "国语罗马字 guóyǔ luómǎzì" system.) However, political and social disruptions during the 1920s kept the Romanization program from being widely adopted.

4. The New National Phonetic System: 新国音 xīn guóyīn

Between 1924 and 1926, the National Language Planning Committee was reconvened with the goal of adapting the old system of phonetic letters to fit the actual pronunciation of Beijing dialect. The new system was called, appropriately, the New Phonetic System, "新国音 xīn guóyīn". It is still in use in Taiwan today, where it goes under the name of "注音符号 zhùyīn fúhào", or more colloquially, "bo po mo fo" – the names of its first four "letters".

5. 拼音 pīnyīn

In 1955 the Bureau of Education of the People's Republic of China held a "National Conference on Chinese Character Reform". Delegates at that conference decided to change the name of the national language from "国语 guóyǔ" (National Language) to "普通话 pǔtōnghuà" (Common Speech). Putonghua is defined as being based on the pronunciation of contemporary Beijing speech, the lexical usage of the northern dialects, and the grammatical norms of "白话 báihuà", the vernacular, literary language. Ultimately, in 1958, the conference issued two proposals, one entitled *Pinyin: A Plan for a Chinese Phonetic Alphabet* (《汉语拼音方案》《Hànyǔ Pīnyīn Fāng'àn》) and the other, *A Plan for Simplifying Chinese Characters* (《汉字简化方案》《Hànzì Jiǎnhuà Fāng'àn》). *Pinyin* became the official system for indicating the pronunciation of standard Chinese in mainland China. Later, it was recognized by the United Nations, and it is now accepted by most countries in the world, including the United States.

Chinese governments have consistently recognized the Beijing dialect as the basis for standard pronunciation. However, standard Chinese, as represented by *Pinyin*, does not always follow Beijing speech. For example, the word for "dumplings" (饺子) is pronounced "jiǎoza" in Beijing speech, but "jiǎozi" in standard Chinese; the word for "[muscle] cramp" (抽筋) is pronounced "chōujīnr" in Beijing speech (with the final "r", typical of that dialect), but "chōujīn" (without the final "r") is acceptable in standard Chinese. It is important to recognize that Standard Chinese – Putonghua – does not follow all the idiosyncrasies of Beijing speech.

The *Pinyin* System

In this book, you will be learning to read and write *Pinyin*, which as you now know, is a standard system of representing Chinese pronunciation, either in conjunction with characters, or independent of characters. *Pinyin* was officially adopted by the Chinese government in 1958 with the immediate goal of assisting speakers of other dialects to learn Putonghua, the standard speech. Eventually it also replaced other systems of Romanization for use in foreign language textbooks and reference materials. In modern China, it appears on street and store signs as well as in children's books, in magazines and newspapers, in dictionaries, on business cards and in advertisements aimed at foreign audiences. *Pinyin* is also one type of input for character word-processing systems.

The *Pinyin* Syllable

A *Pinyin* syllable can be divided into an "initial" and a "rhyme" (the latter sometimes called a "final" in linguistic literature). Rhymes contain main vowels, tones, medials and finals. The main vowel bears the tone mark. There are twenty-one possible initials, thirty-eight rhymes, and four tones.

Pinyin makes use of all the letters of the English alphabet, though the letter "v" is only used for spelling foreign words (including words from minority languages) and local dialect words. Some of the letters are used more or less as in English: f, l, m, n, s, w (among others), have more or less their English values. On the other hand, because *Pinyin* was not designed for speakers of English, it sometimes assigns values to letters that are quite unlike those of English. For example, "c" (usually representing [k] or [s] sounds in English) is pronounced "ts" in *Pinyin*, a sound that does not occur at the beginning of words in English. So some *Pinyin* readings will seem quite transparent to speakers of English ("ti" is "t-ee" for example); others will seem quite opaque ("cai" is "ts-eye").

Initials

bo	po	mo	fo
de	te	ne	le
zi	ci	si	
zhi	chi	shi	ri
ji	qi	xi	
ge	ke	he	

With the exception of the consonant "r", which also occurs in final position, and "ng", which **only** occurs in final position, *Pinyin* consonants only appear initially. What is more, there are no consonant clusters of the sort seen in English words li... ..." and "bu-rst". *Pinyin* initials are customarily presented in six ... sounds with shared articulatory characteristics ... owing vowel so that they can be pronou... occur with all initials so the support vo... " (the last with two values). This chart ... er, be recited daily until familiar. Lines 3, 4 and 5 are particularly crucial.

In the tables tha... cribed in precise phonetic terms (on the left), and then approximated in term...

b, p, m, f: th...

		In English terms
b		...lar to "b", but lighter articulation; like the "p" of "spore"
p		...e the "p" of "paw"
m	nasal	like the "m" of "more"
f	labio-dental fricative	like the "f" of "four"

d, t, n, l: the dentals (formed with the tip of the tongue inside the upper teeth)

	Description	In English terms
d	unaspirated stop	similar to "d", but lighter articulation; like the "t" of "store"
t	aspirated stop	like the "t" of "telephone"
n	nasal	like the "n" of "necessary"
l	lateral	like the "l" of "lamp"

z, c, s: the alveolars (pronounced with the tip of the tongue on the lower teeth)

	Description	In English terms
z	unaspirated affricate	like the "ds" of "woods"
c	aspirated affricate	like the "ts" of "cats"
s	fricative	like the "s" of "say"

Notice that *Pinyin* "c" is never a "k" sound, but always a "ts".

zh, ch, sh, r: the retroflexes (produced with the tongue tip raised towards the roof of the mouth)

	Description	In English terms
zh	unaspirated affricate	like "j" with tongue tip raised; cf. the "dge" of "fudge"
ch	aspirated affricate	like "ch" with tongue tip raised; cf. the "ch" of "chart"
sh	fricative	like "sh" with tongue tip raised; cf. the "sh" of "shore"
r	r-like fricative	like "r" with extended friction

The retroflex consonants are formed with the tip of the tongue rolled upward and touching the roof of the mouth, and the lips pursed. Chinese "r" has a lot more friction than most cases of English "r", so that it can sound almost like the buzzing sound of the "s" of "pleasure".

j, q, x: the palatals (formed with the front – rather than the tip – of the tongue behind the upper teeth)

	Description	In English terms
j	unaspirated affricate	like "j", but with tongue forward, as in the "j" of "jeep"
q	aspirated affricate	like "ch" but with tongue forward, as in the "ch" of "cheap"
x	fricative	like "s" with tongue as in "yield", between "sea" and "she"

The palatals "j, q, x" are followed only by rhymes beginning with (written) "i" or "u": "i, ie, ia", etc., or "u, ue, uan", etc. In such cases – after "j, q, x" – "i" is always pronounced "ee" and "u" is always pronounced "ü". Thus "qu" is pronounced with the "ü" vowel; "que" and "quan" are pronounced with "ü" onset. Note that there are no syllables "ja", only "jia", nor "qong", only "qiong".

g, k, h: the velars (formed with back of the tongue raised at the back of the mouth)

	Description	In English terms
g	unaspirated stop	similar to "g" but lighter articulation; like the "k" of "skid"
k	aspirated stop	like the "c" of "curd" or the "k" of "kerchief"
h	fricative	like the "h" in "hurt", but with friction like the "ch" of "Bach"

In English spelling, "b, d, g" represent voiced stops. In *Pinyin* spelling, the same letters represent voiceless (unaspirated) stops, which are between English "b" and "p". As it turns out, English stops after consonants such as "s" (e.g., "sp" or "st") are also in-between, so in that environment, they are a good match to the Chinese (even though *Pinyin* writes them "b, d, g", while English writes them "p, t, k"): i.e. *Pinyin* "bo" is like English "[s]po[re]".

Rhymes

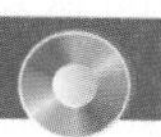

Pinyin rhymes, as noted earlier, are composed of a main vowel (a, e, i, o, u, ü), plus one of three optional elements: a tone (level, rising, low, falling); a medial (i, u, ü); and a final (i, o/u, n, ng), or in the case of the unique "er" final, "-r". Because many of the rhymes of Chinese do not have English equivalents, you will need to rely more than ever on listening to the recordings. Possible rhymes are listed below, with examples and with pronunciation indicated in English terms. Under the heading "in English terms", brackets indicate parts of words to be excluded from the equation (*Pinyin* "ta" is like English "ta[r]" – without the "r"). Parentheses enclose cases in which no word is available and pronunciation can only be approximated by English spelling: *Pinyin* "ke" is like English "k-uh". Tones are not indicated, but all syllables can be pronounced on the first, or high level tone (even though in a few cases, such as "rēn", the language does not actually have a high toned version of the syllable).

Pinyin final	Examples	Examples in English terms
a	ta, ca	ta[r], tsa[r]
ai	tai, hai	tie, hi
an	tan, chan	(t-ah-n, ch-ah-n)
ang	tang, chang	(t-ah-ng, ch-ah-ng)
ao	kao, hao	cow, how
e	ke, che	(k-uh, ch-uh)
ei	lei, pei	lay, pay
en	ren, fen	(r-uh-n, f-uh-n)
eng	leng, teng	lung, tongue
er	er	[f]ur, [h]er

续表 Continued

Pinyin final	Examples	Examples in English terms
i	ti, qi	T, chee[se]
ia	jia, xia	(j-yah, hs-yah)
ian	xian, jian	(hs-yen, j-yen)
iang	jiang, yang	(j-yah-ng, y-ah-ng)
iao	jiao, qiao	(j-ya-oo, ch-ya-oo,) rhymes with cow
ie	qie, lie	(ch-yeh, l-yeh)
in	pin, qin	(p-een, ch-een)
ing	ping, jing	(p-eeng, j-eeng)
iong	xiong	(hs-yoo-ng)
iu	liu	Leo
o	po, mo	[s]po[re], mo[re]
ong	kong, long	(k-oo-ng, l-oo-ng)
ou	tou, mou	toe, moe
u	chu, tu	chew, two
ua	hua, gua	(h-wah, g-wah)
uai	kuai, huai	qui[te], h-why
uan	huan	(h-won)
uang	chuang, kuang	(ch-wah-ng, k-wah-ng)
ueng	weng	(wuh-ng)
ui	sui, tui	sway (, t-way)
un	sun	swoon (but short)
uo	ruo, luo	raw (, l-woh)
u (ü)	qu, lü	(ch-yew, l-yew)
uan (üan)	quan	(ch-yuan)
ue (üe)	xue, lüe	(hs-yweh, l-yweh)
un (ün)	xun	(hs-yu-n)

Notes

1. Syllables are generally composed of an initial and a rhyme:

j + iā = jiā　　　t + ài = tài
h + uán = huán　　　d + ǒng = dǒng

However, the rhymes "a, ai, ao, an, ang, e, en, ou" (i.e., rhymes without an initial "i" or "u") can occur without an initial: "ài" (love), "è" (hungry).

2. *Pinyin* "i" and "u" do not appear in initial position in *Pinyin* syllables. Instead, their consonantal equivalents, "y" or "w" either precede them (if no other written vowel follows) or replace them (if another written vowel follows), according to the following rules: i → y; u (that is pronounced "ü") → y; u (that is pronounced "oo") → w. Examples are shown below:

a. Add "i" to "y"

i → yi　　in → yin　　ing → ying

b. Change "i" to "y"

ia → ya　　ie → ye　　ian → yan　　iang → yang
iao → yao　　iong → yong　　iou → you

c. Add "w" to "u" ("oo")

u → wu

d. Change "u" ("oo") to "w"

ua → wa　　uen → wen　　uan → wan　　ueng → weng
uang → wang　　uo → wo　　uei → wei　　uai → wai

e. Add "y" to "u" ["ü"]

u [ü] → yu　　ue [üe] → yue　　uan [üan] → yuan　　un [ün] → yun

3. In *Pinyin* syllables composed of, or beginning with, "ju", "qu" or "xu", the written "u" is pronounced "ü", never "oo". Below, the arrow (→) means "is pronounced as".

ju → jü　　juan → jüan　　jue → jüe　　jun → jün
qu → qü　　quan → qüan　　que → qüe　　qun → qün
xu → xü　　xuan → xüan　　xue → xüe　　xun → xün

4. "r" appears as a final only in the rhyme "er":

èr (two)　　érzi (son)

In northern Mandarin speech, a suffix "r" – related to the first syllable of "érzi" (son) – occurs with many of the simple nouns of everyday existence. This r-suffix has an affect on the whole syllable: "píng" is pronounced "peeng" but "píngr" – with the r-suffix – is pronounced [pjər] ("pyuhr" in English terms). Some examples:

huār (flower)　　xiǎoháir (child)　　ménr (door)　　yìdiǎnr (a little)

Tones

Chinese is a tonal language, which means that words may differ only in the contour of their pitch: "shū", with high level pitch is "book"; but "shù" with falling pitch is "tree". Getting the tone wrong in Chinese is comparable to getting the consonant or vowel wrong in English, e.g., saying "god" instead of "cod" or "fit" instead of "fat". In Chinese, for example, "qù" means "to go", but "qǔ" means "to marry"; "mǎi" means "to buy", but "mài" means "to sell".

There are four tones in Chinese: (high) level, rising, low (with rise) and falling. These are often labeled by number: first, second, third and fourth. In isolated syllables, they have the following characteristics:

First tone (yīshēng) is a high, flat pitch (ā)

Second tone (èrshēng) rises from mid to high (á)

Third tone (sānshēng) is low with final rise when it is not followed by another syllable (ǎ)

Fourth tone (sìshēng) falls from high to low (à)

The four tones can be contrasted in single syllables:

mā	má	mǎ	mà
妈 mother	麻 hemp	马 horse	骂 to curse

However, tones are more naturally studied in disyllabic sets. In the first set shown below, the main variable is the second syllable. (For the change of tone on "bù" before "lèi", cf. the section on tone shifts, below.)

bù gāo (not tall)   bù máng (not busy)   bù hǎo (not good)   bú lèi (not tired)

In the second set, the main variable is the first syllable:

chī fàn (eat)   niúròu (beef)   chǎofàn (fried rice)   zàijiàn (goodbye)

Awareness of tones, plus constant monitoring of your speech will help you improve your pronunciation, and reduce your foreign accent. Note that tone is not intonation. Intonation is a sentence element independent of particular words: Thus "horse", uttered with a rising intonation might indicate doubt: "Did you say 'horse'?" The response, uttered with falling intonation ("Yes, I did.") indicates certainty. Chinese also has intonation, as you will discover. It interacts with pitch but preserves the distinguishing characteristics of the tones, so they remain recognizable even in emotional language with strong intonational contours.

The Neutral Tone (轻声 qīngshēng)

In addition to the four tones that appear with stressed syllables, there is a neutral tone, called "轻声 qīngshēng" (light tone), that is characteristic of unstressed syllables. The neutral tone is signalled by the absence of a tone mark: "xíngli" (baggage); "dōngxi" (thing). Neutral tones always follow full toned syllables or other neutral tones within a tone group. In the following examples, the neutral toned syllable is preceded by a dot:

tā · de (his)   zhuō · zi (table)   chī · le (have eaten)   tā · men · de (their, theirs)

A neutral tone is shorter and lighter than a full tone syllable. Two levels of pitch for neutral tone can be distinguished, each conditioned by the tone of the preceding syllable:

1. Low neutral tone

When a neutral tone follows a first, second, or fourth tone, it is pronounced on a relatively lower pitch:

gēge (elder brother) bízi (nose) dà de (the big one)

2. High neutral tone

When a neutral tone follows a third tone (a "low" tone), it is pronounced on a relatively higher pitch:

jiějie (elder sister) wǒ de (mine)

Tone Shifts

1. Shifts involving the third tone

a. If a third tone is followed in close juncture by another third tone, the first third tone shifts to second:

Nǐ hǎo (hi) is pronounced: Ní hǎo.
Hěn hǎo (very good) is pronounced: Hén hǎo.

This shift is general, affecting all combinations of low tone in close juncture, so it is not usually indicated in *Pinyin*. It applies, but is not written.

b. When a third tone is followed by a first, second or fourth tone, the third tone is pronounced as a half third tone (low, without rise):

lǎoshī (teacher) low + high
mǎi cài (to buy vegetables) low + falling

2. Shifts involving "yī" (one) and "bù" (not)

The common words "yī" (one, once, a) and "bù" (no, not) also show tonal shifts: Both "yī" and "bù" followed by a first, second, or third tone syllable are pronounced on the fourth tone:

yī → yì (before tones 1, 2, 3)
yì tiān (one day) yì jīn (half kilo)
yì rén (one person) yì pán (one dish)
yì jiǎo (10 cents [formal]) yì máo (10 cents [colloquial])

bù → bù (before tones 1, 2, 3)
bù gāo (not tall)
bù máng (not busy)
bù hǎo (not good)

Before fourth tone words, both are pronounced on second tone:

yī → yí (before tone 4)
yí cì (one time)
yíwàn (10,000)

bù → bú (before tone 4)
bú lèi (not tired)
bú xiè (you're welcome)

Otherwise, "yī" is pronounced on first tone (e.g., in counting): yī èr sān sì wǔ; èrshíyī; sānbǎi sìshíyī.

Tone Marks

1. Where to put tone marks

Tone marks are written over the main vowel. Where there are sequences of vowel letters ("ia, iu, ui, iao", etc.), the main vowel can be determined by ruling out the medials ("i, u", and the rare "ü"). Thus in "ia, iu, ui, iao", the first letters are medials, so the second vowel letters get the tone: iǎ, iū, uì, iāo. With "ao, ei, ou", the first letters are not possible medials, so they must be main vowels – and get the tone: ǎo, èi, ōu.

2. Indicating syllable divisions

In cases where syllables beginning with "a, o, e" are not separated from a previous syllable by a space, a syllable division mark " ' " needs to be inserted to indicate the syllable boundary, e.g.: Xī'ān (the name of the city) – not "Xīān"; hǎi'ōu (seagull) – not "hǎiōu".

3. Other *Pinyin* conventions

Pinyin uses the period (or full stop), the comma, the capital letter and some other forms of punctuation familiar to English users. It also makes limited use of the hyphen, e.g in certain kinds of collective expressions (e.g., "zhōng-xiǎoxué", primary and middle schools); and four-syllable idioms that divide logically into two pairs of syllables (e.g., "láilái-wǎngwǎng", to walk to and fro). Finally, although the notion of the "word" (as opposed to the character or syllable) is not as clearcut in Chinese as in English and other European languages, *Pinyin* places spaces around words rather than syllables (following dictionary precedent).

Please speak standard Chinese.

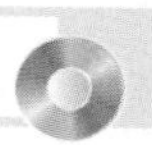

Pronunciation Exercises

1. In each of the groups below, combine the initial with the rhyme, then read the syllable aloud

Group A	Group B	Group C
w - àn	zh - āng	ch - én
j - iāng	l - ín	x - iè
m - èng	d - ù	f - āng

2. Read out the common Chinese surnames listed below. Although the pronunciation of Chinese names can seem difficult at first, you will be glad to know that there are far fewer Chinese surnames than there are English ones

(1) Chén	(7) Jiǎ	(13) Liú	(19) Xiè
(2) Dèng	(8) Jīn	(14) Mèng	(20) Yáng
(3) Féng	(9) Kǒng	(15) Shěn	(21) Zhāng
(4) Gāo	(10) Lǐ	(16) Sūn	(22) Zhào
(5) Guō	(11) Liáng	(17) Tián	(23) Zhèng
(6) Huáng	(12) Lín	(18) Wú	(24) Zhōu

3. Below, you will find a list of countries. Try pronouncing them

1	Fǎguó	France
2	Yīngguó	England, the United Kingdom
3	Déguó	Germany
4	Jiānádà	Canada
5	Yìdàlì	Italy
6	Àodàlìyà	Australia
7	Àodìlì	Austria
8	Měiguó	the United States
9	Xībānyá	Spain
10	Xīlà	Greece
11	Xīnxīlán	New Zealand
12	Ài'ěrlán	Ireland

13	Sūgélán	Scotland
14	Ruìshì	Switzerland
15	Ruìdiǎn	Sweden
16	Nuówēi	Norway
17	Éluósī	Russia
18	Rìběn	Japan
19	Yìndù	India
20	Xīnjiāpō	Singapore

4. Read each of the following compounds aloud at least three times, paying special attention to tones

1+1

fēijī (airplane) shāfā (sofa) shūbāo (school bag)

Xiāng Shān (The Fragrant Hills) huāshēng (peanut) Xī'ān (the name of the city)

1+1+1

Zhījiāgē (Chicago) shōuyīnjī (radio) chāshāobāo (steamed buns)

2+2

Chángchéng (The Great Wall) shítáng (cafeteria) yínháng (bank)

yóutiáo (fried dough sticks) Huáng Hé (The Yellow River) nánrén (men)

2+2+2

Yíhé Yuán (The Summer Palace) Yánhú Chéng (Salt Lake City)

4+4

fàndiàn (hotel) sùshè (dormitory) diànhuà (telephone)

bàogào (report) zàijiàn (goodbye)

4+4+4

diànshìjù (soap opera) yùndònghuì (sports meet)

Listening Comprehension

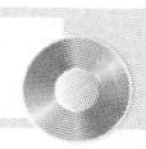

1. Listen to the Chinese version of these country names (plus Scotland and Hong Kong — parts of countries) and write them in *Pinyin* (with tones). Pay special attention to the sounds represented by lines 3, 4 and 5 of the initial chart: z c s, zh ch sh r, j q x

(1) China

(2) Singapore

(3) Korea

(4) Switzerland

(5) Spain

(6) New Zealand

(7) South Africa

(8) Hong Kong

(9) Sweden

(10) Japan

(11) Canada

(12) Scotland

(13) Saudi Arabia

2. Listen to the city names and put the correct tone mark over the appropriate vowel in each word

(1) Xi'an
(2) Wuhan
(3) Nanjing
(4) Guilin
(5) Chengdu
(6) Changchun
(7) Wulumuqi
(8) Shenyang
(9) Shijiazhuang
(10) Zhengzhou
(11) Hefei
(12) Nanchang
(13) Changsha
(14) Hangzhou
(15) Taiyuan
(16) Fuzhou
(17) Guangzhou
(18) Kunming
(19) Guiyang
(20) Nanning
(21) Lanzhou
(22) Xining
(23) Lasa
(24) Yinchuan
(25) Shenzhen
(26) Suzhou
(27) Shanghai

3. Identifying initial sounds. Listen to the syllables spoken on the CD and draw a circle around the *Pinyin* that matches what you heard

(1) a. ce b. che
(2) a. se b. ze
(3) a. zi b. ci
(12) a. xu b. shu
(13) a. shui b. xue
(14) a. ji b. chi

(4) a. zhi b. ri
(5) a. zu b. zhu
(6) a. she b. re
(7) a. se b. ce
(8) a. chi b. ri
(9) a. rui b. shui
(10) a. xi b. shi
(11) a. jia b. zha
(15) a. chuan b. quan
(16) a. ju b. zhu
(17) a. ji b. zi
(18) a. xia b. sha
(19) a. jiong b. zhong
(20) a. qie b. che
(21) a. xia b. sha

4. Identifying rhymes. Listen to the syllables spoken on the CD and draw a circle around the *Pinyin* that matches what you heard

(1) a. dōu b. duō
(2) a. nüè b. niè
(3) a. zǎo b. zǒu
(4) a. zhào b. zhòu
(5) a. lǔ b. lǚ
(6) a. cì b. cè
(7) a. zé b. zì
(8) a. yuè b. yè
(9) a. mǎi b. měi
(10) a. rén b. rán
(11) a. kōng b. kāng
(12) a. lín b. líng
(13) a. gǒu b. gǎo
(14) a. dōu b. diū
(15) a. chāo b. chōu
(16) a. zuó b. zé
(17) a. xù b. shù
(18) a. mén b. méng
(19) a. juān b. jūn
(20) a. wèn b. wàn
(21) a. rè b. rì

5. Identifying tones. Listen to the syllables spoken on the CD and draw a circle around the *Pinyin* that matches the tone that you heard

(1) a. lǎoshī b. lǎoshi
(2) a. fēijī b. Fēijì
(3) a. zhīdao b. zhǐdǎo
(4) a. shuìjiào b. shuǐjiǎo
(5) a. bèijǐng b. Běijīng
(6) a. fèichú b. fēichū
(12) a. rìjì b. rìjí
(13) a. qūxī b. qǔ xí
(14) a. cízhí b. cǐzhì
(15) a. mōsuǒ b. mósuō
(16) a. yǐngxiǎng b. yìngxiàng
(17) a. qiángshǒu b. qiǎngshōu

(7) a. rèhuǒ b. rěhuò

(8) a. shíjiān b. shìjiàn

(9) a. sān kē b. sǎnkè

(10) a. dǎ qiú b. Dàqiū

(11) a. zìjǐ b. zìjì

(18) a. chāoshēng b. cháoshèng

(19) a. lièshí b. lièshì

(20) a. zìsī b. zǐsì

(21) a. yǎnjing b. yǎnjìng

Communication Activities

Pair Work

1. Ask at least four of your classmates for their Chinese names and write them down in *Pinyin* (with tone marks and correct spacing)

2. Have one person read out a province or city name from the list below and another point to it on a map of China

(1) Héběi	(11) Gānsù	(21) Fújiàn
(2) Hénán	(12) Qīnghǎi	(22) Yúnnán
(3) Shānxī	(13) Xīnjiāng	(23) Guǎngdōng
(4) Shǎnxī	(14) Sìchuān	(24) Guǎngxī
(5) Hēilóngjiāng	(15) Ānhuī	(25) Xīzàng
(6) Jílín	(16) Húběi	(26) Nèiměnggǔ
(7) Shāndōng	(17) Húnán	(27) Běijīng
(8) Liáoníng	(18) Zhèjiāng	(28) Shànghǎi
(9) Jiāngsū	(19) Jiāngxī	(29) Tiānjīn
(10) Níngxià	(20) Guìzhōu	(30) Chóngqìng

Review Exercises

I. Underline the initials of the following words

(1) Beijing
(2) Beijing Daxue (Peking University)
(3) Gu Gong (The Palace Museum)
(4) Qian Men (The Front City-Gate)
(5) Yihe Yuan (The Summer Palace)
(6) dashiguan (embassy)
(7) Changcheng (The Great Wall)
(8) Lugou Qiao (The Marco Polo Bridge)
(9) Chang Jiang (The Yangtze River)
(10) Shanghai
(11) Tian Tan (The Temple of Heaven)
(12) Tian'an Men (The Gate of Heavenly Peace)
(13) Shisan Ling (The [13] Ming Tombs)
(14) Xiushui Dongjie (The Silk Market)
(15) Hongqiao Shichang (The Pearl Market)
(16) Panjiayuan (The "Mud" Market)
(17) Huang He (The Yellow River)

II. Underline each of the rhymes in the following words

(1) Yǒuyì Shāngdiàn (The Friendship Store)
(2) Hǎidiàn (a district in Beijing)
(3) Gù Gōng (The Palace Museum)
(4) Tiān'ān Mén (The Gate of Heavenly Peace)
(5) Tiān Tán (The Temple of Heaven)
(6) Cháng Jiāng (The Yangtze River)
(7) Xiùshuǐ Dōngjiē (The Silk Market)
(8) Yíhé Yuán (The Summer Palace)
(9) Chángchéng (The Great Wall)
(10) Shísān Líng (The [13] Ming Tombs)
(11) dàshǐguǎn (embassy)
(12) Pānjiāyuán (The "Mud" Market)
(13) Lúgōu Qiáo (The Marco Polo Bridge)
(14) Běihǎi Gōngyuán (Beihai Park)
(15) Hóngqiáo Shìchǎng (The Pearl Market)
(16) Huáng Hé (The Yellow River)

(17) Qīnghuá Dàxué (Tsinghua University)

(18) Běijīng Shīfàn Dàxué (Beijing Normal University)

III. Identify the tone, then write the tone mark over the correct vowel

(1) Hunan
(2) Chang Jiang
(3) Guizhou
(4) Liaoning
(5) Hubei
(6) Guangxi
(7) Neimenggu
(8) Fujian
(9) Jiangsu
(10) Xizang
(11) Yuenan
(12) Zhongguo
(13) Xianggang
(14) Meiguo
(15) Jianada
(16) Taiwan
(17) Xinjiapo
(18) Ruishi
(19) Yindu
(20) Faguo

IV. The following words are all spelled with initial vowel letters instead of consonants. Change them to regular *Pinyin* spelling

(1) īngguó (England)............
(2) iángzhōu (a city)............
(3) Uáng (a surname)............
(4) uǒ (I, me)............
(5) üènán (Vietnam)............
(6) iě (also)............
(7) üè (moon)............
(8) uèi (hello)............
(9) ī (one)............
(10) üán (¥)............
(11) iǒu (to have)............
(12) īn-iáng (female-male principles)............

V. Practice reading the following words aloud, paying special attention to the high-low distinction of the neutral tone

(1) māma (mother)
(2) yéye (grandpa)
(3) dìdi (younger brother)
(4) gēge (older brother)
(5) háizi (children)
(6) bàba (father)
(7) shūshu (uncle, father's younger brother)
(8) bóbo (uncle, father's older brother)
(9) jiějie (older sister)
(10) mèimei (younger sister)
(11) nǎinai (grandma)

VI. Each of the following words or phrases contains a neutral tone. Identify which ones are relatively high, and which are relatively low

(1) kànle (saw)
(2) jīnzi (gold)
(3) yínzi (silver)
(4) xièxie (thank you)
(5) xiānsheng (Mister)
(6) shénme (what)
(7) zuòzhe (sitting)
(8) nǐ de (your, yours)
(9) wǒ de (my, mine)

Culture Notes

1. Chinese phonetic systems

In addition to *Pinyin*, there are two other Chinese systems of transcription still in use today:

Wade-Giles (威妥玛式拼音 Wēituǒmǎshì Pīnyīn)

The Wade-Giles system was created by Thomas F. Wade, a British diplomat and scholar. In 1867 he published a Mandarin textbook using the Romanized phonetic system he devised. Later, Wade's system was modified by another British diplomat-scholar, Herbert A. Giles. The Wade-Giles system was the standard system for transcribing Chinese words in English printed works until 1978, when the United Nations recognized *Pinyin* as the standard and most other institutions followed suit. For English speakers, the Wade-Giles system is, in many respects, more transparent for those without instruction in *Pinyin*, so even after 1978, books on Chinese history as well as some other subjects often transcribe Chinese into the Wade-Giles system. The system also survives in some current spellings of Chinese names and places (such as Tsinghua University).

Chinese National Phonetic Alphabet (CNPA), also known as "bo po mo fo"

The Chinese National Phonetic Alphabet (CNPA) is made up of thirty-nine symbols that are based mostly on simple characters no longer in use in the modern language. A first draft of the CNPA appeared in 1913, though it was not adopted until later. In Chinese, it is known as "注音符号 zhùyīn fúhào" (phonetic symbols), or more colloquially, as "bo po mo fo", the names of its first four "letters".

Pinyin, Wade-Giles, and the National Phonetic Alphabet (as well as other systems not discussed) all represent (with one or two minor exceptions) the same standard pronunciation.

English	*Pinyin*	Wade-Giles	CNPA
China	Zhōngguó	Chung^1-kuo^2	ㄓㄨㄥ ㄍㄨㄛˊ
Chinese	Hànyǔ	Han^4-yu^3	ㄏㄢˋ ㄩˇ

The following is a comparison between CNPA and *Pinyin*:

注音 CNPA	汉语拼音 *Pinyin*	例子 Samples（注音，汉语拼音）
ㄅ	b	八（ㄅㄚ, bā）
ㄆ	p	爬（ㄆㄚˊ, pá）
ㄇ	m	马（ㄇㄚˇ, mǎ）
ㄈ	f	法（ㄈㄚˇ, fǎ）
ㄉ	d	地（ㄉㄧˋ, dì）
ㄊ	t	提（ㄊㄧˊ, tí）
ㄋ	n	你（ㄋㄧˇ, nǐ）
ㄌ	l	利（ㄌㄧˋ, lì）

续表 Continued

注音 CNPA	汉语拼音 *Pinyin*	例子 Samples（注音，汉语拼音）
ㄍ	g	告（ㄍㄠˋ, gào）
ㄎ	k	考（ㄎㄠˇ, kǎo）
ㄏ	h	好（ㄏㄠˇ, hǎo）
ㄐ	j	叫（ㄐㄧㄠˋ, jiào）
ㄑ	q	巧（ㄑㄧㄠˇ, qiǎo）
ㄒ	x	小（ㄒㄧㄠˇ, xiǎo）
ㄓ	zhi / zh	主（ㄓㄨˇ, zhǔ）
ㄔ	chi / ch	出（ㄔㄨ, chū）
ㄕ	shi / sh	束（ㄕㄨˋ, shù）
ㄖ	ri / r	入（ㄖㄨˋ, rù）
ㄗ	zi / z	在（ㄗㄞˋ, zài）
ㄘ	ci / c	才（ㄘㄞˊ, cái）
ㄙ	si / s	塞（ㄙㄞ, sāi）
ㄚ	a	大（ㄉㄚˋ, dà）
ㄛ	o	多（ㄉㄨㄛ, duō）
ㄜ	e	得（ㄉㄜˊ, dé）
ㄧㄝ	ie	爹（ㄉㄧㄝ, diē）
ㄞ	ai	晒（ㄕㄞˋ, shài）
ㄟ	ei	谁（ㄕㄟˊ, shéi）
ㄠ	ao	少（ㄕㄠˇ, shǎo）
ㄡ	ou	收（ㄕㄡ, shōu）
ㄢ	an	山（ㄕㄢ, shān）
ㄣ	en	申（ㄕㄣ, shēn）
ㄤ	ang	上（ㄕㄤˋ, shàng）
ㄥ	eng	生（ㄕㄥ, shēng）
ㄦ	er	而（ㄦˊ, ér）
ㄧ	yi / i	逆（ㄋㄧˋ, nì）

续表 Continued

注音 CNPA	汉语拼音 *Pinyin*	例子 Samples（注音，汉语拼音）
ㄧㄣ	yin / in	音（ㄧㄣ, yīn）
ㄧㄥ	ying / ing	英（ㄧㄥ, yīng）
ㄨ	wu / u	努（ㄋㄨˇ, nǔ）
ㄨㄣ	wen / un	文（ㄨㄣˊ, wén）
ㄨㄥ	weng / ong	翁（ㄨㄥ, wēng）
ㄩ	yu / u / ü	女（ㄋㄩˇ, nǚ）
ㄩㄣ	yun / ün	韵（ㄩㄣˋ, yùn）
（ㄨㄥ）	yong / iong	永（ㄨㄥˇ, yǒng）

2. The major dialects of Chinese

The Northern Dialects

The Northern dialect group (北方方言 Běifāng fāngyán) is native to 71.4% of the Chinese people. Speakers mainly reside in an area ranging from the southwest to the north and northeast, including the provinces of Héběi, Hénán, Shāndōng, Shānxī, Shǎnxī, Yúnnán, Guìzhōu, Sìchuān, Ānhuī, Húběi, and northern Jiāngsū. Standard Chinese – Mandarin – has its roots in the northern group.

The "Wú" Dialects

The "吴 Wú" dialects, spoken by 6.4% of Chinese people, are spoken in the area around Jiāngsū, Zhèjiāng and Shànghǎi. "Wú" is the old name of Jiāngsū province.

The "Xiāng" Dialects

The "湘 Xiāng" dialects, spoken by 3% of Chinese people, are spoken in and around Húnán province. "Xiāng" is the old name of Húnán.

The "Yuè" Dialects

The "粤 Yuè" dialects, or Cantonese (广东话 Guǎngdōnghuà), spoken by 5.5% of Chinese people, are spoken in Guǎngdōng, Xiānggǎng, Àomén as well as in many parts of Southeast Asia, in North America, and elsewhere in the Chinese diaspora.

The Hakka Dialects

The Hakka dialects (客家话 Kèjiāhuà), spoken by 3.5% of Chinese people, are spoken in parts of Guǎngxī, Fújiàn, and Táiwān, as well as in parts of Southeast Asia.

The "Gàn" Dialects

The "赣 Gàn" dialects (江西话 Jiāngxīhuà), spoken by 4% of Chinese people, are spoken in and around Jiāngxī province. "Gàn" is the old name of Jiāngxī.

The "Mǐn" Dialects

The "闽 Mǐn" dialect group is divided into five Min dialect areas. 6.2% of Chinese people speak Min dialects, mostly in Fújiàn and Táiwān.

Lesson Two Chinese Characters

第二课 汉 字

Dì-èr Kè Hànzì

This lesson deals with the following topics

- Chinese characters
- How characters evolved
- The simplified and traditional character sets
- Types of strokes used to compose characters
- The order of strokes
- The structure of characters
- Radicals and phonetic elements

This lesson also provides practice in

- Identifying types of strokes, stroke order, and character structure
- Writing characters

Culture Notes

- Names of some common radicals

Introduction to Chinese Characters

Chinese is written in "汉字 Hànzì" (Chinese characters). Characters represent syllables, most of which are also words or meaningful components of compound words. For this reason, the Chinese script is often called morphosyllabic, that is, it represents syllables that are mostly morphemes – word elements. Because they do not represent individual sounds, characters cannot (except in some marginal cases) be sounded out like unknown words in more alphabetic languages such as English. For students used to alphabetic writing, this presents serious difficulties!

Characters are not entirely devoid of sound indicators, but one needs a lot of experience to know how to utilize the phonetic hints available. It is, in fact, the phonetic components of characters that makes the script learnable. Here is an example: The character for oxygen is written "氧" and pronounced "yǎng". It is composed of two parts that can also stand alone as characters: "气" and "羊". The latter is pronounced "yáng" (on rising tone). You might not recognize the rather rare character "氧"; but if you know that "羊" (a common character meaning "goat" or "sheep") is pronounced "yáng", you have a phonetic hint. The tones do not match ("yǎng" versus "yáng"), but it may be enough to jog your memory (just as English "ox" might remind you of "oxygen"), and it is enough to let you look up the character under "yang" (without any particular tone) in the dictionary.

The element "羊 yáng" turns out to be a fairly reliable phonetic hint for characters that contain it, e.g.: 洋 yáng; 样 yàng; 痒 yǎng. You still have to match the sounds to meanings, but the context will help with that: "洋" is "seas"; "样" is "type; pattern"; "痒" is "itch". Unfortunately, just as you gain confidence in the equation "羊 = yang" (on some tone), you encounter "祥" and "详", which turn out to be pronounced not "yang", but "xiáng" – close, but not identical. That is the way that sound is encoded within the Chinese writing system: it is present, but takes experience to exploit it. You should keep this in mind as you begin to learn the script.

Another difficulty: Chinese contains many homophones. For example, the characters "一", "衣", and "医", representing words (or parts of words) for "one", "clothing" and "doctor" respectively, are all pronounced "yī" (just as English "to", "too" and "two" are all pronounced the same).

Since the pronunciation of characters is not reliably related to their form (though, as we showed above, the form of characters does contain phonetic hints), it can be a slow business learning to associate sound as well as meaning with a particular character. The process can be speeded up by providing an unambiguous representation of sound alongside the characters. This is one function of *Pinyin*. In this book, *Pinyin* is mostly written directly below the characters. When learning to read (in characters), it is important to cover the *Pinyin* line (a pencil serves quite well), uncovering it only to check on your pronunciation as you go. Your goal is to wean yourself from *Pinyin* and read directly through the characters to sound and ultimately, meaning.

The other function of *Pinyin* is to provide a way of transcribing speech (words or phrases overheard) while you are learning the spoken language and before you have the ability to write such material down in characters. This use of *Pinyin* will last you through your Chinese learning life, since there will always be local and regional expressions – to say nothing of more ordinary material – for which characters do not come easily to mind. The solution: write it down in accurate *Pinyin* and look it up in a dictionary later.

The Evolution of Chinese Characters

Legend has it that Chinese characters were created by "仓颉 Cāng Jié", the official historian of "黄帝 Huángdì", the mythical Yellow Emperor, who is traditionally said to have reigned from 2698 – 2599 BCE. "Cāng

Jié" is supposed to have been inspired by hoof prints to design a writing system based on the unique characteristics of things. However, modern scholars believe it more likely that the Chinese script evolved piecemeal, with more than one person contributing to its development.

Early Chinese documents mention three sources of characters: (1) The Eight Trigrams (八卦 bāguà) from the *Book of Changes*, which are the eight combinations of three broken (yīn) or whole (yáng) lines that represented elements in an ancient system of divination. (2) Drawings depicting things, relationships or events, used to represent words. (3) Symbols, known as "书契 shūqì" (titles, deeds) that appear on pottery up to 6,000 years old, found in places such as Dawenkou (Shandong) and Majiayao (Gansu).

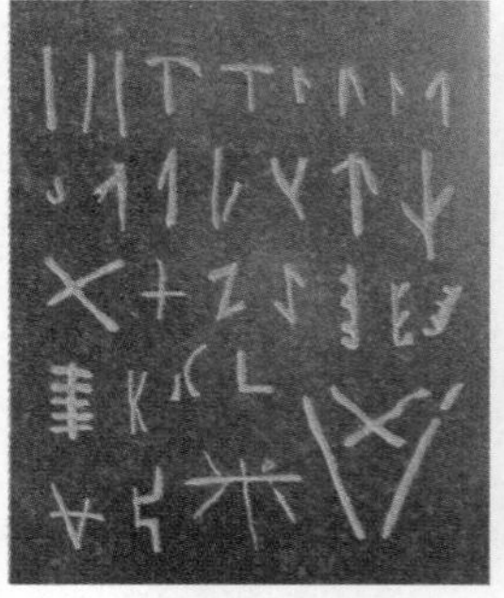
刻画符号 kèhuà fúhào

甲骨文 jiǎgǔwén

金文 jīnwén

Because they represented words rather than things, characters soon lost their pictorial qualities, becoming conventionalized in their modern straight-lined, square-shaped forms at least by the 5th century, and evolving new, non-representational ways of representing words even earlier.

The history of characters is often divided into three periods. The first covers the period from the "oracle bone inscriptions" (甲骨文 jiǎgǔwén) to the appearance of the "small seal" script (from the 14th century to, roughly, the 3rd century BCE).

The oracle bone inscriptions are the earliest extant Chinese writing of significant quantity. The script was engraved mostly on turtle plastrons (the flat shell on the underside) and ox scapulae (the shoulder blade), as part of a process of divination. The characters are archaic, and roughly etched, but many are clearly relatable to modern forms.

小篆 xiǎozhuàn

隶书 lìshū

The second period runs from the development of the "small seal script" to the adoption of the "official script". The former, called "小篆 xiǎozhuàn" in Chinese, is a more balanced and artistically pleasing script that became standard during the unification of the Qin dynasty (221 – 206 BCE).

Though informal scripts co-existed with official ones, eventually, the "official script" (known as "隶书 lìshū"), which was a leaner, more horizontal script, gained currency in the Han period (206 BCE – 220 CE) and eventually became the standard.

The third stage was the development of the "regular" or "model" script, called "楷书 kǎishū", which was created during the Wei and Jin dynasties (220 – 420 CE). By the Song Dynasty, "楷书 kǎishū" had become the standard printed script and it continues to be used today.

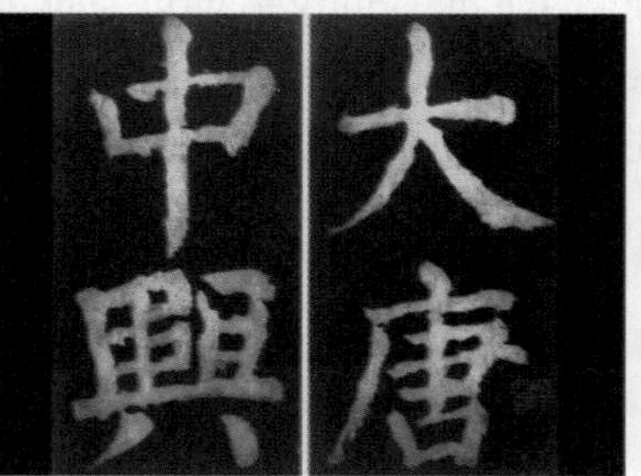

楷书 kǎishū

The following chart shows the development of some "pictographic" characters from the earliest forms to the forms in use today.

Archaic form	Modern form	Meaning
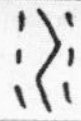	水	water
	日	sun
	月	moon
	牛	ox
	火	fire

Simplified and Complex Forms of Chinese Characters

From ancient times, there have been two co-existing forms of character writing: a formal system, that made use only of standardized characters (正体字 zhèngtǐzì) that was used for serious or official purposes; and an informal system that made use of many non-standard characters (俗体字 sútǐzì), which were simpler to write, and which were used for informal purposes, such as letters to friends, journals, menus and shop signs.

In 1956, in order to promote literacy, a Character Reform Committee was formed with the goal of simplifying the writing system. The committee, made up of Chinese linguists, collected and collated the simplified, unofficial forms of characters used by people in daily life. The reformers then further simplified the most frequently used characters, reducing the number of strokes by an average of one half. Lists of simplified Chinese characters were promulgated, leading to the publication in 1964 of *A Conversion Table of Simplified Chinese Characters*, later revised, in 1986. It contained 2,235 simplified Chinese characters that formed the basis of the simplified character set that is now standard on the Mainland, in Singapore, and in many overseas communities. However, Taiwan and Hong Kong and some overseas communities still use the traditional, complex characters.

Here are some examples from the two sets:

mā	媽/妈	mother
yuán	圓/圆	circle; *a unit of currency*
Hàn	漢/汉	Chinese

The majority of simplifications, even if they reduce the number of strokes significantly as in the first of the examples above, have little effect on the general shape of the character. It is mostly more common characters that have significantly altered shapes (like the third above). Literate Chinese, after a short period of adjustment, have little trouble reading in both character sets – though they might not find writing both so easy. Learners too, after a relatively short period, can learn to switch from one set and another for reading – though most stick to one for writing. This book uses simplified characters because it is designed for learners living in China.

Strokes

Chinese characters are formed from eight basic strokes:

Stroke name	Stroke	Stroke direction	Example
1. Horizontal stroke (横 héng)	一	left to right	三
2. Vertical stroke (竖 shù)	丨	top to bottom	中
3. Left downward stroke (撇 piě)	丿	top-right to bottom-left	人
4. Right downward stroke (捺 nà)	㇏	top-left to bottom-right	八
5. Dot (点 diǎn)			
left dot	㇀	upper right to lower left	小
right dot	丶	upper left to lower right	卜
bottom dots	灬	from left to right	点
6. Many strokes are completed with a hook (钩 gōu), formed just before lifting the writing instrument. The hook is part of the following strokes:			
Left vertical hook	亅	From top down, then a hook to the left	了
Right downward bending hook	乚	From top down, a turn to the horizontal then a hook upwards	七
Horizontal hook	乛	From left to right, then a hook down	买
Arm-hook	㇆	From left to right, then straight down ending with a leftwards hook	勺
Dragon-tail hook	㇂/乙	From top down with upwards hook	戈 九
	㇇	Horizontal line first, then a turn	又
7. Turning stroke (折 zhé)	㇄/𠃊	Vertical line first, then a turn	区 山
	㇛	Left-downward, then right-downward	女
8. Rising stroke (提 tí)	㇀	Rising from bottom left	冲

Stroke Order

The strokes that form a character follow a fixed order (though in some cases, there may be alternate orderings). Having a fixed order of strokes not only streamlines writing, it also creates a physical memory of how to write a character that can support visual and cognitive recall.

Stroke order can be generalized as follows:

1. Top before bottom

If a character contains two or more strokes, proceed from the topmost down. If it has two or more parts, proceed from the top part down (and within each part, from the top down).

毛：三 → 毛
分：丿 → 八 → 分
曼：日 → 昌 → 曼

2. From left to right

If a character contains two or more strokes, proceed from left to right. If it contains two or more parts, complete the leftmost first and proceed rightwards (and from left to right within each part).

人：丿 → 人
什：亻 → 仁 → 什
谁：讠 → 讠亻 → 谁

3. Horizontal strokes first, then verticals

干：一 → 二 → 干
万：一 → 丆 → 万
下：一 → 丅 → 下

4. In symmetrical characters with a dominant central stroke, the central stroke is written first, then strokes to the left, and to the right

小：亅 → 小 → 小
子：了 → 子
水：亅 → 水 → 水

5. Outside first, then inside

月：丿 → 冂 → 月
问：丶 → 门 → 问
风：丿 → 几 → 风

6. Complete the innards before closing the square

回：冂 → 回 → 回
国：冂 → 国 → 国
园：冂 → 园 → 园

Some Chinese characters are simplex (with only one component), but most are composed of two or more components. The following are the four basic structures of Chinese characters.

1. Simplex

毛 máo / Máo (¥0.10; body hair; a surname)

2. a. Left-right structure

块 kuài (*a unit of currency*; piece; cube)

b. Left-center-right structure

谢 xiè (to thank)

3. a. Top-bottom structure

员 yuán (personnel, staff, member of)

b. Top-center-bottom structure

曼 màn (graceful)

4. Outer-inner structure

圆 yuán (circle; *a unit of currency*)

Radicals

In alphabetic languages, words can be ordered alphabetically. In English, all you need to know is the order of the 26 letters of the alphabet to be able to look up any word. Even if you do not know how to spell it exactly, you can usually locate the word you want quite quickly.

In Chinese, an entirely different mechanism has to be employed. In the earliest dictionaries (which date from over 2,000 years ago), characters were assigned a signifier, now generally called a radical. The Chinese term is "部首 bùshǒu", literally, a "component-head", that is, the part that serves as the identifier. Radicals are mostly components that can – or could at one time – appear as independent characters. In characters with two components – the majority – the radical is relatively easy to identify: "化，休，仁" are all assigned the radical "亻" – a combining form of "人" (person); "鸭，鸽，莺" (all representing bird names) are all assigned the bird radical "鸟". The last example illustrates the fact that many radicals have meanings that can be related to the characters they appear in. As another example, the following characters containing "女 nǚ" (woman) all pertain to females: "妈 mā" (mother), "她 tā" (she, her), "姐 jiě" (older sister), "妹 mèi" (younger sister).

Simplex characters may themselves be radicals: 人, 鸟, 木, 口. Or one part of them is designated as radical: for "州", the first dot is the radical; for "卵", it is the right-hand part, but without the dot. The fact that all characters have an assigned radical provides a basis for retrieval in dictionaries and other reference books organized by characters.

In dictionaries, radicals are presented in tables following a fixed order based on number of strokes: two for "亻", five for "鸟", and so on. Page numbers given with each radical refer either to a table of all characters with that radical which, in turn, provide page numbers to the appropriate listings; or they refer directly to the section of the dictionary where the listings for that radical begin. In either case, characters under each radical are listed by number of additional strokes needed to form them: within the "亻" radical, "化" and "仁" would be listed under two strokes, "休" under four, and "儒" – to cite a complicated example – under fourteen.

The radical method not only provides a way of retrieving words from a dictionary, it provides a way of ordering written material of any kind, whether books, files, or personal names. Nowadays, however, many dictionaries are organized first by *Pinyin* pronunciation, which can be alphabetized, with other lookup methods available as fall back for those cases when the pronunciation of a character is not known.

Radicals, which indicate broad semantic categories (such as "fish", "bird", "wood", "cover"), are often paired with an element that provides a phonetic hint – a so-called phonetic component. The examples cited in the first paragraph of this lesson illustrate: "洋 yáng", "样 yàng", and "痒 yǎng". All contain the phonetic component, "羊 yáng" (matching the pronunciation of the whole in all but tone). The radicals, in turn, often provide a semantic hint: "洋 yáng", with "氵", the water radical (a combining form of "水 shuǐ" – water) means "sea"; "样 yàng", with "木", the wood radical (inspired by the form of a tree), originally meant a wooden mold, which creates shapes – hence its modern meaning of "type"; and "痒 yǎng", with "疒", the illness radical, means "itch" – a symptom of many kinds of ailments. Here are some other examples:

Character	Radical (semantic)		Other (phonetic)
们 (mén, collective for people)	亻 (human)	+	门 (mén)
妈 (mā, mother)	女 (woman)	+	马 (mǎ)
圆 (yuán, circle; *a unit of currency*)	囗 (enclosure)	+	员 (yuán)

In 1983, the Chinese Character Reform Committee published a list of 227 radicals to be used as the official system for indexing characters in Chinese dictionaries, such as the standard *Modern Chinese Dictionary* (《现代汉语词典》《Xiàndài Hànyǔ Cídiǎn》).

To conclude: knowing the more common components that make up characters provides learners – and even mature speakers – with a great deal of useful information. Knowing which radical a particular character is categorized under will allow you to retrieve characters of unknown pronunciation in dictionaries and other reference works. Knowing the general meaning associated with common radicals often provides semantic hints as to the meaning of compound characters (characters with two components). Knowing how to recognize phonetic components often helps you to recall pronunciation.

Listening Comprehension

The neutral tone

The following words or phrases each contain a syllable with neutral tone. Listen to them and indicate whether the neutral tone is high or low. Check your pronunciation against that on the CD.

(1) māma (mother)

(2) shūshu (uncle, father's younger brother)

(3) gēge (older brother)

(4) jīnzi (gold)

(5) xiānsheng (mister)

(6) yéye (grandpa)

(7) bóbo (uncle, father's older brother)

(8) háizi (children)

(9) yínzi (silver)

(10) shénme (what)

(11) dìdi (younger brother)

(12) kànle (saw)

(13) bàba (father)

(14) xièxie (thank you)

(15) wǒ de (my, mine)

(16) nǎinai (grandma)

(17) nǐ de (yours)

(18) jiějie (older sister)

Communication Activities

Pair Work

1. Take turns reading aloud each tone group and correcting each other

1+1

pīnyīn (*Pinyin*) kāixīn (happy) yīshēng (doctor) chūzū (for rent)

1+2

jīnnián (this year) Zhōngguó (China) āyí (aunt) fēicháng (extremely)

1+3

kāishǐ (to start) duō měi (how beautiful) zhōngwǔ (noon) shānshuǐ (landscape)

1+4

chī fàn (to eat) shuōhuà (to speak) fānyì (to translate) xīwàng (to hope)

2+1

shíjiān (time) guójiā (country) qiántiān (day before yesterday) huí jiā (to return)

2+2

míngnián (next year) qiánnián (year before last) qíshí (actually) shíxí (internship)

2+3

érqiě (besides) rénkǒu (population) tángguǒ (candy) wúbǐ (incomparable)

2+4

hánjià (winter break) májiàng (mahjang) xíguàn (habit) qiángdà (formidable)

3+1

huǒchē (train) lǎoshī (teacher) hǎotīng (pleasing to the ear) cǎobāo (good-for-nothing)

3+2

hǎorén (good person) jǐngchá (police) xǐ yá (dental cleansing) yǐqián (before)

3+3

nǐ hǎo (hi, hello) zhǐhǎo (may as well) suǒyǐ (so) shǐguǎn (embassy)

3+4

kǎoshì (test) gǎnmào (to catch a cold) nuǎnqì (heat) kě'ài (cute)

4+1

niànshū (to study) Gù Gōng (The Palace Museum) zhàngdān (bill) hòutiān (day after tomorrow)

4+2

àiqíng (love) bìngrén (patient) zìrán (natural) fù qián (to pay)

4+3

dàjiě (older sister) diànyǐng (movie) fùmǔ (parents) fànguǎn (restaurant)

4+4

diànhuà (telephone) fàndiàn (hotel) Hànzì (Chinese characters) yùndòng (sports)

1+1+1

Zhāng yīshēng (Dr. Zhang) fā gōngzī (to issue wages) zhēn shāngxīn (to feel really sad)

2+2+2

Qín Chángchéng (Qin Wall) Yíhé Yuán (The Summer Palace) chéngniánrén (adults)

3+3+3

nǚ zǒngtǒng (woman president) zhǐlǎohǔ (paper tiger) xiǎo lǎoshǔ (little mouse)

4+4+4

jiù shèhuì (old days) zhèng jiàoshòu (proper professor) Yìdàlì (Italy)

1+2+3+4

xīqí gǔguài (strange) jījí kěngàn (ready to get to work)

4+3+2+1

mèngxiǎng chéng zhēn (dreams come true) yìqǔ-tónggōng (different approach, same result)

2. In pairs, one person say a name on the following list in Chinese, then see if the other can guess the English

Kèlíndùn	Mòduōkè	Bùshí	Àiyīnsītǎn
Kěnnídí	Bèiduōfēn	Sàkēqí	Shāshìbǐyà
Kǎméilún	Dáfēnqí	Bǐ'ěr Gàicí	Hālì Bōtè

Group Work

Form groups of three; then each choose a Chinese surname and take turns introducing yourselves by saying: 我姓 Wǒ xìng……

Zhào (赵)	Qián (钱)	Sūn (孙)	Lǐ (李)
Zhōu (周)	Wú (吴)	Zhèng (郑)	Wáng (王)
Féng (冯)	Chén (陈)	Chǔ (褚)	Wèi (魏)
Jiǎng (蒋)	Shěn (沈)	Hán (韩)	Yáng (杨)

Review Exercises

I. Place tone marks on the following city names; the tones are given in the parentheses

(1) Beijing (3, 1)
(2) Xi'an (1, 1)
(3) Xiamen (4, 2)
(4) Kunming (1, 2)
(5) Guangzhou (3, 1)
(6) Wuhan (3, 4)
(7) Xianggang (1, 3)
(8) Shenyang (3, 2)
(9) Dongjing (1, 1)
(10) Lundun (2, 1)
(11) Shanghai (4, 3)
(12) Nanjing (2, 1)
(13) Hangzhou (2, 1)
(14) Chengdu (2, 1)
(15) Chongqing (2, 4)
(16) Tianjin (1, 1)
(17) Aomen (4, 2)
(18) Taibei (2, 3)
(19) Huashengdun (2, 4, 4)
(20) Duolunduo (1, 2, 1)

II. Read out the stroke orders of the following characters, using the Chinese names for the strokes, héng, shù, piě, nà, diǎn, **etc.**

三　小　六　丁　勺　九　八　人
女　水　山　买　又　冲　永

III. Indicate the order of strokes for each of the following characters

毛	六	二	丁	什	人	八	儿
十	千	万	寸	小	水	子	永
月	风	问	用	国	圆	目	四

IV. Using the terms such as simplex, left-right, top-bottom, outer-inner, label the structure of each of the following characters

四	九	他	零	你	是	圆	好
五	很	六	们	谢	慢	谁	喜

simplex .... left-right ....

top-bottom .... outer-inner ....

V. Identify radicals, and, in the spaces provided, give the total number of times each occurs

草	你	英	话	妈
讲	钟	好	说	花
他	钱	何	婚	银
请	茶	休	铭	她

Radical	Number of times

VI. The characters listed below all contain two components, one of which – the radical – relates to the (original) meaning of the character. First identify the radicals by drawing an oval around each, then try to assign a general meaning to each of them

湖 lake	岭 ridge	泪 tears	雾 fog	峻 steep	清 clear
峦 hill	晴 sunny	露 dew	屿 island	晨 morning	雪 snow
雷 thunder	洗 wash	雹 hail	晒 shine	霜 frost	暑 summer
暖 warm	汤 soup	岱 mountain	旦 dawn	河 river	巅 summit (of mountain)

VII. Identify the radicals of the characters in the following business cards

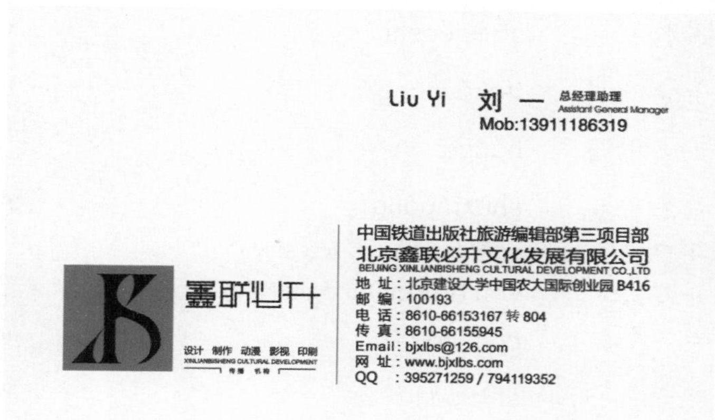

Culture Notes

Names of some common radicals

Radical	Chinese name		Semantic meaning
亻	单人旁	dānrénpáng	human
彳	双人旁	shuāngrénpáng	slow steps
刂	立刀旁	lìdāopáng	knife
讠/言	言字旁	yánzìpáng	word
辶	走之	zǒuzhī	walk
冫	两点水	liǎngdiǎnshuǐ	ice
氵	三点水	sāndiǎnshuǐ	water
扌	提手旁	tíshǒupáng	hand
宀	宝盖	bǎogài	roof
忄	竖心旁	shùxīnpáng	mood
阝	左耳刀 右耳刀	zuǒ'ěrdāo (on left side) yòu'ěrdāo (on right side)	mountain county
艹	草字头	cǎozìtóu	grass
礻	示字旁	shìzìpáng	notify
衤	衣字旁	yīzìpáng	cloth
子	子字旁	zǐzìpáng	son, child
土	提土旁	títǔpáng	earth
口	口字旁	kǒuzìpáng	mouth
禾	禾木旁	hémùpáng	grain
日	日字旁	rìzìpáng	sun
月	月字旁	yuèzìpáng	moon
木	木字旁	mùzìpáng	wood
火	火字旁	huǒzìpáng	fire
灬	四点底	sìdiǎndǐ	fire
山	山字旁	shānzìpáng	mountain
纟/糸	绞丝旁	jiǎosīpáng	silk
钅/金	金字旁	jīnzìpáng	gold
罒	四字头	sìzìtóu	net

Lesson Three How Do You Do?

第三课 你 好

Dì-sān Kè Nǐ Hǎo

In this lesson you will learn how to do the following

- Greet people
- Introduce yourself
- Pose questions
- Invite people to do things with you

Grammar

- "好 hǎo" (good, well)
- "姓 xìng" (to be surnamed); "叫 jiào" (to call, to be called)
- "是 shì" (to be, to be the case)
- "也 yě" (also, too)
- "吗 ma" (question particle for yes-no questions)
- "呢 ne" (question particle for follow-up questions)
- "什么 shénme" (question word for "what" questions)
- "好吗 hǎo ma" (tag question: "OK?")

Culture Notes

- Greetings
- Conventional greetings in daily life

Dialogue

A: 钱民 Qián Mín　　**B:** 谢中 Xiè Zhōng

A: 你好[G1]！我叫[G2]钱民。
Nǐ hǎo[G1]! Wǒ jiào[G2] Qián Mín.

B: 你好！我姓[G2]谢，叫谢中。
Nǐ hǎo! Wǒ xìng[G2] Xiè, jiào Xiè Zhōng.

A: 我是[G3]美国人。你也[G4]是美国人吗[G5]？
Wǒ shì[G3] Měiguórén. Nǐ yě[G4] shì Měiguórén ma[G5]?

B: 我不是美国人，我是英国人。我是老师，你呢[G6]？
Wǒ bú shì Měiguórén, wǒ shì Yīngguórén. Wǒ shì lǎoshī, nǐ ne[G6]?

A: 我不是老师，我是学生。
Wǒ bú shì lǎoshī, wǒ shì xuésheng.

B: 你学什么[G7]？
Nǐ xué shénme[G7]?

A: 我学中文。你教什么？
Wǒ xué Zhōngwén. Nǐ jiāo shénme?

B: 我教英文。
Wǒ jiāo Yīngwén.

A: 我们一起去学校，好吗[G8]？
Wǒmen yìqǐ qù xuéxiào, hǎo ma[G8]?

B: 好。
Hǎo.

New Words

1	你好	nǐ hǎo	Phrase	How do you do?
	你	nǐ	Pron	you
	好	hǎo	Adj	good, OK, fine
2	我	wǒ	Pron	I, me
3	叫	jiào	V	to call, to be called
4	姓	xìng	V / N	to be surnamed; surname
5	是	shì	V	am, are, is, were, was; yes; certainly
6	美国人/美國人	Měiguórén	PropN	American (person)
	美国/美國	Měiguó	PropN	U.S.A.
	人	rén	N	person, people, humans
7	也	yě	Adv	also, too
8	吗/嗎	ma	Part	*turns a declarative sentence into a question*
9	不	bù	Adv	no, not
10	英国人 / 英國人	Yīngguórén	PropN	English, British
	英国/ 英國	Yīngguó	PropN	England, Britain, U.K.
11	老师/ 老師	lǎoshī	N	teacher
12	呢	ne	Part	*forms follow-up questions*
13	学生/ 學生	xuésheng	N	student
14	学 / 學	xué	V	to study
15	什么/ 甚麽	shénme	IntPron	what (in questions)
16	中文	Zhōngwén	PropN	Chinese (language)
17	教	jiāo	V	to teach
18	英文	Yīngwén	PropN	English (language)
19	我们/ 我們	wǒmen	Pron	we, us
20	一起	yìqǐ	Adv	together
21	去	qù	V	to go
22	学校/ 學校	xuéxiào	N	school

Re-enacting the Dialogue*

A: Qian Min **B: Xie Zhong**

A: How do you do? I'm Qian Min.

B: How do you do? My surname is Xie, my full name is Xie Zhong.

A: I'm American. Are you also American?

B: No, I'm not, I'm British. I'm a teacher, and you?

A: I'm not a teacher. I'm a student.

B: What do you study?

A: I study Chinese. What do you teach?

B: I teach English.

A: Let's go to school together, OK?

B: Fine.

---

* The dialogues are not reading exercises; they provide conversational material. For this reason, they are designed for you to be able to access them easily, with *Pinyin* provided along with vocabulary and grammatical explanations. A first step in trying to internalize the conversational material is to practice re-enacting the dialogues. To help you do this, a translation is provided. You can glance at the English to remind yourself of what you want to say, then try to say it, and finally, check yourself against the Chinese. The first time you do this, you will find it quite difficult; but by the third time, you should find yourself close to fluency. Once you reach that point, you will be much more successful in trying out variations on the basic themes in and out of class.

Grammar

▶ G1. "好 hǎo" (good, well)

"好 hǎo" is an adjective. In Chinese, adjectives function like verbs, so that "很好 hěn hǎo" (with the subject "understood") can mean "He's quite well" or "I'm quite well". As that example shows, adjectives can be modified by adverbs of degree, such as "很 hěn" (quite, very) or "也 yě" (also): "很好 hěn hǎo" (It's fine); "我们也好 wǒmen yě hǎo" (We're well too). "不 bù" (no, not) is also a kind of adverb. It negates adjectives (as well as other verbs): "不好 bù hǎo" ([It]'s not good; [He]'s not well).

▶ G2. "姓 xìng[1]" (to be surnamed); "叫 jiào" (to call, to be called)

"姓 xìng" introduces a surname. For example:

① 我姓谢。My surname is Xie.
Wǒ xìng Xiè.

② 你姓什么？What is your surname?
Nǐ xìng shénme?

③ A: 我姓谢，你姓什么？My surname's Xie. What's yours?
Wǒ xìng Xiè, nǐ xìng shénme?

B: 我也姓谢。I'm also surnamed Xie.
Wǒ yě xìng Xiè.

"叫 jiào" (to call, to be called) takes either a full name as object (Wǒ jiào Xiè Wéndé), or two syllables (the "míngzi") of a two syllable name (Wǒ jiào Wéndé).

④ A: 我叫钱英。你叫什么？My name is Qian Ying. What's yours?
Wǒ jiào Qián Yīng. Nǐ jiào shénme?

B: 我叫 Tom。My name is Tom.
Wǒ jiào Tom.

▶ G3. "是 shì" (to be, to be the case)

"是 shì" is one of the most common of Chinese verbs, meaning "to be" or "to be the case". Typically it connects two nouns (or noun phrases) to indicate identity (=) or class inclusion (⊃). In that role, it is often unstressed and therefore untoned (with "qīngshēng").

① 我是学生。I'm a student.
Wǒ shì xuésheng.

② 我是美国人。I'm American.
Wǒ shì Měiguórén.

[1] "姓 xìng", and polite forms such as "贵姓 guìxìng", which makes use of the honorific "guì" (be valued).

Like all verbs (and in fact, like almost all words) in Chinese, "是 shì" does not change its form for tense, number, person, mood or any other of the grammatical categories so familiar to students of European languages. In different contexts, "是 shì" may be translated as "be, am, are, is, was, were". Chinese has its complexities, but grammatical form is not one of them.

The negative of "是 shì" is formed with "不 bù", just as with adjectives: "不是 bú shì".

③ 我不是老师，我是学生。I'm not a teacher. I'm a student.
Wǒ bú shì lǎoshī, wǒ shì xuésheng.

"是 shì", "不是 bú shì", "是吗 shì ma" and so on, are common as expressions of agreement, disagreement, or questioning. In such cases, "是 shì" is often best translated as "be the case; right; correct": "是吗? Shì ma?" (Is [that] so?) "是。Shì." ([It] is.)

▶ G4. "也 yě" (also, too)

"也 yě" is also an adverb. It expresses inclusion (like English "also, too, as well").

① 我也是美国人。I'm American too.
Wǒ yě shì Měiguórén.

② 你也去学校。You're also going to the school.
Nǐ yě qù xuéxiào.

Notice that some of the English equivalents of "也 yě" have quite different properties. "Also", for example, when it means "in addition" or "moreover" can appear before the subject – often at the beginning of the sentence: "Also – I have to go to school." "也 yě" is more constrained. It is an adverb and like other adverbs in Chinese, appears only directly before the verb or before another adverb. English also allows sentences like "Me too", where "too" appears without a verb of any kind. Again, because "也 yě" is an adverb and adverbs generally require an explicit verb, Chinese has to express "me too" more specifically, as "我也是 Wǒ yě shì" (I am too) or "我也去 Wǒ yě qù" (I'm going too).

▶ G5. "吗 ma" (question particle for yes-no questions)

Yes-no questions (i.e. questions that seek yes or no answers) are formed by adding a question particle "吗 ma" to a statement. ("Particles" in Chinese are bound and toneless.)

Subject + Predicate + 吗 ma?

① 你也是英国人吗？Are you English too?
Nǐ yě shì Yīngguórén ma?

Notice that there is no rearrangement of words in questions as there would be in English. The order of words in the response is the same as that in the question. In general, questions with "吗 ma" are spoken with slightly rising question intonation. In fact, in the right contexts, it is possible to ask such questions with intonation alone, without the final particle. Responses tend to repeat the verb, either alone in the affirmative, or with "不 bù" in the negative:

② A：你也去学校吗？Are you also going to school? (Question)
Nǐ yě qù xuéxiào ma?

B1：我也去学校。Yes, I am. (Affirmative answer)
Wǒ yě qù xuéxiào.

B2：不去。/我不去学校。No. / No, I'm not. (Negative answer)
Bú qù. / Wǒ bú qù xuéxiào.

▶ G6. "呢 ne" (question particle for follow-up questions)

The particle "呢 ne" is used in follow-up questions:

Subject_1 + Predicate, Subject_2 + 呢 ne?

我是老师，你呢？I'm a teacher. How about you?
Wǒ shì lǎoshī, nǐ ne?

▶ G7. "什么 shénme" (question word for "what" questions)

Notice that "什么 shénme" is pronounced "shémme" or "shéme" in normal speech. (The reason the first syllable is written with an "n" is because the character "什" is pronounced "shen" in citation form.) "什么 shénme" is a question word (or more formally, an interrogative pronoun) functioning like English "what". However, unlike the English case where the question word often does not appear in the same place as the information provided in the response (What do you teach? / I teach English.), in Chinese, the two occupy the same position in sentence structure (as if saying "You teach what?" / "I teach English.").

A：你教什么？What do you teach?
Nǐ jiāo shénme?

B：我教英文。I teach English.
Wǒ jiāo Yīngwén.

▶ G8. "好吗 hǎo ma" (tag question: "OK?")

"好吗 hǎo ma" may be added to a statement as a tag question, seeking confirmation or agreement: "OK?" "Is that good?"

A：我们一起去学校，好吗？Let's go to school together, OK?
Wǒmen yìqǐ qù xuéxiào, hǎo ma?

B：好，我们一起去。Fine. Let's go together.
Hǎo, wǒmen yìqǐ qù.

Consolidation & Practice

1. Complete the following dialogues, following the sense of the English provided and incorporating the phrase "(很) 好 (hěn) hǎo"

(1) A：你好！
Nǐ hǎo!

B：________________！(How do you do?)

(2) A：你好吗？
Nǐ hǎo ma?

B：________________，你呢？(I'm fine.)

________________, nǐ ne?

A：____________________！(I'm fine, too.)

(3) A：我们一起学中文，好吗？
Wǒmen yìqǐ xué Zhōngwén, hǎo ma?

B：____________________！(Great!)

2. Complete the following sentences, using "是 shì" and whatever else is indicated

(1) 我 ______________。(name)

Wǒ ______________.

(2) 我 _________ 美国人。

Wǒ _________ Měiguórén.

(3) 老师 _________ 英国人。

Lǎoshī _________ Yīngguórén.

(4) 我 _________ 中国人。(not)

Wǒ _________ Zhōngguórén.

(5) 我 _________ 学生，我 _________ 老师。(not a teacher)

Wǒ _________ xuésheng, wǒ _________ lǎoshī.

3. Interview a classmate by asking questions with "姓 xìng" and "叫 jiào"

(1) 你的老师
(2) 你的中国朋友（péngyou, friend）
(3) 你爸爸（bàba, dad）
(4) 你妈妈（māma, mom）
(5) 你哥哥（gēge, elder brother）
(6) 你姐姐（jiějie, elder sister）
(7) 你弟弟（dìdi, younger brother）
(8) 你妹妹（mèimei, younger sister）

4. Insert "也 yě" in the correct place

(1) ________ 我 ________ 很好 ________。
________ wǒ ________ hěn hǎo ________ .
(2) ________ 我 ________ 是 ________ 美国人。
________ wǒ ________ shì ________ Měiguórén.
(3) ________ 我学中文，________ 教 ________ 英文。
________ wǒ xué Zhōngwén, ________ jiāo ________ Yīngwén.
(4) ________ 我 ________ 不 ________ 是老师 ________。
________ wǒ ________ bù ________ shì lǎoshī ________.

5. Turn the following sentences into questions with "吗 ma"

(1) 你好。→
Nǐ hǎo.

(2) 谢中也学英文。→
Xiè Zhōng yě xué Yīngwén.

(3) 老师好！→
Lǎoshī hǎo!

(4) 钱民好。→
Qián Mín hǎo.

(5) 我们一起去学校。→
Wǒmen yìqǐ qù xuéxiào.

6. Ask follow-up questions with "呢 ne"

(1) 我很好，____________?
Wǒ hěn hǎo, ____________?

(2) 我是谢中，____________?
Wǒ shì Xiè Zhōng, ____________?

(3) 我去学校，____________?
Wǒ qù xuéxiào, ____________?

(4) 我教英文，____________?
Wǒ jiāo Yīngwén, ____________?

7. Make tag questions with "好吗 hǎo ma"

(1) Check with your classmate to see if you can study together.
(2) Check with your classmate to see if you can go to school together.
(3) Check with your classmate to see if you can go together to ask the teacher some questions. (wèn, to ask)

8. Ask questions with "什么 shénme", and answer the questions based on the given English

(1) A：你教 ____________?
Nǐ jiāo ____________?
B：我教 ____________。(English)
Wǒ jiāo ____________.

(2) A：你学 ____________?
Nǐ xué ____________?
B：我学 ____________。(Chinese)
Wǒ xué ____________.

(3) A：谢中是 ____________ 老师？
Xiè Zhōng shì ____________ lǎoshī?
B：谢中是 ____________ 老师。(English)
Xiè Zhōng shì ____________ lǎoshī.

(4) A：钱民去 ____________ 学校？
Qián Mín qù ____________ xuéxiào?
B：钱民去 ____________ 学校。(Chinese)
Qián Mín qù ____________ xuéxiào.

Pronunciation Notes

1. Tonal modification (I): 3 + 3 → 2 + 3

If a third tone is followed by another third tone in close juncture, the first third tone becomes a second (rising):

Nǐ hǎo. → Ní hǎo. (Hi)		jǐ diǎn → jí diǎn (what time)	
hěn hǎo → hén hǎo (fine)		yěxǔ → yéxǔ (maybe)	

2. Tone changes (I): "不 bù" (no, not)

"不 bù" has two possible tones, depending on context.

a. When it is followed by a fourth tone, it is second (rising): bú.

bú qù	不去	not go
bú yào	不要	not want
bú duì	不对	not correct
bú shì	不是	not the case

b. Otherwise – alone or followed by a first, second or third tone, it is fourth tone (falling): bù.

bù	不	no
bù chī	不吃	not eat
bù xué	不学	not study
bù hǎo	不好	not good

Pronunciation Exercises

1. Read the following compounds and indicate the changed tones

hěn shǎo (very few)	ǎixiǎo (short)	yǔfǎ (grammar)
zuǒshǒu (left hand)	yǔsǎn (umbrella)	dǎrǎo (to trouble)
gǔdǒng (antiques)	shuǐguǒ (fruit)	hěn lǎo (very old)
xǐ shǒu (to wash hand)	suǒyǐ (therefore)	zhǐhǎo (have to)

2. Read these common expressions aloud

谢谢。Thank you.
Xièxie.

不客气 You're welcome./ Not at all.
Bú kèqi.

对不起。I'm sorry.
Duìbuqǐ.

没关系。Never mind.
Méi guānxi.

再见。Goodbye.
Zàijiàn.

我忘了。I forgot.
Wǒ wàng le.

我不知道。I don't know.
Wǒ bù zhīdào.

我听不懂。I don't understand what you said.
Wǒ tīng bu dǒng.

请说慢一点儿。Speak more slowly, please.
Qǐng shuō màn yìdiǎnr.

请再说一遍。Please say it again. / Please repeat.
Qǐng zài shuō yí biàn.

对。That's correct.
Duì.

不对。That's not right.
Bú duì.

不要了。I don't want any more.
Bú yào le.

好吃！Delicious!
Hǎochī!

请帮帮忙。Could you give me a hand please?
Qǐng bāngbang máng.

Listening Comprehension

1. Listen to the names of the countries, then write them in *Pinyin* (with tones, of course)

(1) ______ (9) ______
(2) ______ (10) ______
(3) ______ (11) ______
(4) ______ (12) ______
(5) ______ (13) ______
(6) ______ (14) ______
(7) ______ (15) ______
(8) ______

2. Listen to the conversation on the CD and answer the questions

(1) What is the relationship between the two people in the conversation?

- A. They are friends.
- B. They are student and teacher.
- C. They are classmates.

(2) What is true about these two people?

- A. They both study Chinese.
- B. They both teach English.
- C. They go to the same school.

3. Listen to the passage on the CD

(1) Circle True or False, based on what you hear

	T	F
① They are both students.		
② None of them is Chinese.		
③ One teaches the other.		
④ Qian Min is teaching Xie Zhong how to speak English.		
⑤ They are going to the same place.		

(2) Based on the passage, answer the following questions

① What is the nationality of the two people?
② What are each of them doing in China?
③ Where do Xie Zhong's students come from?
④ Where are they going together?
⑤ Why doesn't Qian Min learn English from Xie Zhong?

Communication Activities

Pair Work/Role Play

Scenario I: On the first day of class, you are excited and want to get to know all your classmates. Greet each of them and find out what their Chinese names are. Use "好 hǎo", "姓 xìng", and "叫 jiào".

Scenario II: In pairs, take the part of an American student who is studying Chinese and a British student who is teaching English. You are meeting for the first time (in Beijing). Greet each other, introduce yourselves, then explain what you do in Beijing. Use "姓 xìng", "叫 jiào", "是 shì", "去 qù", "教 jiāo", "不 bù", and "也 yě"。

Scenario III: Imagine you have run into one of your Chinese friends on campus. Greet him/her, and ask three or four questions using "什么 shénme", "吗 ma", "呢 ne". Then suggest that the two of you go together to the school, and have a brief exchange, making use of "好吗 hǎo ma".

Review Exercises

I. Match the words in the left-hand list with appropriate words in the right-hand list

(1) 很 hěn	A. 中文 Zhōngwén
(2) 我是 wǒ shì	B. 学校 xuéxiào
(3) 学 xué	C. 什么 shénme
(4) 去 qù	D. 好 hǎo
(5) 教 jiāo	E. 老师 lǎoshī
(6) 我不是 wǒ bú shì	F. 美国人 Měiguórén
(7) 叫 jiào	G. 谢 Xiè
(8) 姓 xìng	H. 谢英 Xiè Yīng

II. Complete the following dialogues by selecting the question words that best fits the context: "吗 ma", "呢 ne", "好吗 hǎo ma", or "什么 shénme"

1. A：我姓谢，叫谢中。你姓 ______________?
   Wǒ xìng Xiè, jiào Xiè Zhōng. Nǐ xìng ____________?

   B：我姓钱，叫钱英。我学中文，你也学中文 ___________?
   Wǒ xìng Qián, jiào Qián Yīng. Wǒ xué Zhōngwén, nǐ yě xué Zhōngwén ___________?

   A：我不学中文, 我学英文。
   Wǒ bù xué Zhōngwén, wǒ xué Yīngwén.

2. A：____?

B：我很好。你________？
Wǒ hěn hǎo. Nǐ ________?

A：我也很好。
Wǒ yě hěn hǎo.

3\. A：谢老师____________________？
Xiè lǎoshī ____________________?

B：谢老师教英文，钱老师________________？
Xiè lǎoshī jiāo Yīngwén, Qián lǎoshī ________________?

A：钱老师也教英文。
Qián lǎoshī yě jiāo Yīngwén.

4\. A：你学中文________________？
Nǐ xué Zhōngwén ________________?

B：我学中文，________________？
Wǒ xué Zhōngwén, ________________?

A：我也学中文，我们一起学中文，________________？
Wǒ yě xué Zhōngwén, wǒmen yìqǐ xué Zhōngwén, ________________?

B：好。
Hǎo.

III. Answer the questions below following the English cues

1\. A：你是学生吗？
Nǐ shì xuésheng ma?

B：________________________。(No.)

2\. A：你去学校吗？
Nǐ qù xuéxiào ma?

B：________________________？(Yes, together with…, OK?)

3\. A：我也学中文。
Wǒ yě xué Zhōngwén.

B：________________________？(study together, OK?)

IV. Complete the following sentences with “也 yě”, “好 hǎo”, “是 shì”, or “不是 bú shì”

1\. A：我是英国人，你呢？
Wǒ shì Yīngguórén, nǐ ne?

B：________________________________。

2. A：你是老师吗？
Nǐ shì lǎoshī ma?

B：________________________________。

3. A：我很好，你呢？
Wǒ hěn hǎo, nǐ ne?

B：________________________________。

4. A：我们一起学中文，好吗？
Wǒmen yìqǐ xué Zhōngwén, hǎo ma?

B：________________________________。

V. Complete the following dialogue based on the English cues

A：你好！我__________钱中，你叫__________？(am, what)
Nǐ hǎo！Wǒ __________ Qián Zhōng, nǐ jiào __________?

B：__________________钱英。(My name is…)
__________________ Qián Yīng.

A：__________英国人__________？(Are you British?)
__________ Yīngguórén __________?

B：不是，我是美国人。
Bú shì, wǒ shì Měiguórén.

A：你学中文吗？
Nǐ xué Zhōngwén ma?

B：______________ (Yes.)

A：我也学中文。中国老师教我。
Wǒ yě xué Zhōngwén. Zhōngguó lǎoshī jiāo wǒ.

B：我的老师______________中国人。(is also)
Wǒ de lǎoshī ______________ Zhōngguórén.

A：我也教中国老师学英文。
Wǒ yě jiāo Zhōngguó lǎoshī xué Yīngwén.

B：是吗？中国老师是好学生吗？
Shì ma? Zhōngguó lǎoshī shì hǎo xuésheng ma?

A：是。我__________好老师。 (am also)
Shì. Wǒ __________ hǎo lǎoshī.

VI. Interview at least two of your classmates and report the information to the class. Your interview and report should be conducted in Chinese, and should include the following information

1. Names (including family names and given names).

2. How the classmates are (feeling) at the time of the interview.

3. Their status (teacher, student, etc.) and what they do (teach English, etc.).

Culture Notes

1. Greetings

Chinese utter greetings when they meet, or they may shake hands; but they do not usually kiss or hug (unless, occasionally, to anticipate foreign customs).

2. Conventional greetings in daily life

In daily life in China, when neighbors, friends, or colleagues greet each other, they do not usually say "你好 nǐ hǎo" (which can be translated as "Hi") but rather something like: "你/您吃饭了吗? Nǐ / Nín chī fàn le ma?" (Have you eaten yet?) "你/您去哪儿? Nǐ / Nín qù nǎr?" (Where are you going?). The younger generation may regard such questions as too intrusive, in which case they might say: "你/您最近忙吗? Nǐ / Nín zuìjìn máng ma?" (Are you busy these days?) or "天气真热啊! Tiānqì zhēn rè a!" (It's really hot today!). These conventional gambits can be answered in a perfunctory way: "嗯，很忙。Ǹg, hěn máng." (Uhuh, I am.) "嗯，真热。Ǹg, zhēn rè." (Uhuh, it sure is.)

Lesson Four　Counting

第四课　计 算

Dì-sì Kè　　Jìsuàn

In this lesson you will learn how to do the following

- Count in Chinese
- Buy fruit

Grammar

- Numbers
- Verbs in series
- Measure words
- "二 èr" and "两 liǎng" (two)
- The adverb "还 hái" (still, yet, in addition, also, too)
- The question word "多少 duōshao" (how much, how many)
- When "零 líng" (zero) and "一 yī" (one) need to be expressed

Culture Notes

- Formal written numbers
- Chinese hand numbers
- Lucky and unlucky numbers
- Using an abacus

Chant

(Counting rhymes, and buying fruit)

一，二，三，四，五，六，七[G1]，
Yī, èr, sān, sì, wǔ, liù, qī[G1],

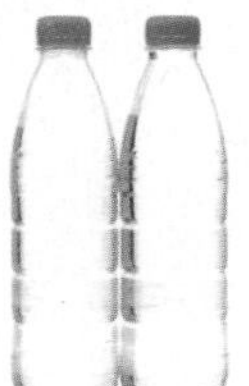

我去商店买东西[G2]。
wǒ qù shāngdiàn mǎi dōngxi[G2].

一瓶[G3]可乐，两[G4]瓶水，
Yì píng[G3] kělè, liǎng[G4] píng shuǐ,

三斤[1]葡萄，四个[2]梨；
sān jīn[1] pútao, sì ge[2] lí;

五个苹果，六个桃，
wǔ ge píngguǒ, liù ge táo,

七个橘子，八两[1]草莓；
qī ge júzi, bā liǎng[1] cǎoméi;

还[G5]要九根香蕉，十片西瓜。
hái[G5] yào jiǔ gēn xiāngjiāo, shí piàn xīguā.

一共[3]多少[G6]钱？
Yígòng[3] duōshao[G6] qián?

一百一十块[4]零[G7]七毛[4]。
Yìbǎi yīshí kuài[4] líng[G7] qī máo[4].

Notes

1. "斤 jīn" (a "catty"; 0.5 kilogram or 10 liǎng) and "两 liǎng" (often translated "ounce"; 0.05 kilogram) are Chinese units of weight that are often used in markets. Kilogram is "公斤 gōngjīn".
2. "个 gè", with neutral tone in unstressed position (yí ge), is the most frequently used measure word (see G3 behind). It is also a default measure, used when a more specific measure word is not required, or not known.
3. "一共 yígòng" (altogether) is a "moveable adverb". Moveable adverbs have freer distribution than regular adverbs, not requiring a verb, for example, "一共 yígòng" frequently occurs immediately before numbers: "一共两块五 yígòng liǎng kuài wǔ" (two fifty altogether).
4. There are eight denominations of paper currency and six values of coins. The paper currency denominations are 100 *yuan* (¥ 100), 50 *yuan* (¥ 50), 20 *yuan* (¥ 20), 10 *yuan* (¥ 10), 5 *yuan* (¥ 5), 1 *yuan* (¥ 1), 5 *jiao* (¥ 0.5), and 1 *jiao* (¥ 0.1). The coins are 1 *yuan* (¥ 1), 5 *jiao* (¥ 0.5), 1 *jiao* (¥ 0.1), 5 *fen* (¥ 0.05), 2 *fen* (¥ 0.02), and 1 *fen* (¥ 0.01). The dimensions of paper currency and of coins are scaled, large to small, according to their denominations.

New Words

1	计算/計算	jìsuàn	V	to count, to calculate
2	一	yī	Num	one
3	二	èr	Num	two
4	三	sān	Num	three
5	四	sì	Num	four
6	五	wǔ	Num	five
7	六	liù	Num	six
8	七	qī	Num	seven
9	商店	shāngdiàn	N	shop, store
10	买东西/買東西	mǎi dōngxi	Phrase	to go shopping
	买/買	mǎi	V	to buy
	东西/東西	dōngxi	N	things
11	瓶	píng	N	bottle
12	可乐/可樂	kělè	N	cola
13	两/兩	liǎng	Num	two
14	水	shuǐ	N	water
15	斤	jīn	Meas	*0.5 kilo* (*unit of weight* = 10 两 liǎng)
16	葡萄	pútao	N	grape
17	个/個	gè	Meas	*the most common measure word, used for various things and for people*
18	梨	lí	N	pear
19	苹果/蘋果	píngguǒ	N	apple
20	桃	táo	N	peach
21	橘子	júzi	N	orange, tangerine
22	八	bā	Num	eight
23	两/兩	liǎng	Meas	*a unit of weight* (*0.05 kilo or 1.33 ounces*)
24	草莓	cǎoméi	N	strawberry
25	还/還	hái	Adv	also, still, even more, in addition

26	要	yào	V	to want, to need (*the negative is "*不要 bú yào*", not want to*)
27	九	jiǔ	Num	nine
28	根	gēn	Meas	*used for long, thin objects*
29	香蕉	xiāngjiāo	N	banana
30	十	shí	Num	ten
31	片	piàn	Meas	piece, slice, flakes
32	西瓜	xīguā	N	watermelon
33	一共	yígòng	Adv	altogether
34	多少	duōshao	IntPron	how much, how many
	多	duō	Adj	a lot, many, more than
	少	shǎo	Adj	little, a few
35	钱/錢	qián	N	money, cash
36	百	bǎi	Num	hundred
37	块/塊	kuài	Meas	*unit of Chinese currency, used colloquially for yuan*
38	零	líng	Num	zero
39	毛	máo	Meas	*unit of Chinese currency, used colloquially for 10 cents*

The Chant in English

(Counting rhymes, and buying fruit)

One, two, three, four, five, six, seven.
I'm going to the store to buy some things:
One bottle of cola and two bottles of water,
three catties of grapes and four pears;
five apples and six peaches,
seven oranges and eight ounces of strawberries;
I also want nine bananas and ten pieces ofwatermelon.
How much is that altogether?
One hundred ten *yuan* and seventy *fen*.

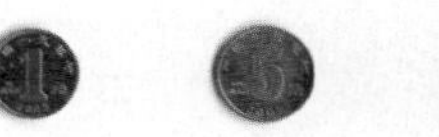

Grammar

▶ G1. Numbers

(1) The basic numbers are:

yī 一　　èr 二 / liǎng 两　　sān 三　　sì 四　　wǔ 五
liù 六　　qī 七　　bā 八　　jiǔ 九　　shí 十
bǎi 百 (100)　　qiān 千 (1,000)　　wàn 万 (10,000)
yì 亿 (100 million)

(2) Other numbers are formed by combinations of the basic numbers plus "零 líng".

shíyī 十一　　èrshí 二十　　sānshíwǔ 三十五
yìbǎi sì(shí) 一百四（十）　　wǔqiān líng liùshí 五千零六十
yíwàn qīqiān bābǎi jiǔ(shí) 一万七千八百九（十）

Details:

a. The teens (11-19) are formed with "十 shí" (10) plus basic numbers:

shíyī 十一　　shíliù 十六　　shíjiǔ 十九

b. Multiples of ten, are formed with basic numbers plus "十 shí":

èrshí 二十　　sānshí 三十　　sìshí 四十……jiǔshí 九十

c. The rest of the numbers are formed by combining a. and b.:

èrshíyī 二十一　　sānshí'èr 三十二　　sìshíliù 四十六……jiǔshíjiǔ 九十九

(3) "百 bǎi" (hundred)

a. Multiples of hundred are formed with basic numbers plus "百 bǎi" (hundred):

èrbǎi 二百　　sānbǎi 三百　　jiǔbǎi 九百

b. The numbers from 101 to 109 require "零 líng" (zero) to fill the empty tens slot:

103	yìbǎi líng sān	一百零三
109.70 *yuan*	yìbǎi líng jiǔ kuài qī	一百零九块七

(4) Large numbers are read from large units to small. Large numbers are:

yì 亿 (a hundred million)
qiānwàn 千万 (ten million)
bǎiwàn 百万 (million)

shíwàn 十万 (hundred thousand)

wàn 万 (ten thousand)

qiān 千 (thousand)

bǎi 百 (hundred)

shí 十 (ten)

gè 个 (unit)

They are read as in English, except that Chinese never expresses a larger unit in terms of a smaller one if the larger one is available: never "sixteen hundred", always "one thousand six hundred". However, above "万 wàn" (at least until "亿 yì" – 100 million), higher units have to be expressed in terms of "万 wàn" (ten thousand) : "百万 bǎiwàn" (million, i.e., 100 × 10000), etc. (Even 100 million can be expressed as "万万 wànwàn" as well as "亿 yì".)

3,895: sānqiān bābǎi jiǔshíwǔ
3 千 8 百 9 十 5

▶ G2. Verbs in series

In the sentence "我去商店买东西 Wǒ qù shāngdiàn mǎi dōngxi", a single subject performs two actions, in temporal order – one after the other: "去商店 qù shāngdiàn" (to go to a store) and "买东西 mǎi dōngxi" (to buy things). The English equivalent (I'm going to the store to buy some things) requires the explicit connector "to", which shows that the second verb is not the main verb (i.e., it cannot change tense). Chinese has quite a different structure. Chinese simply juxtaposes the two verb phrases with no intervening words, in a pattern called "verbs in series". Verbs in series are a characteristic feature of Chinese sentence organization. Notice that a single subject applies to both the verb phrases (which often have the form of verb+object – VO).

Subject	+	VO	+	VO.
我 Wǒ		去商店 qù shāngdiàn		买东西。 mǎi dōngxi.

▶ G3. Measure words

English distinguishes between count nouns that can be counted directly (apples, ideas, days, etc.) and non-count nouns that can only be counted if they are measured (a canister of air, a bottle of water, an item of information, etc.). For Chinese, all nouns are non-count and require a measure word to be counted, even those cases that would be count nouns in English: "三个苹果 sān ge píngguǒ" (three apples); "八根香蕉 bā gēn xiāngjiāo" (eight bananas).

All measure words are bound forms (BFs), and appear only with numbers or, as you will see later, demonstratives, like "this" and "that". In appropriate contexts, a measure word can stand in for a noun: "八根 bā gēn" (eight of them [bananas understood]).

In addition to measure words for nouns, there are also verbal measure words, that are used for counting frequency of actions, e.g., "三次 sān cì" (three times). You will see examples of these in subsequent lessons.

The measure words in this lesson are: "瓶 píng" (bottle); "个 gè", for people, and a host of other nouns, including certain fruits; and "根 gēn", mostly for nouns that denote long, thin things. "个 gè" is a default measure, used when a more specific measure is not needed, or not know.

▶ G4. "二 èr" and "两 liǎng" (two)

"Two" is "二 èr" in counting, but is "两 liǎng" before measure words (a little bit like English "two" and "a couple of"). Thus, in the dialogue, you have: "两瓶水 liǎng píng shuǐ". "二 èr" is a free form (as in counting), but "两 liǎng", like all measure words, is bound.

"二 èr" is usual in sequences of numbers, such as house numbers like "二三零 èr-sān-líng" (230) or telephone numbers, like "二零三二八八四 èr-líng-sān-èr-bā-bā-sì". When two is part of a large number, such as 22 or 102, it is still "二 èr", even when followed by a measure word – after all, "两 liǎng" is "two" and 22 is not 2. So: "两个人 liǎng ge rén" (two people), but "二十二个人 èrshí'èr ge rén" (22 people), and "一百四十二个苹果 yìbǎi sìshí'èr ge píngguǒ" (142 apples).

"二 èr" is also used in the names of months, and in other places where the meaning is "second" not "two":

èryuè	二月	February	èrjiě	二姐	second sister
èr céng	二层	second floor	dì-èr	第二	second

Contrast "二层 èr céng" (second floor) with "两层 liǎng céng" (two floors): "层 céng" (floor) is a measure word only in the second case, where it is counting the number of floors.

There are a few cases of high numbers when either "二 èr" or "两 liǎng" can be used:

(1) For the numbers 200, 2,000, and 20,000, etc., either "二 èr" or "两 liǎng" can be used, with northern and southern Chinese speakers having different preferences:

200	èrbǎi 二百	liǎngbǎi 两百
2,000	èrqiān 二千	liǎngqiān 两千
20,000	èrwàn 二万	liǎngwàn 两万

(2) With measure words of length, capacity (volume) or weight, both "二 èr" and "两 liǎng" are used, depending on region, and personal preferences:

Two *jin* (weight): liǎng jīn 两斤 èr jīn 二斤

Twenty *mao* (always counted in "dimes"): liǎng máo 两毛 èr máo 二毛

▶ G5. The adverb "还 hái" (still, yet, in addition, also, too)

"还 hái" is a common adverb with the general meaning of "even up to this time", often corresponding to English adverbs such as "still", "yet", or "also":

① A：你好吗？How are you?
Nǐ hǎo ma?

B：还好。Still OK.
Hái hǎo.

② A：你还要什么？ What else do you want?
Nǐ hái yào shénme?

B：还要一斤草莓。I also want a catty of strawberries.
Hái yào yì jīn cǎoméi.

"还 hái" should be distinguished from the adverb "也 yě", introduced in Lesson 3. The distinction can be illustrated by the following pair of sentences:

③ 我也要买东西。I too want to do some shopping. ("just as you do")
Wǒ yě yào mǎi dōngxi.

④ 我还要买东西。I need to do some shopping, too. ("in addition to other things")
Wǒ hái yào mǎi dōngxi.

▶ G6. The question word "多少 duōshao" (how much, how many)

"多少 duōshao", the question word for quantity, contains the roots "多 duō" (a lot, many) and "少 shǎo" (a few) – the latter with neutral tone. As with other question words in Chinese, it is not fronted, but rather, remains in the position where the amount would appear in a statement:

A：要多少？ How many do you want?
Yào duōshao?

B：要二十五个。I'd like 25 of them.
Yào èrshíwǔ ge.

"多少 duōshao" may modify measure words (cf. "瓶 píng", below); but if a noun is available, the measure word will usually be omitted:

Duōshao píng?	多少瓶？	How many bottles (of something)?
Duōshao qián?	多少钱？	How much money?
Duōshao xuésheng?	多少学生？	How many students?
Duōshao Hànzì?	多少汉字？	How many characters?

▶ G7. When "零 líng" (zero) and "一 yī" (one) need to be expressed

(1) "零 líng" (zero) in numbers

"零 líng" is used in numbers (including prices) whenever one or both of the tens or hundreds slots are empty, but not the last slot – the units: 201, but not 200; ¥ 3.05, but not ¥ 3.50.

301	sānbǎi líng yī	三百零一
¥ 10.08	shí kuài líng bā fēn	十块零八分

For numbers in the thousands (with "千 qiān") or ten thousands (with "万 wàn"), when there is only one empty slot, "零 líng" is not required (as with the first of the two zeroes below):

30,102	sānwàn yībǎi líng èr	三万一百零二

However, when such numbers contain two empty slots in succession, then “零 líng” is included, but only once:

50,067	wǔwàn líng liùshíqī	五万零六十七

(2) “一 yī” (one) in numbers

As you know, the number ten is read “十 shí” in citation. However, in large numbers ending in 10 (210, 1210, etc.), the tens units are read “一十 yīshí”:

213	èrbǎi yīshísān	二百一十三
3,516	sānqiān wǔbǎi yīshíliù	三千五百一十六

Consolidation & Practice

1. Practice with numbers

(1) Recite the numbers 0 to 10 aloud, forwards and backwards

0	líng	零	4	sì	四	8	bā	八
1	yī	一	5	wǔ	五	9	jiǔ	九
2	èr	二	6	liù	六	10	shí	十
3	sān	三	7	qī	七			

(2) Recite the multiples of ten aloud

20	èrshí	二十	60	liùshí	六十
30	sānshí	三十	70	qīshí	七十
40	sìshí	四十	80	bāshí	八十
50	wǔshí	五十	90	jiǔshí	九十

(3) Intermediate numbers

11	shíyī	十一
21	èrshíyī	二十一
34	sānshísì	三十四
42	sìshí'èr	四十二

And continue to sample numbers up to 99

(4) Numbers above a hundred

101	yìbǎi líng yī	一百零一
102	yìbǎi líng èr	一百零二
105	yìbǎi líng wǔ	一百零五
202	èrbǎi líng èr	二百零二
303	sānbǎi líng sān	三百零三

Continue with 404, 506, etc.

(5) Counting from a hundred in tens and units

111	yìbǎi yīshíyī	一百一十一
112	yìbǎi yīshí'èr	一百一十二
116	yìbǎi yīshíliù	一百一十六

122	yìbǎi èrshí'èr	一百二十二

Continue sampling: 132, 145, 163, etc.

(6) Two hundred up to a thousand

200	èrbǎi	二百
212	èrbǎi yīshí'èr	二百一十二
371	sānbǎi qīshíyī	三百七十一
537	wǔbǎi sānshíqī	五百三十七
699	liùbǎi jiǔshíjiǔ	六百九十九
747	qībǎi sìshíqī	七百四十七
862	bābǎi liùshí'èr	八百六十二
999	jiǔbǎi jiǔshíjiǔ	九百九十九
1,000	yìqiān	一千

(7) Try reading these large numbers aloud

6,440   2,195   10,420   13,444   24,000   1,030   8,475

2. Practice using verbs in series by rearranging the given phrases based on the English meaning

(1) 商店　我去　买东西 (I'm going to the store to buy things.)
shāngdiàn wǒ qù mǎi dōngxi

→ ……………………………………………………………………

(2) 去学校　学中文　他 (He's going to school to learn Chinese.)
qù xuéxiào xué Zhōngwén tā

→ ……………………………………………………………………

(3) 老师　买苹果　去商店 (The teacher is going to the store to buy apples.)
lǎoshī mǎi píngguǒ qù shāngdiàn

→ ……………………………………………………………………

(4) 教英文　英国老师　去学校
jiāo Yīngwén Yīngguó lǎoshī qù xuéxiào
(The English teacher is going to the school to teach English.)

→ ……………………………………………………………………

(5) 买橘子　吗　去商店　你 (Are you going to the store to buy oranges?)
mǎi júzi ma qù shāngdiàn nǐ

→ ……………………………………………………………………

3. Fill in the blanks with the appropriate measure word: 瓶 píng, 个 ge, 片 piàn, 两 liǎng, 斤 jīn, 块 kuài, 根 gēn

(1) 我买三______可乐，一______水。
Wǒ mǎi sān ______ kělè, yì ______ shuǐ.

(2) 我要四______橘子，五______桃。
Wǒ yào sì ______ júzi, wǔ ______ táo.

(3) A：你要多少草莓？ B：我要六______草莓。
Nǐ yào duōshao cǎoméi? Wǒ yào liù ______ cǎoméi.

(4) A：你要多少葡萄？ B：我要一______葡萄。
Nǐ yào duōshao pútao? Wǒ yào yì ______ pútao.

(5) 美国学生要买七______梨，三______香蕉。
Měiguó xuésheng yào mǎi qī ______ lí, sān ______ xiāngjiāo.

(6) 我也要七______梨。
Wǒ yě yào qī ______ lí.

(7) 我还要一______西瓜，两______苹果。
Wǒ hái yào yí ______ xīguā, liǎng ______ píngguǒ.

4. Practice using “二 èr” versus “两 liǎng”

(1) 二 èr

èryuè	二月	February
èr céng	二层	second floor
èrjiě	二姐	second sister
èr lóu	二楼	second floor or second building
èr mén	二门	second door
èr bān	二班	second section
dì-èr	第二	second

(2) 两 liǎng

liǎng ge rén	两个人	two people
liǎng kuài qián	两块钱	two dollars
liǎng céng lóu	两层楼	a two story building
liǎng píng shuǐ	两瓶水	two bottles of water
liǎng bēi píjiǔ	两杯啤酒	two glasses of beer

liǎng ge mén	两个门	two doors

(3) "两 liǎng" or "二 èr"

èrbǎi	二百	liǎngbǎi	两百
èrqiān	二千	liǎngqiān	两千
èrwàn	二万	liǎngwàn	两万

5. In the following sentences, place a caret (^) where the adverb "还 hái" can be inserted

(1) 她 要 买 东西。
Tā yào mǎi dōngxi.

(2) 我 要 一个 西瓜。
Wǒ yào yí ge xīguā.

(3) 学生 要 去 商店。
Xuésheng yào qù shāngdiàn.

(4) 我 买 两个 苹果，要 一个 西瓜。
Wǒ mǎi liǎng ge píngguǒ, yào yí ge xīguā.

(5) 我 买 三瓶 水，要 六瓶 可乐。
Wǒ mǎi sān píng shuǐ, yào liù píng kělè.

(6) 我 要 两个 橘子，要 两根 香蕉。
Wǒ yào liǎng ge júzi, yào liǎng gēn xiāngjiāo.

(7) 他 明天 要 去 学校。
Tā míngtiān yào qù xuéxiào.

6. Practice using the question word "多少 duōshao" by asking your classmate(s) the following questions

(1) How much does a pound of banana cost?

(2) How many bottles of water do you drink everyday?

(3) How much money do you have?

(4) How many friends do you have in China?

(5) How many apples do you want to buy?

(6) How much does a *jin* of grapes cost?

7. Read the following numbers aloud, using "零 líng" and "一 yī"

101	105	107	109	104	108
202	209	207	201	206	208
300	900	708	602	500	801
506	509	607	400	703	902

11	111	212	315	518
115	118	419	514	613
911	814	718	216	916

Pronunciation Notes

Tone changes (II): "一 yī" (one)

The number "一 yī" can have three different tones.

It is first tone (level) when used in counting:

yī 一　　shíyī 十一　　xīngqīyī 星期一

It is second tone (rising) when followed in close juncture with a fourth tone word, typically – but not always – a measure word:

yí kuài 一块　　yíwàn 一万　　yí cì 一次 (one time)

It is fourth tone (falling) when followed in close juncture (e.g., by a measure word) that is not fourth tone, i.e., by first, second or third tones:

yì jīn 一斤　　yì máo 一毛　　yì liǎng 一两　　yìbǎi 一百

In other words, except for having first tone in counting, "一 yī" shows the same tonal shifts as "不 bù" (not).

Pronunciation Exercises

1. Read the following phrases aloud and place the appropriate tone mark on "一 yī"

	Pinyin	Characters	English meaning
1	dì-yi	第一	the first
2	yi tiān	一天	one day
3	yi píng	一瓶	one bottle
4	yi běn	一本	one copy
5	yi ge	一个	one piece
6	yi bēi	一杯	one glass, one cup
7	yi wǎn	一碗	one bowl (of something)
8	yi huà	一画	one stroke

2. Read the numbers and the *Pinyin* below

(1) 6845 9059 3737 2000 2001
1999 1959 1995 9595 5959

(2) cèsuǒ (bathroom) xīmén (west gate) sì jiào (the fourth building)
Sháo Yuán (Spoon Garden) qī hào lóu (Building # 7)

3. Here are the numbers arranged by tone group; read them out

First tone	yī 一	sān 三	qī 七	bā 八
Second tone	líng 零	shí 十		
Third tone	wǔ 五	jiǔ 九		
Fourth tone	èr 二	sì 四	liù 六	

4. In each group, read out the initials with the rhymes, as indicated; assume high level tone (first tone)

j q x — ie iu ia	z c s — u ui un
zh ch sh r — i ang en an	b p m — o ao ai

5. Read the following pairs of words aloud, being careful to distinguish them

(1) yīshí 一十	yìshí 一时	yímín 移民	yìmíng 一鸣
"yī" zì "一"字	yǐzi 椅子	yì tiān 一天	yǐqián 以前
(2) èr zǐ 二子	érzi 儿子	èr nǚ 二女	érnǚ 儿女
èr duǒ 二朵	ěrduo 耳朵	érqiě 而且	yú'ěr 鱼饵
(3) sān rén 三人	shànrén 善人	sān diǎn 三点	sǎndiǎn 散点
dà sān 大三	dǎ sǎn 打伞		
(4) sìzhōu 四周	sīchóu 丝绸	Sì Shū 四书	sǐ shù 死树
sìshí 四十	sīshì 私事		
(5) wǔ tiān 五天	wùtiān 雾天	Wǔ-Sì 五四	wúsī 无私
wǔ huí 五回	wùhuì 误会		
(6) Liù Shū 六书	liǔshù 柳树	liù píng 六瓶	liūbīng 溜冰
liù jīn 六斤	liúxīn 留心		
(7) qīshí 七十	qíshì 歧视	qī míng 七名	qǐ míng 起名
qī zhé 七折	qìchē 汽车		
(8) bābǎi 八百	bàba 爸爸	bāzì 八字	bǎzi 靶子
bālù 八路	bá shù 拔树		
(9) jiǔshí 九十	jiùshì 旧事	jiǔzhōu 九州	jiùjiu 舅舅
jiǔ jīn 九斤	jiūxīn 揪心		
(10) shí fú 十幅	shīfu 师父	"shí" zì "十"字	shìzi 柿子
yīshí 一十	yíshì 一世		

Listening Comprehension

1. Listen to the numbers on the CD and then write them down in *Pinyin* (with tones) in the spaces provided

(1) ______ (6) ______

(2) ______ (7) ______

(3) ______ (8) ______

(4) ______ (9) ______

(5) ______ (10) ______

2. Listen to the conversation between two foreigners in China and answer the following questions

(1) What do the people in the conversation want to do?

- A. Buy some fruit.
- B. Buy water.
- C. Go shopping together.

(2) What does the man want to buy?

- A. Fruit.
- B. Some things.
- C. Drinks.

(3) What things are they *not* planning to buy?

- A. Water.
- B. Bananas.
- C. Cola.

(4) How much is the woman going to spend?

- A. Less than ¥ 2.50.
- B. ¥ 2.50.
- C. More than ¥ 2.50.

3. Listen to the passage on the CD and indicate True or False

	T	F
(1) Qian Min is going to buy three kinds of things.		
(2) He is going to buy a whole watermelon.		
(3) He is not going to buy any grapes.		
(4) He is going to spend more than ¥ 20.00.		

Communication Activities

Pair Work

Scenario I: One person recites a number, the other identifies the tone. Then reverse roles.

Scenario II: Count off (in sequence). Take turns and repeat.

Scenario III: Tell each other your (or other) telephone numbers and write them down. Check each other's numbers to see if they are correct.

Scenario IV: One person recites the names of fruit or other items (water, apple, banana, orange, watermelon, strawberries, grapes, etc.), the other repeats the item with a number, using an appropriate measure word: píngguǒ → sān ge píngguǒ, etc.

Group Work

Every morning, in schools in China, the students stand up and do physical exercise with their teachers while counting off the sets. Give it a try. Repeat a movement while counting off in Chinese following the sequence below:

1-2-3-4-5-6-7-8 2-2-3-4-5-6-7-8 3-2-3-4-5-6-7-8 4-2-3-4-5-6-7-8

Review Exercises

I. Fill in the blanks with the measure word for each thing listed below

(1) 一 ______ 草莓
yī ______ cǎoméi

(2) 两 ______ 西瓜
liǎng ______ xīguā

(3) 三 ______ 香蕉
sān ______ xiāngjiāo

(4) 四 ______ 梨
sì ______ lí

(5) 五 ______ 葡萄
wǔ ______ pútao

(6) 六 ______ 水
liù ______ shuǐ

(7) 七 ______ 钱
qī ______ qián

(8) 八 ______ 桃
bā ______ táo

(9) 九 ______ 苹果
jiǔ ______ píngguǒ

II. Match the characters in the left-hand list with the *Pinyin* on the right

(1) 瓶 A. gè
(2) 百 B. jīn
(3) 个 C. bǎi
(4) 斤 D. liǎng
(5) 零 E. píng
(6) 两 F. líng

III. Read from 111 to 999 using the following chart

一		一		一
二		二		二
三		三		三
四		四		四
五	百	五	十	五
六		六		六
七		七		七
八		八		八
九		九		九

IV. Answer the questions according to the English cues, and if "two" is involved, select between "二 èr" and "两 liǎng"

1. A：草莓多少钱一斤？
   Cǎoméi duōshao qián yì jīn?

   B：______________________________。(18 *yuan*)

2. A：你要什么？
   Nǐ yào shénme?

   B：我要________瓶水、________个苹果。(2, 2)
   Wǒ yào ________ píng shuǐ、________ ge píngguǒ.

3. A：三根香蕉多少钱？
   Sān gēn xiāngjiāo duōshao qián?

   B：______________________________。(9.80 *yuan*)

V. Answer the following questions with a sentence containing "一共 yígòng"

1. A：我要一斤香蕉、三斤苹果，多少钱？
   Wǒ yào yì jīn xiāngjiāo、sān jīn píngguǒ, duōshao qián?

   B：______________________________。

2. A：这是两斤三两葡萄。
   Zhè shì liǎng jīn sān liǎng pútao.

B：______________________________。

3\. A：我买七个橘子、三瓶水，还要一个西瓜，一共多少钱？
Wǒ mǎi qī ge júzi、sān píng shuǐ, hái yào yí ge xīguā, yígòng duōshao qián?

B：______________________________。

VI. Answer the following questions using verbs in series

1\. A：你去学校做什么？
Nǐ qù xuéxiào zuò shénme?

B：____________________。(to go to school to study Chinese)

2\. A：你去商店做什么？
Nǐ qù shāngdiàn zuò shénme?

B：____________________。(to go to the store to buy some things)

3\. A：你去商店买什么？
Nǐ qù shāngdiàn mǎi shénme?

B：____________________。(to go to the store to buy cola)

4\. A：谢中老师去学校做什么？
Xiè Zhōng lǎoshī qù xuéxiào zuò shénme?

B：____________________。(to go to the school to teach English)

VII. Find out from each other: (a) why he/she came to China, (b) why he/she came to school, and why he/she will go to the store, using the pattern: Subject + VO + VO

....

....

....

VIII. Answer the following questions in Chinese based on your own situation. The exercise can be written out, or presented orally

1. How do you count from 101 to 109?

2. How do you invite your friend to go shopping with you?

3. How do you ask your friend what to buy at the store?

4. How do you ask how much for half a kilo of grapes?

5. How do you ask how much for two bottles of coke?

6. How do you say 2.22?

Culture Notes

1. Formal written numbers

Just when you think you have learned all the numbers, you will notice that the numbers on Chinese coins and currency are written with characters different from the ones you have just learned. These are the formal characters for writing the numbers. They have been in use for many years, particularly in banking (e.g., on checks, payment orders, and receipts), where they are used to avoid the problems of misreading or alteration. Using the regular characters for numbers, it would be very easy to alter "一 yī" (one) to "十 shí" (ten) or "千 qiān" (thousand). Here are the formal versions of the numbers; in some cases, you will be able to see the connections, but not in all:

壹	贰	叁	肆	伍	陆	柒	捌	玖	拾	佰	仟
1	2	3	4	5	6	7	8	9	10	100	1000

2. Chinese hand numbers

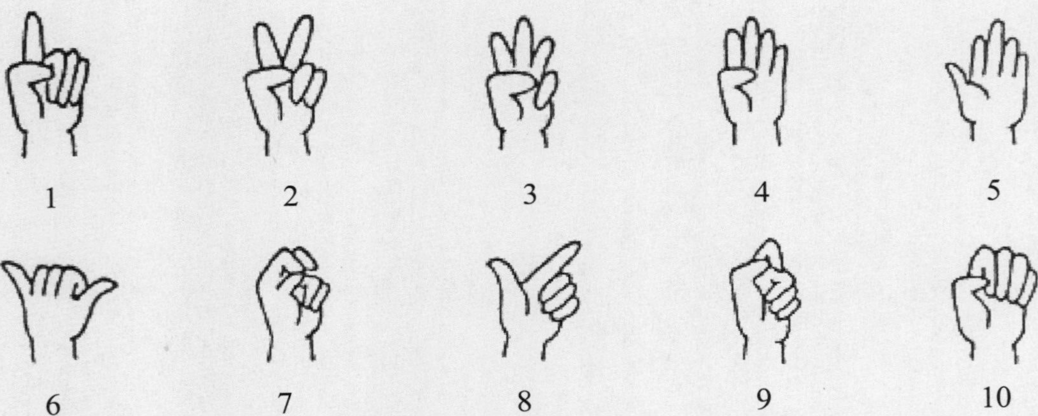

3. Lucky and unlucky numbers

Many Chinese words are near homophones, which means that one word often suggests another, making word play and punning particularly easy. For instance, "sì" (four) sounds like "sǐ" (death), so many people avoid the number four. On the other hand, "bā" (eight) sounds quite like "fā" (which is associated with compounds meaning "to become rich"), so the number eight is a favorite. The expression "èr bā" (two eights) suggests "both becoming rich". In the business world numbers such as 28, 88, and 888 are favorites. In the south of China an automobile license plate with the number "888" sells for a high price.

Another lucky number is nine. By *yin-yang* principles, it is the fullest number. When *yin* or *yang* reaches the value of nine, any further increase will bring it to ten, where *yin* turns into *yang* and *yang* turns into *yin*. For that reason, nine represents completeness or fullness in Chinese culture. Nine dragons are a symbol of the emperor. Some people have nine in their names.

Chinese often categorize things in sets of a specific number, such as "a student with all three modes of success"

(三好学生 sān hǎo xuésheng), or "may the four happinesses come to your door" (四喜临门 sì xǐ línmén) or "having five children all making the grade" (五子登科 wǔ zǐ dēngkē).

4. Using an abacus

The Chinese abacus has been in use for many hundreds of years. It has nine rows of beads on rods in an upper rack and a lower. The two beads in the upper rack of each row each represent fives; the five beads on the lower rack of each row each represent units – ones. By simply extending the process you learned in counting to 999 in Exercise III, you can represent very large numbers. The columns on the abacus signify, from left to right: "个 gè" (units), "十 shí" (tens), "百 bǎi" (hundreds), "千 qiān" (thousands), "万 wàn" (ten thousands), "十万 shíwàn" (hundred thousands), "百万 bǎiwàn" (millions), "千万 qiānwàn" (ten millions), and "亿 yì" (hundred millions).

yì	qiānwàn	bǎiwàn	shíwàn	wàn	qiān	bǎi	shí	gè
↓	↓	↓	↓	↓	↓	↓	↓	↓
4	7	5,	6	2	3,	4		
1	9							

It is read: sìyì qīqiān wǔbǎi liùshí'èr wàn sānqiān sìbǎi yīshíjiǔ

You start from the left, reading each number followed by the appropriate power of ten, as indicated. Since there are no unitary words for powers of ten between "万 wàn" (10,000) and "亿 yì" (100 million), the powers of ten (10 million, million, 100 thousand) have to be given in terms of "万 wàn" – which means holding off on saying "万 wàn" until you have passed through four columns (i.e. 7000, 500, 60 and 2): qīqiān wǔbǎi liùshí'èr wàn (i.e., 7562,0000, or in English terms, 75,620,000). Then, having completed the ten thousands, you continue with the thousands, hundreds, tens and units.

Lesson Five At a Restaurant

第五课 在餐馆

Dì-wǔ Kè Zài Cānguǎn

In this lesson you will learn how to do the following

- Request a particular seat in a restaurant
- Order drinks
- Order dishes for a meal
- Ask for, and pay the bill

Grammar

- Auxiliary verbs: "能 néng" (can, be able to), "可以 kěyǐ" (can, may) and "要 yào" (want to, would like to, need to, will)
- "(一) 点儿 (yì) diǎnr" (a little, a bit, a small amount)
- Sentences with subjects omitted
- Verb-not-verb questions, e.g.: "要不要 yào bu yào" "喝不喝 hē bu hē"
- The particle "了 le"
- Prices and units of money

Culture Notes

- Addressing strangers
- Types of restaurants
- "小费 xiǎofèi" (tipping)
- "食堂 shítáng" (cafeterias)
- Foreign currency exchange

Dialogue

A：服务员 fúwùyuán **B**：钱民 Qián Mín

A：请[1]进。请这边[2]坐。
Qǐng[1] jìn. Qǐng zhèbian[2] zuò.

B：我们能[G1]坐那边吗？
Wǒmen néng[G1] zuò nàbian ma?

A：可以[G1]。请。你们喝点儿[G2]什么？
Kěyǐ[G1]. Qǐng. Nǐmen hē diǎnr[G2] shénme?

B：有咖啡吗[G3]？
Yǒu kāfēi ma[G3]?

A：没有。我们有红茶、绿茶、冷饮和啤酒。
Méiyǒu. Wǒmen yǒu hóngchá、lǜchá、lěngyǐn hé píjiǔ.

B：要一壶绿茶，还要两瓶啤酒和一杯可乐。有英文菜单吗？
Yào yì hú lǜchá, hái yào liǎng píng píjiǔ hé yì bēi kělè. Yǒu Yīngwén càidān ma?

A：这是菜单，有图片。你们现在要[G1]点菜吗？
Zhè shì càidān, yǒu túpiàn. Nǐmen xiànzài yào[G1] diǎn cài ma?

B：好。要这个炒辣子鸡丁，不要太辣。一个糖醋鱼。那个是牛肉[3]吗？
Hǎo. Yào zhège chǎo làzi-jīdīng, bú yào tài là. Yí ge tángcùyú. Nàge shì niúròu[3] ma?

A：那个是铁板牛肉。
Nàge shì tiěbǎn-niúròu.

B：要一个。你们有什么素菜[4]？
Yào yí ge. Nǐmen yǒu shénme sùcài[4]?

A：我们有白菜、豆苗、芥蓝和油麦菜。
Wǒmen yǒu báicài、dòumiáo、jièlán hé yóumàicài.

Notes

1. "请 qǐng" is a verb meaning, literally "to invite", but here used for politeness, like "please". Cf. "请进 qǐng jìn" (Come in, please), "请坐 qǐng zuò" (Sit down, please). "请 qǐng" can also be used alone (often with an appropriate hand gesture) as an invitation to proceed, implying "after you", "go ahead", "help yourself", according to context.
2. "这边 zhèbian" (on this side) – "zhèbianr" in northern speech – indicates a location. The location of a verbal event generally comes before the associated verb in Chinese.
3. "肉 ròu" (meat) alone implies "pork" in Chinese. Other kinds of meat add the animal name before "肉 ròu", e.g., "鸡肉 jīròu" (chicken), "牛肉 niúròu" (beef), "羊肉 yángròu" (lamb, mutton).
4. "素菜 sùcài" denotes either vegetarian dishes, made with vegetables or beancurd but no meat, or vegetable dishes that are primarily vegetables.

B：要一个清炒豆苗，一个蒜蓉芥蓝。
Yào yí ge qīngchǎo-dòumiáo, yí ge suànróng-jièlán.

A：点不点[G4]汤？
Diǎn bu diǎn[G4] tāng?

B：要一个鸡蛋汤。
Yào yí ge jīdàntāng.

A：您要点什么主食？
Nín yào diǎn shénme zhǔshí?

B：你们有什么主食？
Nǐmen yǒu shénme zhǔshí?

A：米饭、馒头、葱油饼、饺子、面条都[5]有。
Mǐfàn、mántou、cōngyóubǐng、jiǎozi、miàntiáo dōu[5] yǒu.

B：每人来一碗米饭吧。
Měi rén lái yì wǎn mǐfàn ba.

A：还要什么？
Hái yào shénme?

B：不要了[G5]。谢谢。
Bú yào le[G5]. Xièxie.

B：服务员，买单[6]。一共多少钱？
Fúwùyuán, mǎidān[6]. Yígòng duōshao qián?

A：一共一百七十元五角。
Yígòng yìbǎi qīshí yuán wǔ jiǎo.

B：这是两百块。
Zhè shì liǎngbǎi kuài.

A：找您二十九块五毛[G6]。
Zhǎo nín èrshíjiǔ kuài wǔ máo[G6].

B：谢谢。再见。
Xièxie. Zàijiàn.

A：再见。
Zàijiàn.

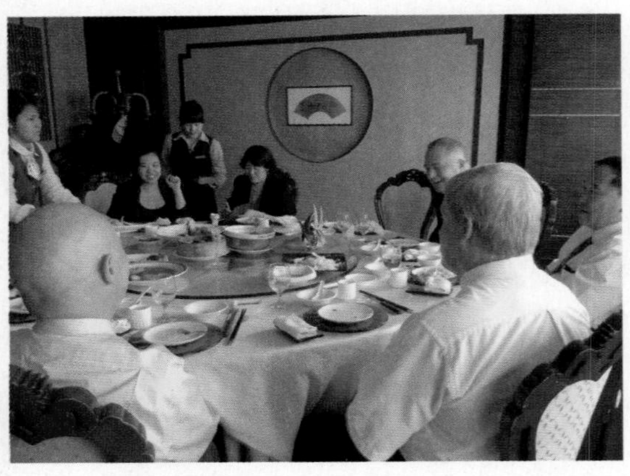

5. The adverb "都 dōu" (all) is, like other adverbs, placed immediately before a verb. Unlike English "all", which can modify nouns ("all dishes"), "都 dōu" only modifies verbs, not nouns.
6. "买单 mǎidān", literally "buy-list", that is, the record of purchases, is used to call for the bill or check in restaurants and bars. The word has spread to northern Chinese speech from Cantonese. The term "结账 jiézhàng" (to settle accounts) is also used.

New Words

1	餐馆/餐館	cānguǎn	N	restaurant
2	服务员/服務員	fúwùyuán	N	attendant, service person
3	请/請	qǐng	V	to invite, to treat (sb. to dinner, etc.), please
4	进/進	jìn	V	to enter, to go or come in
5	这边/這邊	zhèbian	Pron	this side, over here
	这/這	zhè	Pron	this
	边/邊	bian	Suf	side
6	坐	zuò	V	to sit (cf. "请坐 qǐng zuò", *please sit down*)
7	能	néng	Aux	can, may, be able to
8	那边/那邊	nàbian	Pron	that side, over there
	那	nà	Pron	that
9	可以	kěyǐ	Aux	may, can, to be fine, OK
10	你们/你們	nǐmen	Pron	you (plural)
11	喝	hē	V	to drink
12	（一）点儿/（一）點兒	(yì) diǎnr	Q	a little, a bit, slightly
13	有	yǒu	V	to have, there is/are
14	咖啡	kāfēi	N	coffee
15	没有	méiyǒu	V/Adv	to not have, there is / are not; did not, has not (= 没 méi)
16	红茶/紅茶	hóngchá	N	black tea (*literally* "*red-tea*")
	茶	chá	N	tea
17	绿茶/綠茶	lǜchá	N	green tea
18	冷饮/冷飲	lěngyǐn	N	cold drinks, soft drinks
	饮/飲	yǐn	BF	drink
19	和	hé	Conj	and, together with
20	啤酒	píjiǔ	N	beer
21	要	yào	Aux	would like to

22	壶/壺	hú	N	pot, kettle
23	杯/盃	bēi	N	cup
24	菜单/菜單	càidān	N	menu
25	图片/圖片	túpiàn	N	picture, illustration
26	现在/現在	xiànzài	N	now, at present, today
27	点菜/點菜	diǎn cài	Phrase	to order (food, dishes)
	点/點	diǎn	V	to order
28	这个/這个	zhège	Pron	this one
29	炒	chǎo	V	to stir-fry
30	辣子鸡丁/辣子鷄丁	làzi-jīdīng	Phrase	chili chicken
	辣子	làzi	N	hot pepper, chili
	鸡丁/雞丁	jīdīng	N	diced chicken
	鸡/雞	jī	N	chicken
	丁	dīng	N	cube-shaped pieces
31	太	tài	Adv	too, extremely
32	辣	là	Adj	spicy, hot
33	糖醋鱼/糖醋魚	tángcùyú	N	sweet and sour fish
	糖	táng	N	sugar, candy, sweets
	醋	cù	N	vinegar
	鱼/魚	yú	N	fish
34	那个/那個	nàge	Pron	that one
35	牛肉	niúròu	N	beef
36	铁板/鐵板	tiěbǎn	N	iron plate
37	素菜	sùcài	N	vegetarian food
38	白菜	báicài	N	Chinese cabbage, bok choy
39	豆苗	dòumiáo	N	pea sprouts
40	芥蓝/芥藍	jièlán	N	Chinese broccoli
41	油麦菜/油麥菜	yóumàicài	N	Chinese lettuce, Chinese greens

42	清炒	qīngchǎo	V	to sautée or fry, without additional ingredients
43	蒜蓉	suànróng	N	mashed or chopped garlic
44	汤/湯	tāng	N	soup
45	鸡蛋/雞蛋	jīdàn	N	(chicken) egg
46	您	nín	Pron	you (polite form)
47	主食	zhǔshí	N	principle food, staple
48	米饭/米飯	mǐfàn	N	cooked rice
49	馒头/饅頭	mántou	N	steamed bun
50	葱油饼/蔥油餅	cōngyóubǐng	N	scallion pancake
51	饺子/餃子	jiǎozi	N	stuffed dumplings
52	面条/麵條	miàntiáo	N	noodles
53	都	dōu	Adv	all
54	每	měi	Pron	every, each (cf. "每人 měi rén", *each/every person*)
55	来/來	lái	V	to bring, to take, to have (to cause to) come, to arrive
56	碗	wǎn	N	bowl
57	吧	ba	Part	suggestive, why don't [we]… (cf. "就这样吧 jiù zhèyàng ba", *let's do it that way, then*)
58	了	le	Part	*post-verbal, indicating successful action, sentence final, indicating new state, new phase, up to now, etc.*
59	谢谢/謝謝	xièxie	V	thank you, thanks
60	买单/買單	mǎidān	VO	to pay the bill (in a restaurant, etc.)
61	元	yuán	Meas	Renminbi (cf. "美元 měiyuán", *U.S. dollar*)
62	角	jiǎo	Meas	*unit of Chinese currency, used formally for 10 cents*
63	再见/再見	zàijiàn	V	good-bye, see you again

Re-enacting the Dialogue

A: a service person **B: a customer named Qian Min**

A: Come in, please. Please sit over here.

B: Is it possible for us to sit over there?

A: Sure, as you like. What would you like to drink?

B: Do you have coffee?

A: No, we don't. We have black tea, green tea, soft drinks and beer.

B: We'll take a pot of green tea, two bottles of beer and a glass of cola. Do you have a menu that's in English?

A: This is our menu – it has illustrations. Would you like to order now?

B: Okay. We'll have this stir-fried spicy diced chicken – but don't make it too spicy; and a hot and sour fish. Is that one a beef dish?

A: That's sizzling beef cooked on an iron pan.

B: We'll have that. What do you have in the way of vegetable dishes?

A: We have bok choy, pea sprouts, Chinese broccoli, and Chinese greens.

B: We'll have the sautéed pea sprouts, and the Chinese broccoli with mashed garlic.

A: Do you want soup?

B: We'll have egg-drop soup, please.

A: What (staple) would you like the food with?

B: What sorts do you have?

A: We have rice, steamed bread, scallion pancakes, stuffed dumplings and noodles.

B: We'll each have a bowl of rice.

A: Anything else?

B: That's it. Thank you.

B: Waitress, the bill please. What's the total?

A: The total is ¥ 170.50.

B: Here's ¥ 200.00.

A: Here is ¥ 29.50 in change.

B: Thank you. G'bye.

A: Bye.

Grammar

▶ G1. Auxiliary verbs: "能 néng" (can, be able to), "可以 kěyǐ" (can, may) and "要 yào" (want to, would like to, need to, will)

Auxiliary verbs is the name given to a disparate group of verbs that are used in conjunction with a following verb (which can be regarded as their object). Their meanings typically have to do with ability, permission, possibility, intention and obligation.

Three auxiliary verbs are introduced in this lesson. Two of them, "能 néng" and "可以 kěyǐ" can both be translated "can" or "able to"; but the first, "能 néng", typically refers to external circumstances or physical ability, whil the second "可以 kěyǐ" signifies permission. The example in the dialogue illustrates:

① A：我们能坐那边吗？ Is it possible for us to sit over there?
Wǒmen néng zuò nàbian ma?

B：可以 (坐)。请。 Sure, as you like.
Kěyǐ (zuò). Qǐng.

The first sentence, with "能 néng", questions whether the physical setting makes it possible for them to sit there. The response with "可以 kěyǐ" states that it is all right to do so.

Negation is with "不 bù", as you would expect: "不能 bù néng" (not able to); "不可以 bù kěyǐ" (not permitted to).

The third auxiliary introduced in the lesson is "要 yào" (want, would like to, need to, will).

② 你们现在要点菜吗？ Would you like to order now?
Nǐmen xiànzài yào diǎn cài ma?

③ 要不要买东西？ Do (you) need to do any shopping?
Yào bu yào mǎi dōngxi?

When followed by another verb, "要 yào" functions as an auxiliary. It may also function as a plain verb, with a noun object expressed (or implied), as in this example from Lesson 4:

④ 还要九根香蕉，十片西瓜。 I also want nine bananas and ten pieces of watermelon.
Hái yào jiǔ gēn xiāngjiāo, shí piàn xīguā.

▶ G2. "(一) 点儿 (yì) diǎnr" (a little, a bit, a small amount)

In the sentence "你们喝点儿什么？Nǐmen hē diǎnr shénme?" (What would you like to drink?), "(一) 点儿 (yì) diǎnr" appears as a modifier of "什么 shénme", literally, "a bit of what". (The "一 yī" is often elided when the phrase occurs in object position.) It is best to think of "点儿什么 diǎnr shénme" as a unit – a more casual form of "什么 shénme". Later, you will see examples of "(一) 点儿 (yì) diǎnr" used in more representative fashion, in expressions such as "她会说一点儿中文 Tā huì shuō yìdiǎnr Zhōngwén" (She can speak a little Chinese) or "我喝一点儿绿茶 Wǒ hē yìdiǎnr lǜchá" (I'll have some green tea).

▶ G3. Sentences with subjects omitted

When the context makes it clear who or what is being talked about, Chinese often omits the subject where English would have a pronoun. In the dialogue for this lesson, for example, the question "有咖啡吗? Yǒu kāfēi ma?" (Do you have coffee?) omits any mention of the subject, which if it were present, would probably be "你们 nǐmen" (you). The answer, "没有 méiyǒu" (we don't) also makes no mention of the subject (cf. English "we" in the translation). That response also introduces the only exception to the use of "不 bù" to negate verbs: "有 yǒu" (have; there is/are) is negated as "没有 méiyǒu" (not have; there isn't/aren't) – with "没 méi" rather than "不 bù".

▶ G4. Verb-not-verb questions, e.g.: "要不要 yào bu yào" "喝不喝 hē bu hē"

Yes-no questions can be formed with the sentence-final particle "吗 ma", as you learned earlier. Yes-no questions can also be formed by combining positive and negative versions of a verb: "有没有 yǒu méiyǒu" "是不是 shì bu shì" "能不能 néng bu néng".

A：要不要汤？ Would you like soup?
Yào bu yào tāng?

B：要。/不要。 Yes, I would. / No, I wouldn't.
Yào. / Bú yào.

The pattern applies to two-syllable verbs as well: "可以不可以 kěyǐ bu kěyǐ". With two-syllable verbs, a reduced version is also common: "可不可以 kě bu kěyǐ". (The reduced pattern is probably a result of the influence of Cantonese, in which the reduced pattern is more usual.)

▶ G5. The particle "了 le"

The particle "了 le" has a number of grammatical functions. It may be attached to the end of the sentence (sentence-le); or it may be attached to the verb (verb-le). This lesson illustrates sentence-le, which indicates a change of state, a new phase. In English, the sense of sentence "了 le" can be captured by words such as "now" in the positive, or "no more" or "anymore" in the negative.

① A：还要什么？ Would you like anything else?
Hái yào shénme?

B：不要了。谢谢。 No more, thanks.
Bú yào le. Xièxie.

② 现在好了。 It's fine now.
Xiànzài hǎo le.

③ 来了，来了。 Here they are!
Lái le, lái le.

④ 不能再喝了。 I can't drink any more.
Bù néng zài hē le.

With more examples, you will see that neither this function of "了 le", nor other functions to be introduced later, correspond to what in English is called tense. Instead, Chinese is sensitive to what is usually called "aspect", that is, whether the verbal event is beginning, ongoing, changed or complete.

▶ G6. Prices and units of money

Most of the units of money have both a colloquial form and a formal or written form. In the dialogue for this lesson, the waiter gives the total in the more formal register, using "元 yuán" for dollars and "角 jiǎo" for "units of ten cents" (i.e. in terms of dimes). The customer, on the other hand, responds using the colloquial (spoken) forms, "块 kuài" and "毛 máo", and the rest of the conversation follows accordingly.

A：服务员，买单。一共多少钱？ Waitress, the bill please. What's the total?
Fúwùyuán, mǎidān. Yígòng duōshao qián?

B：一共一百七十元五角。The total is ¥170.50.
Yígòng yìbǎi qīshí yuán wǔ jiǎo.

A：这是两百块。Here's ¥200.00.
Zhè shì liǎngbǎi kuài.

B：找您二十九块五毛。Here is ¥29.50 in change. (Find you ¥29.50.)
Zhǎo nín èrshíjiǔ kuài wǔ máo.

The formal terms for units of money, used in banks, businesses, on menus and forms and for almost all written communication, are "元 yuán", "角 jiǎo", and "分 fēn". The colloquial terms are "块 kuài", "毛 máo", and "分 fēn". There is only one term for the smallest unit, "分 fēn". Informal and formal terms would not normally be mixed in a single price – and not usually in a single utterance.

Colloquial usage generally drops the last (smallest) unit – "分 fēn" in the following example:

rénmínbì	Formal	Colloquial
¥29.47	29 元 4 角 7 分 èrshíjiǔ yuán sì jiǎo qī fēn	29 块 4 毛 7 èrshíjiǔ kuài sì máo qī

Consolidation & Practice

1. Ask and answer with "能 néng" or "可以 kěyǐ" (plus verb phrase)

Subject + Aux + Verb + Object + 吗 ma?

Example: A：我们能 /可以坐那边吗？
Wǒmen néng / kěyǐ zuò nàbian ma?

B1：能。/可以。
Néng. / Kěyǐ.

B2: 不能。/不可以。
Bù néng. / Bù kěyǐ.

他 tā	教 jiāo	英文 Yīngwén
我们 wǒmen	一起去 yìqǐ qù	学校 xuéxiào
辣子鸡丁 làzi-jīdīng	不太 bú tài	辣 là
这个菜 zhège cài	不要 bú yào	肉 ròu
现在 xiànzài	点 diǎn	菜 cài
油麦菜 yóumàicài	清炒 qīngchǎo	
我们 wǒmen	坐 zuò	这边 zhèbian

2. You are having dinner at the house of a Chinese friend. Your host asks you what you'd like to drink or eat. Respond, using the pattern "(还) 要 V (一) 点儿 (hái) yào V (yì) diǎnr"

Example: A：你们要喝点儿什么？
Nǐmen yào hē diǎnr shénme?

B：我要喝一点儿绿茶。
Wǒ yào hē yìdiǎnr lǜchá.

A：你们还要喝点儿什么？
Nǐmen hái yào hē diǎnr shénme?

B：我还要喝一点儿红茶。
Wǒ hái yào hē yìdiǎnr hóngchá.

喝	啤酒
hē	píjiǔ

要	糖醋鱼
yào	tángcùyú

喝	红茶
hē	hóngchá

还喝	可乐
hái hē	kělè

还要	素菜
hái yào	sùcài

3. Practice forming sentences with subjects omitted. Form questions and responses along the lines of the model

有 yǒu + Object + 吗 ma?

Example: A：有咖啡吗？
Yǒu kāfēi ma?

B：有。/ 没有。
Yǒu. / Méiyǒu.

面条 miàntiáo	清炒豆苗 qīngchǎo-dòumiáo	铁板牛肉 tiěbǎn-niúròu	蒜蓉芥蓝 suànróng-jièlán
鸡蛋汤 jīdàntāng	辣子鸡丁 làzi-jīdīng	糖醋鱼 tángcùyú	葱油饼 cōngyóubǐng

4. Form verb-not-verb questions, then respond with a negative and an alternative (see model)

Example: A：要不要这个菜？
Yào bu yào zhège cài?

B：不要，要那个菜。
Bú yào, yào nàge cài.

要	米饭	馒头
yào	mǐfàn	mántou

吃	这个菜	那个菜
chī	zhège cài	nàge cài

要	酸辣汤	鸡蛋汤
yào	suānlàtāng	jīdàntāng

吃	饼	面条
chī	bǐng	miàntiáo

吃	鱼	鸡肉
chī	yú	jīròu

喝	茶	可乐
hē	chá	kělè

5. Practice using the sentence particle "了 le". Answer in the negative, following the model

Example: A：你还要菜吗？
Nǐ hái yào cài ma?

B：不要了。
Bú yào le.

(1) 还要主食吗？
Hái yào zhǔshí ma?

(2) 还要饺子吗？
Hái yào jiǎozi ma?

(3) 还吃鱼吗？
Hái chī yú ma?

(4) 还要汤吗？
Hái yào tāng ma?

(5) 还吃面条吗？
Hái chī miàntiáo ma?

6. Report prices

rénmínbì	Formal	Colloquial
¥1.32	1元3角2分 yì yuán sān jiǎo èr fēn	1块3毛2 yí kuài sān máo èr
¥60.70	60元7角 liùshí yuán qī jiǎo	60块7毛 liùshí kuài qī máo

(1) Say these amounts in Chinese

¥8.23 ¥9.56 ¥10.89 ¥19.14 ¥101.00 ¥56.25 ¥210.37 ¥98.48

(2) Ask about amounts with "多少 duōshao"

Example: A：这是多少钱？
Zhè shì duōshao qián?

B：这是一百美元。
Zhè shì yìbǎi měiyuán.

那 nà　人民币 rénmínbì　300 RMB ×3

这 zhè　美元 měiyuán　150 US$

那 nà　港币 (HK$) gǎngbì　500 HK$

这 zhè　钱 qián　1,000 块 kuài ×10

那 nà　钱 qián　95 元 yuán ×2

一共 yígòng　钱 qián　三十五块 sānshíwǔ kuài

Pronunciation Notes

Tonal modification (II): The half-third tone

In Lesson 1, under the heading of "tone shifts", it was noted that the contour of the third tone varies according to what follows. In citation form (before a pause), or at the end of a tone group, it is low with a (often slight) final rise. Followed by another third tone (in close juncture), it is pronounced as a second tone (rising). Followed by any other tone (in close juncture), it is pronounced low (without rise) – the so-called "half-third tone". The following examples illustrate the half-third tone – remember to stay low:

měi tiān	每天	every day
měi nián	每年	every year
měi yuè	每月	every month
měi rén	每人	every person
lǎoshī	老师	teacher
lǎorén	老人	old person
hǎochī	好吃	good to eat
hǎokàn	好看	nice looking
hěn lèi	很累	quite tired
hěn gāo	很高	quite tall

Pronunciation Exercises

1. Recite the following words and phrases – the first syllables are all third tone

	Pinyin	Characters	English meaning
1	wǒ chī	我吃	I eat
2	wǒ lái	我来	I come
3	wǒ yào	我要	I want
4	nǐ hē	你喝	you drink
5	nǐ lái	你来	you come
6	nǐ huàn	你换	you change
7	wǔ tiān	五天	five days
8	wǔ nián	五年	five years
9	wǔ cì	五次	five times
10	lǎoshī	老师	teacher
11	xiǎoháir	小孩儿	children
12	xiě zì	写字	to write characters
13	Wǔchāng	武昌	name of a city
14	Shěnyáng	沈阳	name of a city
15	Bǎodìng	保定	name of a city

2. Recite the following list of words, all with third tone followed by second tone

	Pinyin	Characters	English meaning
1	Měiguó	美国	United States
2	lǎorén	老人	old person
3	zhǎo qián	找钱	to give change
4	gǎigé	改革	to reform
5	hǎiyáng	海洋	ocean
6	yěmán	野蛮	barbarous, savage
7	jiǎngtái	讲台	platform, rostrum

	Pinyin	Characters	English meaning
8	zǒngcái	总裁	company president, CEO
9	jiějué	解决	to solve
10	jǐngchá	警察	police
11	zǔguó	祖国	motherland
12	suǒ mén	锁门	to lock a door
13	lěiqiú	垒球	softball
14	yǒu qián	有钱	to be rich
15	nǎiyóu	奶油	cream

3. Read the following terms aloud — most of them deal with administrative units or organizations

	Pinyin	Characters	English meaning
1	xuéxiào	学校	school
2	xiǎoxué	小学	elementary school
3	zhōngxué	中学	secondary school
4	dàxué	大学	university, college
5	Jiàoyù Bù	教育部	Ministry of Education
6	Jiàoyù Jú	教育局	Bureau of Education
7	Zhōngyāng Zhèngfǔ	中央政府	Central Government
8	shěng	省	province
9	Guówùyuàn	国务院	State Council
10	shì	市	city
11	xiàn	县	county
12	Shāngwù Bù	商务部	Ministry of Commerce
13	shāngdiàn	商店	store
14	Nóngyè Bù	农业部	Ministry of Agriculture
15	nóngcūn	农村	countryside
16	Wénhuà Bù	文化部	Ministry of Culture
17	chāojí shìchǎng / chāoshì	超级市场 / 超市	supermarket

	Pinyin	Characters	English meaning
18	shūdiàn	书店	bookstore
19	zǎoshì	早市	morning market
20	jǐngchájú	警察局	police bureau
21	pàichūsuǒ	派出所	police station
22	gōngsī	公司	company

Listening Comprehension

1. Listen to the dialogue and then answer the questions

(1) What does the woman ask for first?
(2) What else does the woman ask for?
(3) How many dishes does the woman order?
(4) How much is the rice?
(5) What is the total cost?

2. Listen to the dialogue and then answer the questions

(1) What was the first dish requested by the man?
(2) What did the man ask for after that? Why?
(3) What beverages did the man order?
(4) What items were in the final order?

Communication Activities

Pair Work

Scenario I: With a partner, take the roles of customer and waiter/waitress in a restaurant. The customer examines the menu and asks the price of dishes; the waiter/waitress answers:

Example: A：这个菜多少钱？
Zhège cài duōshao qián?

B：这个菜六十六块。
Zhège cài liùshíliù kuài.

(1) $ 200
(2) ¥ 415
(3) ¥ 168
(4) HK$ 344

Scenario II: Again, with a partner, take the roles of (foreign) customer, and waiter/waitress and order one meat dish, two vegetarian dishes, a staple (rice, bread) and a soup. Then pay for them.

The conversation should proceed as follows. First, the customer selects items and checks the price of each:

我要……多少钱？
Wǒ yào……Duōshao qián?

The waiter/waitress gives the price and asks the customer if he/she wants anything else. The customer can respond with the "了 le" pattern:

不要了，谢谢。
Bú yào le, xièxie.

Finally, the customer asks for the check and the waiter/waitress gives the total.

菜单 MENU

炒白菜	chǎobáicài	¥ 15.00
辣子鸡丁	làzi-jīdīng	¥ 23.50
糖醋鱼	tángcùyú	¥ 69.00
铁板牛肉	tiěbǎn-niúròu	¥ 54.00
清炒豆苗	qīngchǎo-dòumiáo	¥ 25.00
蒜蓉芥蓝	suànróng-jièlán	¥ 28.00
鸡蛋汤	jīdàntāng	¥ 20.00
酸辣汤	suānlàtāng	¥ 23.00
米饭	mǐfàn	¥ 1.50 per bowl
馒头	mántou	¥ 1.00 each
饺子	jiǎozi	¥ 15.00 for six

Group Work

Working with a partner, you have a stack of real or hand-drawn RMB bills, as well as a selection of coins. Hold up each one and let your partner identify it using the formal expressions for money (元 yuán, 角 jiǎo, 分 fēn). You repeat, using the colloquial equivalents (块 kuài, 毛 máo, 分 fēn).

Review Exercises

I. Match the words in the left-hand list with the words in the right-hand list

(1) 一杯 yì bēi
(2) 三瓶 sān píng
(3) 一壶 yì hú
(4) 喝（一）点儿 hē (yì) diǎnr
(5) 五 wǔ
(6) 图片 túpiàn

A. 菜单 càidān
B. 绿茶 lǜchá
C. 角 jiǎo
D. 啤酒 píjiǔ
E. 咖啡 kāfēi
F. 什么 shénme

II. Provide translations or descriptions for the following food related terms

素菜 sùcài ....
肉菜 ròucài ....
辣子 làzi ....
清炒 qīngchǎo ....
米饭 mǐfàn ....
主食 zhǔshí ....
油麦菜 yóumàicài ....
糖醋 tángcù ....
铁板 tiěbǎn ....
汤 tāng ....
馒头 mántou ....
面条 miàntiáo ....

III. Complete the following sentences with "了 le"

1. A：你还要什么？
   Nǐ hái yào shénme?

   B：________________________________。(no more)

2. A：你买饺子吗？
   Nǐ mǎi jiǎozi ma?

   B：________________________________。(not any more)

3. A：你还去学校吗？
   Nǐ hái qù xuéxiào ma?

   B：________________________________。(not any more)

4. A：你还来一个葱油饼吗？
   Nǐ hái lái yí ge cōngyóubǐng ma?

   B：________________________________。(no more)

IV. Answer the following questions using "能 néng", "可以 kěyǐ" or "要 yào"

1. A：我可以坐这边吗？
   Wǒ kěyǐ zuò zhèbian ma?

   B：______________________________。(Yes, certainly)

2. A：您要点什么菜？要不要辣子鸡丁？
   Nín yào diǎn shénme cài? Yào bu yào làzi-jīdīng?

   B：那个菜太辣了，______________________________。(don't want it)
   Nàge cài tài là le,

   A：我们要一个牛肉，好吗？
   Wǒmen yào yí ge niúròu, hǎo ma?

   B：好吧！我们__________不__________来一点儿主食？
   Hǎo ba! Wǒmen __________ bu __________ lái yìdiǎnr zhǔshí?

   A：好，每人来一碗米饭吧！
   Hǎo, měi rén lái yì wǎn mǐfàn ba!

3. A：您现在可以点菜吗？
   Nín xiànzài kěyǐ diǎn cài ma?

   B：____________。你有没有英文菜单？(No, I can't)
   ____________. Nǐ yǒu méiyǒu Yīngwén càidān?

   A：没有。这个呢？这个菜单有图片，____________？(Can you read it)
   Méiyǒu. Zhège ne? Zhège càidān yǒu túpiàn, ____________?

   B：可以，可以，太好了！
   Kěyǐ, kěyǐ, tài hǎo le!

V. Complete the following dialogues with "(一)点儿 (yì) diǎnr"

1. A：______________________________？

   B：我们要一壶茶，还要三瓶啤酒。
   Wǒmen yào yì hú chá, hái yào sān píng píjiǔ.

2. A：您要吃点儿什么？
   Nín yào chī diǎnr shénme?

   B：来______________________________。
   Lái ______________________________.

3. A：你现在学什么？
   Nǐ xiànzài xué shénme?

   B：______________________________，也教一点儿英文。
   ______________________________, yě jiāo yìdiǎnr Yīngwén.

4. A：我现在要去商店买东西，你要不要买什么东西？
Wǒ xiànzài yào qù shāngdiàn mǎi dōngxi, nǐ yào bu yào mǎi shénme dōngxi?

B：我要________________，还要________________。
Wǒ yào ________________, hái yào ________________.

VI. Answer these "要不要 yào bu yào" questions in the negative

1. A：我们现在有铁板牛肉，你要不要来一个？
Wǒmen xiànzài yǒu tiěbǎn-niúròu, nǐ yào bu yào lái yí ge?

B：________________，我不吃牛肉。你们有辣子鸡丁吗？
________________, wǒ bù chī niúròu. Nǐmen yǒu làzi-jīdīng ma?

2. A：你要不要学一点儿中文？你可以用（to use）中文点菜。
Nǐ yào bu yào xué yìdiǎnr Zhōngwén? Nǐ kěyǐ yòng Zhōngwén diǎn cài.

B：________________，你点菜，我吃，很好！
________________, nǐ diǎn cài, wǒ chī, hěn hǎo!

3. A：你要不要这个菜单，有图片。
Nǐ yào bu yào zhège càidān, yǒu túpiàn.

B：________________，我可以用中文点菜。
________________, wǒ kěyǐ yòng Zhōngwén diǎn cài.

4. A：你要不要买一点儿喝的东西？他们这边有咖啡、茶，还有啤酒、可乐。
Nǐ yào bu yào mǎi yìdiǎnr hē de dōngxi? Tāmen zhèbian yǒu kāfēi、chá, hái yǒu píjiǔ、kělè.

B：咖啡、茶、啤酒、可乐我都__________，我要一瓶橙汁（orange juice）。
Kāfēi、chá、píjiǔ、kělè wǒ dōu __________, wǒ yào yì píng chéngzhī.

VII. Answer the following questions based on your own situation. This exercise can be written, or presented orally

1. You want to sit at a different table. What do you say to the waitress?
2. How would you ask the waiter for an illustrated menu?
3. It's time to pay the bill. What do you say to the waiter / waitress?
4. How much did you pay for your meal altogether? Give the amount first in colloquial terms, then in formal language.

Culture Notes

1. Addressing strangers

"服务员 fúwùyuán" is the most common term used to address service people in banks, shops, supermarkets, and restaurants, etc. Not so long ago, young women could be addressed as "小姐 xiǎojiě", literally "older sister", but in recent years, the word has become associated with "call girls", so people sometimes use "美女 měinǚ" (pretty girl) or "小妹 xiǎomèi" (little sister), instead. If one is not quite sure how to address a service person, then it is safer to just state a request, e.g.: "I would like to…" Other service people, such as cooks and drivers, can be addressed as "师傅 shīfu" (master). "同志 tóngzhì" (comrade) is still used occasionally as a form of address to strangers amongst Chinese, but like "小姐 xiǎojiě", it too has gained a special association, in this case, with male homosexuals.

2. Types of restaurants

The two basic categories of restaurants are Chinese-style, "中餐 zhōngcān" (Chinese cuisine) and Western-style, "西餐 xīcān" (Western cuisine). Many Chinese restaurants are named after regional cuisines or special dishes. For instance, "Peking duck" restaurants serve dishes made with duck roasted over an open fire, "北京烤鸭 Běijīng kǎoyā" (Beijing roast duck). Restaurants with "四川风味 Sìchuān fēngwèi" (Sichuan taste) serve spicy food from Sichuan. Restaurants in "Guangdong-style", often labeled "粤菜 yuècài" (Cantonese dishes) or "港菜 gǎngcài" (Hong Kong dishes), serve dimsum and other specialties from Guangdong and Hong Kong. In the larger cities in China, there are also vegetarian restaurants. A "Western-style" restaurant usually serves both European and American food. "韩国烧烤 Hánguó shāokǎo" restaurants sell Korean barbecue and other Korean dishes, and "日本料理 Rìběn liàolǐ" restaurants serve Japanese cuisine. "家常菜 jiāchángcài" means "family style", which is usually northern-style.

3. "小费 xiǎofèi" (tipping)

Traditionally, there is no tipping in Chinese restaurants. However, nowadays, restaurants in top-level hotels often add a 15% service charge to the bill.

4. "食堂 shítáng" (cafeterias)

Almost all work places in China have a "食堂 shítáng", which is an employee or student cafeteria or dining hall. Schools also have a "faculty cafeteria" (教师食堂 jiàoshī shítáng); government agencies, companies, and other work places, have an "employee cafeteria" (职工食堂 zhígōng shítáng). The word "食堂 shítáng" usually indicates buffet style: you stand in line and choose from food you see behind a counter, then you carry the food to your seat. Coupons are often used instead of cash, and there is no sit-down table service, but the prices at "食堂 shítáng" are significantly cheaper than at restaurants. Chinese colleges usually have a separate foreigners' cafeteria, called a "留学生食堂 liúxuéshēng shítáng" (foreign students' cafeteria), for all foreigners – students, teachers, and visitors.

Foreigners are expected to eat there rather than at the regular cafeteria. Foreign students' cafeterias usually sell both Chinese-style food and Western-style food. Cafeteria coupons are sold at a counter or office in or near the cafeteria.

5. Foreign currency exchange

Foreign currency can be exchanged at all major banks of China, such as the People's Bank of China (中国人民银行 Zhōngguó Rénmín Yínháng), Bank of China (中国银行 Zhōngguó Yínháng), China Construction Bank (中国建设银行 Zhōngguó Jiànshè Yínháng), Industrial and Commercial Bank of China (中国工商银行 Zhōngguó Gōngshāng Yínháng), Agricultural Bank of China (中国农业银行 Zhōngguó Nóngyè Yínháng), and at international airports, at some large hotels, at some large department stores, and in some tourist areas. To change money, you have to show your passport or your foreign resident's ID. The exchange rate varies slightly from one place to another. A slightly more favorable rate is given for traveler's checks. Traveler's checks from American Express, Citibank, Thomas Cook and Barclays are readily accepted by Chinese banks. To convert RMB back to foreign currency, you need to show your original receipts of exchange – so be sure to keep them. It is illegal to exchange foreign currency on the street – and you are likely to be given counterfeit money if you do so. Foreign credit cards can also be used to obtain RMB from Chinese ATM machines. The Bank of China charges a service fee for those transactions.

Lesson Six Asking for Directions

第六课 问 路

Dì-liù Kè Wèn Lù

In this lesson you will learn how to do the following

- Ask how to get to a certain place
- Give simple directions
- Explain where something is located

Grammar

- "有 yǒu" (there is, there are) expressing existence
- Location phrases
- The interrogative "怎么 zěnme" (how)
- "往 wǎng" (towards) indicating direction
- The particle "的 de" in location phrases
- The copula verb "是 shì"
- "在 zài" (to be at; at, on, in) expressing location
- "从 cóng" (from) indicating place of origin

Culture Notes

- City districts
- Street names and directions

Dialogue

A：谢中 Xiè Zhōng　　**B**：路人 lùrén　　**C**：李远，中国学生 Lǐ Yuǎn, Zhōngguó xuésheng

（马路边 Mǎlù biān）

A：请问[1]，这附近哪儿[2]有[G1]洗手间？
Qǐngwèn[1], zhè fùjìn nǎr[2] yǒu[G1] xǐshǒujiān?

B：马路对面[G2]，麦当劳里有。
Mǎlù duìmiàn[G2], Màidāngláo li yǒu.

A：马路对面哪儿有麦当劳？怎么[G3]走？
Mǎlù duìmiàn nǎr yǒu Màidāngláo? Zěnme[G3] zǒu?

B：您过了马路往[G4]南走，过一个红绿灯，经过一个超市和药店，药店的[G5]旁边是[G6]麦当劳。
Nín guòle mǎlù wǎng[G4] nán zǒu, guò yí ge hónglǜdēng, jīngguò yí ge chāoshì hé yàodiàn, yàodiàn de[G5] pángbiān shì[G6] Màidāngláo.

A：远不远[3]？
Yuǎn bu yuǎn[3]?

B：不太[4]远。
Bú tài[4] yuǎn.

A：谢谢。
Xièxie.

B：不客气[5]。
Bú kèqi[5].

Notes

1. "请问 qǐngwèn", literally "request to ask", is a polite way of getting the attention of a stranger so you can ask a question.
2. "哪儿 nǎr" (where), with the "-r" ending common to northern speech, is the colloquial equivalent to "哪里 nǎli".
3. "远不远 yuǎn bu yuǎn", literally "far or not", is another example of the verb-not-verb question type introduced in Lesson 4 (cf. "要不要 yào bu yào"), the only difference being that "远 yuǎn" is an adjectival verb. Cf. "好不好 hǎo bu hǎo".
4. "太 tài" is an adverb, used to express degree or extent. As with other adverbs, it appears before a verb (adjectival or not) or before another adverb.
5. "不客气 bú kèqi", literally, "don't behave like a guest", i.e. "no need to be polite", is often a response to expressions of thanks, and is equivalent to the English "you're welcome".

（在校园 Zài xiàoyuán）

A：同学，请问，中文系在[G7]哪儿？
Tóngxué, qǐngwèn, Zhōngwénxì zài[G7] nǎr?

C：您是留学生吧？
Nín shì liúxuéshēng ba?

A：不是。我是英文系的外教，去那儿学中文。
Bú shì. Wǒ shì Yīngwénxì de wàijiào, qù nàr xué Zhōngwén.

C：我是中文系的学生，刚从[G8]那边来。中文系在北边，往前一直走。
Wǒ shì Zhōngwénxì de xuésheng, gāng cóng[G8] nàbian lái. Zhōngwénxì zài běibian, wǎng qián yìzhí zǒu.

A：走多远？
Zǒu duō yuǎn?

C：不远。您过了大门，左转，经过银行和书店，右转。中文系在图书馆和教学楼的中间[6]。
Bù yuǎn. Nín guòle dàmén, zuǒ zhuǎn, jīngguò yínháng hé shūdiàn, yòu zhuǎn. Zhōngwénxì zài túshūguǎn hé jiàoxuélóu de zhōngjiān[6].

A：在路的左边还是右边？
Zài lù de zuǒbian háishi yòubian?

C：在右边。
Zài yòubian.

A：谢谢。
Xièxie.

C：不谢。
Bú xiè.

---

6. "中间 zhōngjiān" is a position word that combines with a preceding "在 zài" (at) to mean "the middle of", "the center of'", or "in between". In the dialogue, "中间 zhōngjiān" is the object of "在 zài" (i.e. "at the middle of…") and the whole phrase "图书馆和教学楼的 túshūguǎn hé jiàoxuélóu de" modifies it, literally "at the [the library and classroom building's] center", or in standard English, "between the library and the classroom building". The order of the Chinese is almost opposite to that of the English.

New Words

1	问路/問路	wèn lù	Phrase	to ask the way, to ask (for) directions
	问/問	wèn	V	to ask (a question)
2	马路/馬路	mǎlù	N	road, street
3	请问/請問	qǐngwèn	V	Excuse me, may I ask....
4	附近	fùjìn	N	vicinity, neighborhood, region close by
5	哪儿/哪兒	nǎr	IntPron	where
6	洗手间/洗手間	xǐshǒujiān	N	bathroom, washroom, restroom (cf. "卫生间 wèishēngjiān")
7	对面/對面	duìmiàn	PW	opposite, across from
8	麦当劳/麥當勞	Màidāngláo	PropN	McDonald's
9	里/裡	li	PW	in, inside, the inside
10	怎么/怎麼	zěnme	IntPron	how, in what way
11	走	zǒu	V	to walk ("一直走 yìzhí zǒu", *to go straight on*), to leave
12	过/過	guò	V	to pass, to pass by, to go through, to celebrate
13	往	wǎng	Prep	towards, in the direction of
14	南	nán	PW	south
15	红绿灯/紅綠燈	hónglǜdēng	N	traffic light (red-green-light)
	红/紅	hóng	Adj	red
	绿/綠	lǜ	Adj	green
	灯/燈	dēng	N	light, lamp
16	经过/經過	jīngguò	V / Prep	to undergo, to experience; via, by way of (a place)
17	超市	chāoshì	N	supermarket (cf. "超级市场 chāojí shìchǎng")
18	药店/藥店	yàodiàn	N	drugstore, pharmacy, Chinese medicine shop
19	的	de	Part	signals modification (of) or possession ('s)
20	旁边(儿)/旁邊(兒)	pángbiān (r)	PW	next to, beside
21	远/遠	yuǎn	Adj	far, distant, remote (cf. "不远 bù yuǎn", *not far from, close to*)

22	不客气/不客氣	bú kèqi	Exp	you're welcome, don't mention it
23	校园/校園	xiàoyuán	N	campus, school yard, school compound
24	同学/同學	tóngxué	N	fellow student, classmate
25	系	xì	N	department at a university or college
26	在	zài	V / Prep	to be at, to exist, to be alive; at, in, on
27	留学生/留學生	liúxuéshēng	N	student studying abroad, overseas student
28	外教	wàijiào	N	foreign teacher
29	刚/剛	gāng	Adv	just, exactly, just a short while ago
30	从/從	cóng	Prep	from, through
31	北边(儿)/北邊(兒)	běibian (r)	PW	north side
	北	běi	PW	north
32	前	qián	PW	front, forward, ahead ("往前 wǎng qián", *forward*), before
33	一直	yìzhí	Adv	straight, continuously
34	多远/多遠	duō yuǎn	Phrase	How far?
	多	duō	IntPron	to what degree, how
35	大门/大門	dàmén	N	front door, front gate, main gate
36	左	zuǒ	PW	left (cf. "左边 zuǒbian", *the left side*)
37	转/轉	zhuǎn	V	to turn, to shift, to change, to pass on, to transfer
38	银行/銀行	yínháng	N	bank (financial institution)
39	书店/書店	shūdiàn	N	bookstore
40	右	yòu	PW	right (cf. "右边 yòubian", *the right side*)
41	图书馆/圖書館	túshūguǎn	N	library
42	教学楼/教學樓	jiàoxuélóu	N	classroom building
43	中间/中間	zhōngjiān	PW	in between, in the middle
44	路	lù	N	road, path, (bus) route, line
45	还是/還是	háishi	Adv	still, (in alternative questions) or
46	不谢/不謝	bú xiè	Exp	don't thank me, not at all, it's nothing

Re-enacting the Dialogue

A: Xie Zhong **B: a passerby** **C: Li Yuan, a Chinese student**

(On the street)

A: Excuse me, is there a toilet around here?

B: Across the street, in the McDonald's.

A: Where is the McDonald's across the street? How can I get there?

B: Cross the street and head south; go past the traffic light, pass by the supermarket and the drugstore. There's a McDonald's next to the drugstore.

A: Is it far?

B: Not too far.

A: Thanks.

B: You're welcome.

(On campus)

A: Excuse me, fellow student, where is the Chinese Department please?

C: You're an overseas student, right?

A: No, I'm a foreign teacher in the English Department. I'm going over there to study Chinese.

C: I'm a student in the Chinese Department; I just came from there. The Chinese Department is on the north side (of the campus) – straight ahead!

A: How far is it to walk?

C: Not too far. Go through the main gate, turn left, go by the bank and the bookstore, and turn right. The Chinese Department is between the library and the classroom-building.

A: It is on the left, or right side of the road?

C: On the right.

A: Thank you.

C: You're welcome.

Grammar

▶ G1. "有 yǒu" (there is, there are) expressing existence

The verb "有 yǒu" (to have) can be used to express possession, as in: "我有两个苹果 Wǒ yǒu liǎng ge píngguǒ" (I have two apples); or it can express existence, as in: "北京有很多外国人 Běijīng yǒu hěn duō wàiguórén" (There are a lot of foreigners in Beijing). This lesson focuses on the latter usage. The sentence pattern is:

Place + 有 yǒu + Object.

The place can be represented by a place noun, or by a noun followed by a position word. For example:

① 北京有很多外国留学生。There are many foreign students in Beijing.
Běijīng yǒu hěn duō wàiguó liúxuéshēng.

② 大门旁边有一个餐馆。There is a restaurant next to the main gate.
Dàmén pángbiān yǒu yí ge cānguǎn.

③ 马路对面有一个超市。There is a supermarket on the other side of the street.
Mǎlù duìmiàn yǒu yí ge chāoshì.

④ 饭馆里边有很多人。There are lots of people in the restaurant.
Fànguǎn lǐbian yǒu hěn duō rén.

The place can be questioned with "哪儿 nǎr" ("哪里 nǎli" in more formal registers, or in southern Mandarin). For example:

⑤ 哪儿有洗手间？Where is there a restroom?
Nǎr yǒu xǐshǒujiān?

The scope of the question can be narrowed by specifying a general location first:

⑥ 这附近哪儿有洗手间？Where is there a restroom nearby?
Zhè fùjìn nǎr yǒu xǐshǒujiān?

▶ G2. Location phrases

A location phrase is composed of a place noun (e.g., "药店 yàodiàn", drugstore) and a position word (e.g., "旁边 pángbiān", besides) in the order place noun before position word: 药店旁边 yàodiàn pángbiān (next to the drugstore). Notice that this is the opposite order to that of the English equivalent. Other examples:

Màidāngláo lǐbian	麦当劳里边	inside (the) McDonald's
mǎlù duìmiàn	马路对面	the other side of the road
chāoshì nánbian	超市南边	south of the supermarket
xiàoyuán běibian	校园北边	the north side of the campus

The modifying relation between the place noun (e.g., 马路 mǎlù) and the position word (e.g., 对面 duìmiàn) can be explicitly marked with "的 de" (see G5). For instance, "马路的对面 mǎlù de duìmiàn", literally, "the road's other side", i.e., "the other side of the road".

▶ G3. The interrogative "怎么 zěnme" (how)

"怎么 zěnme" is the question word for manner adverbials and, like them, appears directly before the associated verb.

① 你怎么去学校? How do you go to school?
Nǐ zěnme qù xuéxiào?

② 你怎么走? How do you get there?
Nǐ zěnme zǒu?

As with other question words, the answer appears in the same position as the question word:

③ 我坐车去学校。I go to school by bus.
Wǒ zuò chē qù xuéxiào.

④ 往南走。You head south.
Wǎng nán zǒu.

▶ G4. "往 wǎng" (towards) indicating direction

Prepositions "往 wǎng" and "向 xiàng" (both "towards") combine with position words, such as "前 qián" (in front) or "左 zuǒ" (left), to form prepositional phrases that are placed (as usual) before the verb, where they indicate the direction of movement.

Subject + 往 wǎng/向 xiàng + Position Word + Motion Verb.

wǎng zuǒ zhuǎn	往左转	turn left
xiàng yòu zhuǎn	向右转	turn right
xiàng zuǒ zǒu	向左走	walk to the left
wǎng yòu zǒu	往右走	walk to the right

In the expressions for "turn right" and "turn left", the prepositions can be omitted:

zuǒ zhuǎn	左转	turn left
yòu zhuǎn	右转	turn right

Notice that English words order is, again, quite the opposite of the Chinese: "左转 zuǒ zhuǎn", literally "(to the) left turn", but English "turn (to the) left".

▶ G5. The particle "的 de" in location phrases

"的 de" is commonly used to indicate modification, including the modification of one noun by another: "周老师的学生 Zhōu lǎoshī de xuésheng" (Teacher Zhou's students); "英文系的外教 Yīngwénxì de wàijiào" (foreign teachers in the English Department). The pattern is:

Noun + 的 de + Head Noun → NP

As noted in G2, the modification relationship between place nouns and position words (which is often left implicit in phrases such as "药店旁边 yàodiàn pángbiān", next to the drugstore) can be made explicit by the addition of "的 de":

① 药店的旁边 next to the drugstore
yàodiàn de pángbiān

药店的旁边是麦当劳。Next to the drugstore is a McDonald's.
Yàodiàn de pángbiān shì Màidāngláo.

② 教学楼的前边 in front of the classroom building
jiàoxuélóu de qiánbian

教学楼的前边有一个书店。There's a bookstore in front of the classroom building.
Jiàoxuélóu de qiánbian yǒu yí ge shūdiàn.

③ 图书馆和教学楼的中间 between the library and the classroom building
túshūguǎn hé jiàoxuélóu de zhōngjiān

④ 饭馆在图书馆和教学楼的中间。
Fànguǎn zài túshūguǎn hé jiàoxuélóu de zhōngjiān.
The restaurant is located between the library and the classroom building.

▶ G6. The copula verb "是 shì"

As noted in Lesson 3 (G3), "是 shì" typically links two noun phrases in an identity relationship, e.g., "他是谢中 Tā shì Xiè Zhōng" (He's Xie Zhong); or a relationship of class inclusion, e.g., "我是学生 Wǒ shì xuésheng" (I'm a student).

Subject + 是 shì + Object.

The subject may consist of a simple noun, as above. But it may also be composed of a location phrase, such as "银行的左边 yínháng de zuǒbian" (to the left of the bank).

① 银行的左边是书店。To the left of the bank is the bookstore.
Yínháng de zuǒbian shì shūdiàn.

In this case, "是 shì" (in its identity function) serves to indicate the arrangement of the two entities, the bank and the bookstore. Other examples:

② 银行的右边是超市。To the right of the bank is a supermarket.
Yínháng de yòubian shì chāoshì.

③ 马路的对面是洗手间。On the other side of the street is a restroom.
Mǎlù de duìmiàn shì xǐshǒujiān.

▶ G7. "在 zài" (to be at; at, on, in) expressing location

(1) "在 zài" can be used as a verb, meaning "to be at, to be in, to be on." It functions to link a person or place to a location: "老师在教室里 Lǎoshī zài jiàoshì li" (The teacher is in the classroom); "洗手间在马路对面 Xǐshǒujiān zài mǎlù duìmiàn" (The restroom is on the other side of the street). The usual pattern for "在 zài" is:

Subject + 在 zài + Location.

The subject in such sentences is usually assumed to be identifiable to the hearer, so the English equivalent will often have the definite article, "the".

① 银行在前边。The bank is up ahead.
Yínháng zài qiánbian.

② 教学楼在英文系右边。The classroom building is to the right of the English Department.
Jiàoxuélóu zài Yīngwénxì yòubian.

(2) "在 zài" can be also used as a preposition to introduce a place where an action takes place. In this case the 在-place phrase appears before the verb. The sentence pattern for this usage is:

Subject + 在 zài + Place + V (+ Object).

③ 我在餐馆吃饭。I eat in a restaurant.
Wǒ zài cānguǎn chī fàn.

④ 他在超市买东西。He shops at the supermarket.
Tā zài chāoshì mǎi dōngxi.

⑤ 我在北京学中文。I study Chinese in Beijing.
Wǒ zài Běijīng xué Zhōngwén.

(3) The interrogative word "哪儿 nǎr" (where) can in all cases be used to question the place, as follows:

Subject + 在 zài + 哪儿 nǎr? ("在 zài" as a main verb)

Subject + 在哪儿 zài nǎr + V (+ Object)? ("在 zài" as a preposition)

⑥ A: 洗手间在哪儿？Where is the bathroom?
Xǐshǒujiān zài nǎr?

B: 洗手间在英文教室的旁边。The bathroom is next to the English classroom.
Xǐshǒujiān zài Yīngwén jiàoshì de pángbiān.

⑦ A: 中文书在哪儿？Where's the Chinese book?
Zhōngwén shū zài nǎr?

B: 中文书在桌子下边。The Chinese book's under the desk.
Zhōngwén shū zài zhuōzi xiàbian.

⑧ A: 你在哪儿买东西？Where do you do your shopping?
Nǐ zài nǎr mǎi dōngxi?

B: 我在超市买东西。I shop at the supermarket.
Wǒ zài chāoshì mǎi dōngxi.

(4) 在-sentences are negated, in the usual way, by inserting "不 bù" in the adverbial position before "在 zài":

⑨ 他不在教室。He is not in the classroom.
Tā bú zài jiàoshì.

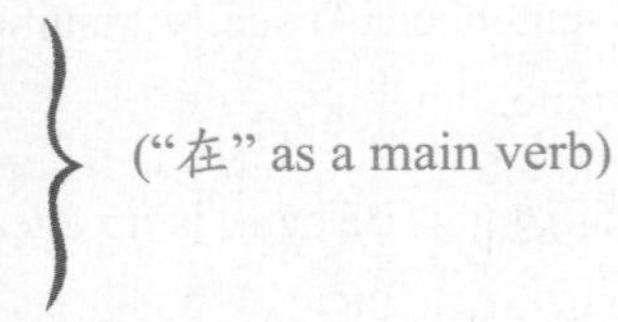

⑩ 妈妈不在家。Mom is not home.
Māma bú zài jiā.

⑪ 我不在超市买东西。I don't shop at the supermarket.
Wǒ bú zài chāoshì mǎi dōngxi.

("在" as a preposition)

⑫ 她不在银行工作。She doesn't work at a bank.
Tā bú zài yínháng gōngzuò.

▶ G8. "从 cóng" (from) indicating place of origin

"从 cóng" is a preposition that introduces the place of origin: 从 cóng+ Place (of origin). For example: "从那边来 cóng nàbian lái" (come from over there); "从图书馆去 cóng túshūguǎn qù" (go from the library). Note that, like other prepositions, "从 cóng" with its object comes before its associated verb:

① A：你从哪儿来？Where are you from?
Nǐ cóng nǎr lái?

B：我从美国来。I am from America.
Wǒ cóng Měiguó lái.

One other point: A person is not usually the beginning point of a movement; rather, it is the place associated with the person. One way to express this in Chinese is to add "这儿 zhèr" or "那儿 nàr" to the person: "从我这儿 cóng wǒ zhèr" (from where I am); "去她那儿 qù tā nàr" (go to where she is).

② 从外教那儿来 come from the foreign teachers
cóng wàijiào nàr lái

③ 从你这儿去 go from where you are
cóng nǐ zhèr qù

Consolidation & Practice

1. Make sentences following the example

(1) Locate the places or people listed below with "在 zài"

Target place + 在 zài + 哪儿 nǎr?

Example: A：超市在哪儿？ Where is the supermarket?
Chāoshì zài nǎr?

B：超市在学校旁边。The supermarket is next to the school.
Chāoshì zài xuéxiào pángbiān.

药店 yàodiàn | 餐馆 cānguǎn | 中国银行 Zhōngguó Yínháng | 谢老师 Xiè lǎoshī | 教学楼 jiàoxuélóu | 你的同学 nǐ de tóngxué | 中文系 Zhōngwénxì

(2) Seek the existence of a place with "有 yǒu"

哪儿 nǎr + 有 yǒu + Target place?

Example: A：哪儿有洗手间？ Where is a toilet?
Nǎr yǒu xǐshǒujiān?

B：前边有。There is one in front.
Qiánbian yǒu.

饭馆 fànguǎn | 银行 yínháng | 厕所 cèsuǒ | 商店 shāngdiàn | 麦当劳 Màidāngláo | 药店 yàodiàn

(3) Ask where something can be done

请问 qǐngwèn, 在 zài + 哪儿 nǎr + Verb + Object?

Example: 请问，在哪儿换钱？ Where can I change money, please?
Qǐngwèn, zài nǎr huàn qián?

买药 mǎi yào | 买书 mǎi shū | 吃饭 chī fàn | 学中文 xué Zhōngwén | 买单 mǎidān | 买西瓜 mǎi xīguā

2. Give directions, with verbs "在 zài", "是 shì", or "有 yǒu"

(1) With "在 zài"

Target place + Verb + Location.

Example: 图书馆在前边。The library is straight ahead.
Túshūguǎn zài qiánbian.

Target place	Location
宾馆 bīnguǎn	马路对面 mǎlù duìmiàn
中国银行 Zhōngguó Yínháng	左边 zuǒbian
厕所 cèsuǒ	大门右边 dàmén yòubian
药店 yàodiàn	那边 nàbian
麦当劳 Màidāngláo	商店旁边 shāngdiàn pángbiān
英文系 Yīngwénxì	教学楼旁边 jiàoxuélóu pángbiān

(2) With "是 shì"

Location + 是 shì + Target place.

Example: 银行的左边是书店。On the left side of the bank is a bookstore.
Yínháng de zuǒbian shì shūdiàn.

Location	Target place
书店的旁边 shūdiàn de pángbiān	商店 shāngdiàn
马路的对面 mǎlù de duìmiàn	洗手间 xǐshǒujiān
教学楼的前边 jiàoxuélóu de qiánbian	中文系 Zhōngwénxì
饭馆的右边 fànguǎn de yòubian	银行 yínháng

(3) With "有 yǒu"

Location + 有 yǒu + Target place.

Example: 教学楼的旁边有一个书店。There's a bookstore next to the classroom building.
Jiàoxuélóu de pángbiān yǒu yí ge shūdiàn.

Location	Target place
麦当劳里边 Màidāngláo de lǐbian	洗手间 xǐshǒujiān
超市的旁边 chāoshì de pángbiān	饭馆 fànguǎn
大门的右边 dàmén de yòubian	书店 shūdiàn
马路的对面 mǎlù de duìmiàn	中国银行 Zhōngguó Yínháng
校园的北边 xiàoyuán de běibian	图书馆 túshūguǎn

3. Ask directions with "请问 qǐngwèn, destination + 怎么走 zěnme zǒu?" and answer questions with "往 wǎng + direction + 走 zǒu"

Destination + IntPron + Verb? Prep + Direction + Verb.

Example: A: 请问，超市怎么走？How do I get to the supermarket?
Qǐngwèn, chāoshì zěnme zǒu?

B: 往前走。Go straight ahead.
Wǎng qián zǒu.

A	B
商店 shāngdiàn	一直 yìzhí
银行 yínháng	南 nán
汽车站 (bus stop) qìchēzhàn	过了商店，往前 guòle shāngdiàn, wǎng qián
医院 yīyuàn	过了麦当劳，左转 guòle Màidāngláo, zuǒ zhuǎn
图书馆 túshūguǎn	经过书店，往右转 jīngguò shūdiàn, wǎng yòu zhuǎn

4. Express place of origin: "从 cóng……来 lái / 去 qù……"

Subject + 从 cóng + Place + 来 lái/ 去 qù (+ Destination).

Example: 外教从美国来。The foreign teachers come from America.
Wàijiào cóng Měiguó lái.

Subject		Place		Destination
学生 xuésheng		学校 xuéxiào		
留学生 liúxuéshēng		英国 Yīngguó	来 lái	
他 tā	从 cóng	图书馆 túshūguǎn		
我们 wǒmen		您这儿 nín zhèr	去 qù	麦当劳 Màidāngláo
他们 tāmen		银行 yínháng		超市 chāoshì

5. Make a turn, with the preposition "往 wǎng" and the verb "转 zhuǎn"

往 wǎng + Direction + Verb.

Example: 往左转。Turn left.
Wǎng zuǒ zhuǎn.

右 yòu	这边 zhèbian	那边 nàbian	后 hòu
北 běi	南 nán	东(east) dōng	西(west) xī

Pronunciation Notes

1. The pronunciation of "j", "q" and "x"

Pinyin "j", "q" and "x" present problems for speakers of English mainly because the letters "q" and "x" (but not "j") have unexpected values: "q" is more like English "chy"; "x" is more like English "sy". So all three match up: "jy", "chy" and "sy". Once you completely sever all associations with English "q" and "x", you will not find the sounds themselves particularly hard to pronounce.

For the first two, "j" and "q", the tip of the tongue is pressed against the back of the lower teeth, while the sides of the upper part of the tongue are pressed against the upper teeth and gum. *Pinyin* "x" is pronounced in a similar position, except that the tip of tongue does not form a complete block; it lets the air through, so that you hear a hissing sound. Contrast "家 jiā" (home), "钱 qián" (money), "虾 xiā" (shrimp) – remember, the position of the tongue hardly changes.

jī 鸡 chicken	jiā 家 home	juān 捐 to donate
qī 七 seven	qiā 掐 to pinch	quān 圈 circle
xī 西 west	xiā 虾 shrimp	xuān 宣 to declare

Notice also that "j", "q" and "x" are always followed immediately by the letters "i" and "u" (e.g. ji, jie, jian; ju, jue, juan); and the "i" and "u" are always pronounced "ee" and "ü".

2. Final "i"

In the previous section, it was noted that "j", "q" and "x" appear only before written "i", and that after those initials, written "i" is only pronounced "ee"; e.g., jī, qī, xī; jiè, qiè, xiè. Written "i" also occurs after other intials, but only by itself, as the full rhyme. You've already encountered the word "shì" many times (e.g., in "shì bu shì"), so you know it is pronounced by extending the "sh" sound into the vowel – with no tongue movement at all. Using English spelling, it can be represented as "shr". Thus: "zhi, chi, shi, ri" – all with the vowel that you hear in "shì". That's quite different from the "ee" vowel of "jī, qī, xī"! "Zi, ci, si" – the only other cases of final "i" – are pronounced in much the same way as "zhi, chi, shi, ri", that is, by extending the initial sound into the vowel, as in the case of the "zì" of "Hànzì" or the "sì" of "yī èr sān sì". So when you see a final "i" in a syllable, first check to see if the initial is "j", "q" or "x". If it is, then it's "ee"; if not, then it's one of those swallowed vowels.

	Pinyin	Characters	English meaning
1	jī	机	machine
2	qī	妻	wife
3	xī	息	to rest
4	zì	字	character
5	cì	次	time, occurrence
6	sì	四	four
7	zhī	知	to know
8	chī	吃	to eat
9	shì	是	to be
10	rì	日	sun

Mixed (watch the tones as well): cì shì sì jī zhī qī zì chī xī rì

Pronunciation Exercises

1. Read the following words aloud. Pay special attention to the differences between "j", "q" and "x"

	Pinyin	Characters	English meaning
1	júzi	橘子	orange
2	jùzi	句子	sentence
3	jiāng	姜	ginger
4	qiū	秋	autumn
5	qiáng	墙	wall
6	xué	学	to study
7	xiān	先	first
8	qúnzi	裙子	skirt
9	Xúnzǐ	荀子	*name of a Chinese philosopher*
10	xiàng	向	towards

2. In each group, combine initial with rhyme and read the syllables aloud

Group A	Group B	Group C	Group D
j - iǔ	zh - è	y (i) - īng	z - ài
q - ián	ch - ǎo	w (u) - ǔ	c - óng
x - iǎo	sh - āng	yu (ü) - án	s - ì

3. Read these words for common items of furniture aloud

	Pinyin	Characters	English meaning
1	jiājù	家具	furniture
2	shāfā	沙发	sofa
3	zhuōzi	桌子	table, desk
4	cānzhuō	餐桌	dining table
5	yǐzi	椅子	chair
6	shūguì	书柜	bookcase
7	chuáng	床	bed

	Pinyin	Characters	English meaning
8	shuāngrénchuáng	双人床	double bed
9	diànshì	电视	TV set

4. Read the following words aloud. Many of them refer to schools and people involved with schools, so you might learn some useful educational vocabulary while you practice pronunciation

	Pinyin	Characters	English meaning
1	xuéxiào	学校	school
2	xiǎoxué	小学	elementary school
3	xiàozhǎng	校长	president, headmaster/headmistress
4	jiàoshòu	教授	professor
5	jiàoshī	教师	teacher
6	xuésheng	学生	student
7	xiǎoxuéshēng	小学生	elementary school student
8	jiāzhǎng	家长	parents
9	zhōngxuéshēng	中学生	secondary school student
10	kēxuéjiā	科学家	scientist
11	dàxuéshēng	大学生	college student
12	xuéxí	学习	to study
13	xiūxi	休息	to rest
14	xīngqī	星期	week
15	jiàqī	假期	holiday

Listening Comprehension

1. Listen to the dialogue between a foreign student and a Chinese student; then answer the questions

   (1) How many libraries are being talked about?

   (2) Where does the man want to go?

   (3) What route does the woman tell him to take?

   (4) Is the library nearer the bank or the classroom building?

2. Listen to the conversation between two females

   (1) What does the first person have to do?

   (2) What is she looking for?

   (3) Where is she told to go?

   (4) Draw a map showing their route.

Communication Activities

Pair Work

Scenario I: Take turns asking questions and giving answers, following the pattern illustrated in the examples. Use the verbs "在 zài", "有 yǒu", and "是 shì".

Example: A：食堂在哪儿？
Shítáng zài nǎr?
B：在前边。
Zài qiánbian.

A：哪儿有厕所？
Nǎr yǒu cèsuǒ?
B：书店后边。
Shūdiàn hòubian.

A：右边是什么？
Yòubian shì shénme?
B：右边是教学楼。
Yòubian shì jiàoxuélóu.

Scenario II: You're new to campus. Your roommate's been there for several years and knows his/her way around. Ask him/her how to get to the places you want to get to, such as the Chinese library, the cafeteria, and the classroom building. He/She will tell you, showing you on the map if necessary. Use expressions like "go forward", "go straight", "turn left", "turn right", "pass the…" and/or "turn back".

Scenario III: Your partner gives you orders, such as "go forward", "go straight", "turn left", "turn right", or "turn back". You act out what he/she says, repeating each order to yourself , e.g., "Wǎng qián zǒu. / Hǎo, wǎng qián zǒu." If walking around is impracticable, move a small object around a table top to simulate walking instead.

Review Exercises

I. Match the verbs in the left-hand list with the nouns in the right-hand list

(1) 去 qù　　　A. 素菜 sùcài
(2) 过 guò　　　B. 路 lù
(3) 往 wǎng　　　C. 银行 yínháng
(4) 问 wèn　　　D. 马路 mǎlù
(5) 要 yào　　　E. 左转 zuǒ zhuǎn

II. Create questions with "怎么 zěnme" based on the answers given

1. A：______________________________?
B：我刚去麦当劳吃了。
Wǒ gāng qù Màidāngláo chī le.

2. A：______________________________?

B：我没有人民币了。
Wǒ méiyǒu rénmínbì le.

3. A：________________？

B：我不吃肉。
Wǒ bù chī ròu.

III. Answer the following questions with a sentence containing an appropriate "location phrase" (= noun + position word)

1. A：药店在前边吗？
Yàodiàn zài qiánbian ma?

B：________________。(across the street)

2. A：图书馆在校园北边吗？
Túshūguǎn zài xiàoyuán běibian ma?

B：________________。(next to the classroom building)

3. A：书店在银行旁边吗？
Shūdiàn zài yínháng pángbiān ma?

B：________________。(on the right side of the store)

4. A：去麦当劳要经过两个红绿灯吗？
Qù Màidāngláo yào jīngguò liǎng ge hónglǜdēng ma?

B：________________。(south of the traffic light)

IV. Re-form the following sentences so you can make use of the words in brackets

Example:

大门对面有网吧。 (在 zài) → 网吧在大门对面。
Dàmén duìmiàn yǒu wǎngbā. Wǎngbā zài Dàmén duìmiàn.

1. 商店旁边是书店。 (有 yǒu) →
Shāngdiàn pángbiān shì shūdiàn.

2. 英文系在教学楼旁边。 (有 yǒu) →
Yīngwénxì zài jiàoxuélóu pángbiān.

3. 银行旁边是邮局。 (在) →
Yínháng pángbiān shì yóujú.

4. 食堂在七号楼旁边。 （是）→
Shítáng zài qī hào lóu pángbiān.

5. 马路对面是中国银行。 （有）→
Mǎlù duìmiàn shì Zhōngguó Yínháng.

6. 书店后面有一个厕所。 （在）→
Shūdiàn hòumiàn yǒu yí ge cèsuǒ.

V. Answer the following questions using "从 cóng……来 lái"

1. A：你是北京人吗？
   Nǐ shì Běijīngrén ma?

   B：不是，________________________________。
   Bú shì, ________________________________.

2. A：我是美国人，你也是吗？
   Wǒ shì Měiguórén, nǐ yě shì ma?

   B：不是，________________________________。
   Bú shì, ________________________________.

3. A：她是你的英国外教吗？
   Tā shì nǐ de Yīngguó wàijiào ma?

   B：对，________________________________。
   Duì, ________________________________.

4. A：请问，学校大门在哪儿？从这儿怎么走？
   Qǐngwèn, xuéxiào dàmén zài nǎr? Cóng zhèr zěnme zǒu?

   B：____________________________________。

VI. Use words from each row to form location phrases. Then reverse their order, and explain how the meanings change

Example: 校园+的+北边；北边+的+校园

Place Nouns	Location Nouns	Place + Location	Location + Place
1. 图书馆 túshūguǎn	前边 qiánbian	(1) __________	(2) __________

2. 麦当劳 Màidāngláo　对面 duìmiàn　(1) ________ (2) ________

3. 厕所 cèsuǒ　里边 lǐbian　(1) ________ (2) ________

4. 超市 chāoshì　东边 dōngbian　(1) ________ (2) ________

5. 银行 yínháng　南边 nánbian　(1) ________ (2) ________

6. 饭馆 fànguǎn　旁边 pángbiān　(1) ________ (2) ________

7. 药店 yàodiàn　外边 wàibian　(1) ________ (2) ________

8. 外教 wàijiào　后边 hòubian　(1) ________ (2) ________

9. 大门 dàmén　西边 xībian　(1) ________ (2) ________

10. 马路 mǎlù　右边 yòubian　(1) ________ (2) ________

VII. Answer the questions with "在 zài + Place Noun + Verb"

1. A：留学生在哪儿学中文？
Liúxuéshēng zài nǎr xué Zhōngwén?

B：________________。(中国 Zhōngguó)

2. A：他在哪儿吃饭？
Tā zài nǎr chī fàn?

B：________________。(饭馆 fànguǎn)

3. A：那个外教在哪儿教英文？
Nàge wàijiào zài nǎr jiāo Yīngwén?

B：________________。(我们学校 wǒmen xuéxiào)

4. A：你去哪儿买苹果？
Nǐ qù nǎr mǎi píngguǒ?

B：________________。(超市 chāoshì)

5. A：你在哪儿住？
Nǐ zài nǎr zhù?

B：我________________________。(学校里边 xuéxiào lǐbian)

Wǒ ________________________.

6. A：你的老师在哪儿住？

Nǐ de lǎoshī zài nǎr zhù?

B：他________________________。(学校外边 xuéxiào wàibian)

Tā ________________________.

VIII. Provide directions based on the given situations, using the items listed below

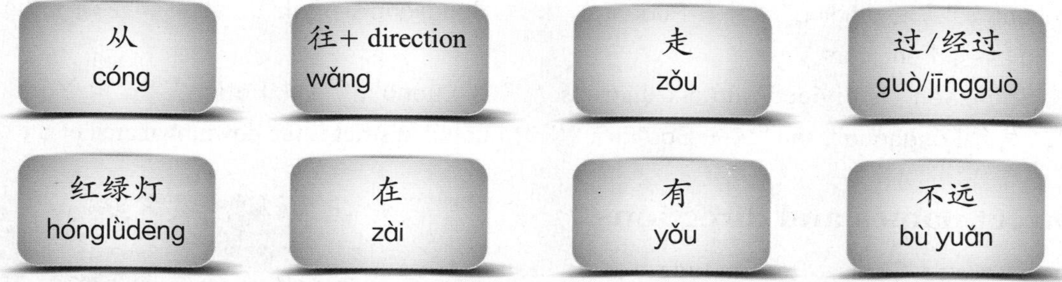

1. You are new to a university in China. Ask where the important places and facilities are: the classroom buildings, cafeterias, shops, banks, etc.

2. Your roommate is sick. Explain to him/her where the nearest drugstore is and what the best way to get there is.

3. Tell your classmate how to get to the teacher's office on campus.

4. Someone stops you on the street, saying that he/she needs to find a public toilet. Direct him/her to one.

Culture Notes

1. City districts

Cities in China are divided into districts, so when you want to find a place in a city, you need to know the name of the district. "北京 Běijīng" has sixteen districts or counties, of which "西城 Xīchéng" and "东城 Dōngchéng", comprise the downtown area. Most foreign embassies and company offices are in the "朝阳 Cháoyáng" district. Most universities, including Peking University and Tsinghua University are located in the "海淀 Hǎidiàn" district.

"上海 Shànghǎi" has 16 administrative districts: "黄浦 Huángpǔ", "卢湾 Lúwān", "徐汇 Xúhuì", "长宁 Chángníng", "静安 Jìng'ān", "普陀 Pǔtuó", "闸北 Zháběi", "虹口 Hóngkǒu","杨浦 Yángpǔ", "宝山 Bǎoshān", "闵行 Mǐnháng", "嘉定 Jiādìng", "浦东 Pǔdōng", "松江 Sōngjiāng", "金山 Jīnshān", "青浦 Qīngpǔ", "南汇 Nánhuì", and "奉贤 Fèngxián".

"深圳 Shēnzhèn" is divided into six districts: "罗湖 Luóhú", "福田 Fútián", "盐田 Yántián", "南山 Nánshān", "龙岗 Lónggǎng", and "宝安 Bǎo'ān". "罗湖 Luóhú" district is the downtown area of the city.

2. Street names and directions

Street names in China often include one of the cardinal directions, north, south, east or west (which in Chinese are ordered EWSN or ESWN). For example, "天安门西大街 Tiān'ānménxī Dàjiē" (Tiananmen West Boulevard) indicates that the boulevard is west of Tiananmen Square. Noting the cardinal directions for street names can be a big help in finding your way.

Lesson Seven At a Hotel

第七课 在宾馆

Dì-qī Kè Zài Bīnguǎn

In this lesson you will learn how to do the following

- Ask about hotel reservations
- Explain what sort of room you would like
- Request that someone clean the room and change the linen
- Ask someone to fix some things that are not working in your room

Grammar

- Question words
- The "是 shì……的 de" construction, for emphasizing attendant circumstances (how, when, where, etc.)
- More on the particle "的 de"
- "给 gěi" as a main verb
- Duration phrases
- "好 hǎo" as a verb complement
- "……的时候 de shíhou" (when, during, while)
- Pivotal constructions

Culture Notes

- Types of hotels
- Taking care of valuables
- Arranging for an Internet connection and making long-distance telephone calls
- Room inspection at checkout

Dialogue

A：李大伟 Lǐ Dàwěi　　B：服务员 fúwùyuán　　C：清洁工 qīngjiégōng

（酒店大厅 Jiǔdiàn dàtīng）

A： 你好。我在你们酒店预订了一个房间。
Nǐ hǎo. Wǒ zài nǐmen jiǔdiàn yùdìngle yí ge fángjiān.

B： 请问，您是用谁的[G1]名字预订的[G2]？
Qǐngwèn, nín shì yòng shéi de[G1] míngzi yùdìng de[G2]?

A： 是朋友订的，用的是他的[G3]名字：李工。
Shì péngyou dìng de, yòng de shì tā de[G3] míngzi: Lǐ Gōng.

B： 对，我们这儿是有您预订的房间。请给[G4]我您的护照。
Duì, wǒmen zhèr shì yǒu nín yùdìng de fángjiān. Qǐng gěi[G4] wǒ nín de hùzhào.

A： 这是我的护照。能不能给我一间单人间，大床房，不要临街的房间？
Zhè shì wǒ de hùzhào. Néng bu néng gěi wǒ yì jiān dānrénjiān, dàchuángfáng, bú yào línjiē de fángjiān?

B： 我尽量给[G4]您安排。您打算住多久？
Wǒ jǐnliàng gěi[G4] nín ānpái. Nín dǎsuàn zhù duō jiǔ?

A： 我住三天[G5]。
Wǒ zhù sān tiān[G5].

B： 您需要付三天的押金。您每天的房费是568元，一共1800元押金。
Nín xūyào fù sān tiān de yājīn. Nín měi tiān de fángfèi shì wǔbǎi liùshíbā yuán, yígòng yìqiān bābǎi yuán yājīn.

A： 我可以用信用卡吗？
Wǒ kěyǐ yòng xìnyòngkǎ ma?

B： 可以。请在这儿签您的名字。这是押金收据，请收好[G6]。这是您的房间钥匙。您的房间号码是1420[1]。房间在14层，电梯在右边。

Notes

1. Reciting numbers in Chinese: A two-digit number is spoken as a number, not digit-by-digit: 18 is "shíbā", 96 is "jiǔshíliù". A three-digit number may be expressed as a number, or digit-by-digit: 405 is "sìbǎi líng wǔ", or "sì-líng-wǔ". Numbers with four digits or more are usually said digit-by-digit: 1420 is "yī-sì-èr-líng" (or "yāo-sì-èr-líng"; on the Mainland, "yī" as a number is often pronounced "yāo" for clarity). Large round numbers, however, are said as whole numbers: ten thousand is "yíwàn", etc.

Kěyǐ. Qǐng zài zhèr qiān nín de míngzi. Zhè shì yājīn shōujù, qǐng shōuhǎo[G6]. Zhè shì nín de fángjiān yàoshi. Nín de fángjiān hàomǎ shì yāo-sì-èr-líng[1]. Fángjiān zài shísì céng, diàntī zài yòubian.

A： 请问餐厅在哪儿？
Qǐngwèn cāntīng zài nǎr?

B： 我们有中餐厅和西餐厅。中餐厅在一楼，西餐厅在二楼。
Wǒmen yǒu zhōngcāntīng hé xīcāntīng. Zhōngcāntīng zài yī lóu, xīcāntīng zài èr lóu.

A： 你们酒店有没有叫醒服务？
Nǐmen jiǔdiàn yǒu méiyǒu jiàoxǐng fúwù?

B： 有。您要我什么时候叫醒您？
Yǒu. Nín yào wǒ shénme shíhou jiàoxǐng nín?

A： 请明天早上六点[2]叫醒我。谢谢。
Qǐng míngtiān zǎoshang liù diǎn[2] jiàoxǐng wǒ. Xièxie.

B： 不客气。
Bú kèqi.

（在房间 Zài fángjiān）

C： 先生，现在[3]可以打扫您的房间吗？
Xiānsheng, xiànzài[3] kěyǐ dǎsǎo nín de fángjiān ma?

A： 请稍等一会儿[4]。……进来吧。请帮忙换床单和杯子。
Qǐng shāo děng yíhuìr[4]. ……Jìnlai ba. Qǐng bāngmáng huàn chuángdān hé bēizi.

C： 没问题。
Méi wèntí.

A： 你打扫洗澡间的时候[G7]，能不能多给我一条毛巾[5]？

---

2. Time expressions begin with the largest unit and proceed to the smallest, e.g., "明天早上六点 míngtiān zǎoshang liù diǎn" (tomorrow morning at 6:00).
3. "现在 xiànzài" is a noun acting as a time word. Time words are placed before the verb: "现在可以打扫您的房间吗？Xiànzài kěyǐ dǎsǎo nín de fángjiān ma? " (May I clean your room now?) If a subject is present, time words may appear before or after the subject, with slight difference in nuance: "我现在可以去 Wǒ xiànzài kěyǐ qù", or "现在我可以去 Xiànzài wǒ kěyǐ qù".
4. "请稍等一会儿 Qǐng shāo děng yíhuìr": "等一会儿 děng yíhuìr" means, literally "wait for a while", but it often implies simply "in a while; shortly". In combination with "稍 shāo" (slightly, a bit), however, the meaning is always "wait for a while".
5. "多给我一条毛巾 duō gěi wǒ yì tiáo máojīn" (give me one more towel) has "多 duō" before the verb, as an adverbial, and the item, "一条毛巾 yì tiáo máojīn", after the verb. This is the standard way of requesting an additional item. Cf. "请多给我一个 Qǐng duō gěi wǒ yí ge" (Please give me one more).

Nǐ dǎsǎo xǐzǎojiān de shíhou[G7], néng bu néng duō gěi wǒ yì tiáo máojīn[5]?

C： 当然可以。您还要什么？
Dāngrán kěyǐ. Nín hái yào shénme?

A： 不要了。我房间的空调好像坏了，屋里很热。
Bú yào le. Wǒ fángjiān de kōngtiáo hǎoxiàng huài le, wū li hěn rè.

C： 我叫人来修[G8]。
Wǒ jiào rén lái xiū[G8].

A： 谢谢。
Xièxie.

C： 不客气。
Bú kèqi.

New Words

1	清洁工/清潔工	qīngjiégōng	N	sanitation worker, street cleaner, garbage collector
2	酒店	jiǔdiàn	N	large hotel (esp. in China)
3	大厅/大廳	dàtīng	N	lobby
4	预订/預訂	yùdìng	V	to book (hotel room, ticket, etc.)
5	房间/房間	fángjiān	N	room (in a hotel, house, etc.)
6	用	yòng	V	to use
7	谁的/誰的	shéi/shuí de	Phrase	whose
	谁/誰	shéi/shuí	IntPron	who (m)
8	名字	míngzi	N	given name, personal name, name
9	朋友	péngyou	N	friend
10	订/訂	dìng	V	to reserve (a room, ticket, etc.)
11	他的	tā de	Phrase	his (cf. "她的 tā de", *hers*)
	他	tā	Pron	he, him, other, another
12	对/對	duì	Adj	correct, right
13	这儿/這兒	zhèr	N	here, this place
14	给/給	gěi	V / Prep	to give; for (the benefit of)

15	您的	nín de	Phrase	(formal-polite) your, yours (cf. "你的 nǐ de")
16	护照/護照	hùzhào	N	passport
17	我的	wǒ de	Phrase	my, mine
18	不能	bù néng	Phrase	cannot, must not, unable
19	间/間	jiān	Meas	*used for rooms*
20	单人间/單人間	dānrénjiān	N	single room, room for one person
21	大床房	dàchuángfáng	N	single room with one large bed
	大	dà	Adj	big
	床	chuáng	N	bed
	房	fáng	BF	room, house, building
22	临街/臨街	línjiē	V	to face the street
23	尽量/儘量	jǐnliàng	Adv	as much as possible, do one's best to
24	安排	ānpái	V/N	to arrange, to make arrangements; arrangements
25	打算	dǎsuàn	V/N	to plan, to intend; plan, intention
26	住	zhù	V	to live, to lodge, to stay at
27	多久	duō jiǔ	Phrase	for how long
28	需要	xūyào	V/N	to need, to be needed, have to; needs
29	付	fù	V	to pay
30	押金	yājīn	N	money deposit, earnest money
31	每天	měi tiān	Phrase	every day, daily
32	房费/房費	fángfèi	N	room rate
	费/費	fèi	N	fees, cost, expenses
33	信用卡	xìnyòngkǎ	N	credit card
34	签/簽	qiān	V	to sign (name), to affix (one's mark)
35	收据/收據	shōujù	N	receipt
36	收	shōu	V	to receive, to accept
37	钥匙/鑰匙	yàoshi	N	a key (to a lock)
38	号码/號碼	hàomǎ	N	number (as in "telephone number")

	号/號	hào	N	number, size (of clothing, etc.), day of the month, street or house number
39	层/層	céng	Meas	floor, story (storey), layer
40	电梯/電梯	diàntī	N	elevator (lift), escalator
41	餐厅/餐廳	cāntīng	N	dining room, dining hall
42	中餐厅/中餐廳	zhōngcāntīng	N	Chinese restaurant, a restaurant serving Chinese food
43	西餐厅/西餐廳	xīcāntīng	N	a restaurant serving Western-style food
44	楼/樓	lóu	N	building, floor ("一楼 yī lóu", *first floor*; "二楼 èr lóu", *second floor*)
45	叫醒服务/叫醒服務	jiàoxǐng fúwù	Phrase	wake-up service
	叫醒	jiàoxǐng	V	to awaken (by calling)
	服务/服務	fúwù	V/N	to serve; service
46	什么时候/甚麽時候	shénme shíhou	Phrase	what time, when
	时候/時候	shíhou	N	time
47	明天	míngtiān	N	tomorrow
48	早上	zǎoshang	N	morning
49	点/點	diǎn	Meas	*used for points* (*on the clock*)
50	先生	xiānsheng	N	sir, preceded by a surname, Mr.
51	打扫/打掃	dǎsǎo	V	to clean, to sweep
52	稍	shāo	Adv	slightly, a little
53	等	děng	V	to wait
54	一会儿/一會兒	yíhuìr	Q	a while, soon, in a while, shortly
55	进来/進來	jìnlai	V	to enter, to come in
56	帮忙/幫忙	bāngmáng	VO	to help out, to lend a hand, to do a favor
57	换/換	huàn	V	to change, to exchange, to convert (currency)
58	床单/床單	chuángdān	N	bed sheet
59	杯子/盃子	bēizi	N	cup, glass
60	没问题/沒問題	méi wèntí	Exp	no problem, sure, certainly
61	洗澡间/洗澡間	xǐzǎojiān	N	bathroom

62	条/條	tiáo	Meas	*used for long, thin objects, such as roads, rivers, trousers, fish, etc.*
63	毛巾	máojīn	N	towel
64	当然/當然	dāngrán	Adv	of course, without doubt
65	空调/空調	kōngtiáo	N	air conditioning, air conditioner
66	好像	hǎoxiàng	Adv	seem, be like, look like, as if
67	坏了/壞了	huài le	Phrase	broken down, gone wrong, spoiled, bad
	坏/壞	huài	Adj	bad, broken
68	屋里/屋裡	wū li	Phrase	inside a house or room
69	很	hěn	Adv	quite, very
70	热/熱	rè	Adj/N	hot, popular; a craze, fad, "fever"
71	修	xiū	V	to fix, to repair

Re-enacting the Dialogue

A: David Lee **B: an attendant** **C: a custodian**

(In the lobby of a hotel)

A: Hi. I reserved a room at this hotel.

B: Whose name did you reserve it under, please?

A: It was booked by a friend, under his own name, Li Gong.

B: Right, we have the room you reserved. May I have your passport, please?

A: Here's my passport. Could you give me a single room with a large bed, not facing the street?

B: I'll do my best to arrange it for you. How long are you planning to stay?

A: I'm staying three days.

B: You'll need to pay a deposit for three days. Your daily rate for the room is ¥568; altogether that's ¥1800 deposit for three days.

A: Can I use a credit card?

B: Sure. Sign your name here, please. Here's a receipt for your deposit; please keep it safe.

Here's the key to your room. Your room number's 1420. The room's on the fourteenth floor – the elevator's on the right.

A: Where's the dining room, please?

B: We have a Chinese dining room and a Western one; the Chinese dining room is on the first floor, the Western one is on the second.

A: Do you have a wake-up service at the hotel?

B: We do. What time do you want us to wake you?

A: Please wake me up at six in the morning; thanks.

B: You're welcome.

(In the room)

C: Sir, may I clean your room now?

A: Would you mind waiting a minute. ... Come on in. Please change the sheets and the cups.

C: No problem.

A: When you clean the bathroom, could you give me an extra towel?

C: Of course. Need anything else?

A: No, but the air conditioning in my room seems to be broken; it's quite hot in the room.

C: I'll have someone come and fix it.

A: Thanks.

C: You're welcome.

Grammar

▶ G1. Question words

A number of common question words or phrases were introduced in earlier lessons: "多少 duōshao" (how many/much); "哪儿 nǎr" (where), "哪里 nǎli" in more formal speech; "什么 shénme" (what); and "怎么 zěnme" (how, in what way). This lesson introduces most of the rest of them: "谁 shéi/shuí" (who, whom) and "谁的 shéi/shuí de" (whose); "多久 duō jiǔ" (for how long); and "什么时候 shénme shíhou" (at what time, when).

① 您是用谁的名字预订的？ Whose name did you use to make the reservation?
Nín shì yòng shéi de míngzi yùdìng de?

Sometimes "谁 shéi/shuí" can be the starting point of a question: "谁是服务员？ Shéi shì fúwùyuán?" (Who is the attendant/steward?) At other times, the category can be the starting point: "服务员是谁？ Fúwùyuán shì shéi?" Both questions seek the identity of someone, but there is a slight difference in nuance. Here are two other examples:

② 您打算住多久？ How long do you plan to stay?
Nín dǎsuàn zhù duō jiǔ?

③ 您要我什么时候叫醒您？ When do you want me to wake you up?
Nín yào wǒ shénme shíhou jiàoxǐng nín?

In English, one of the rules for forming questions is to begin with the question word. In Chinese, this is not the case. Question words appear in the sentence in the place where the answers appear.

▶ G2. The "是 shì……的 de" construction, for emphasizing the attendant circumstances (how, when, where, etc.)

The "是 shì……的 de" construction is used to emphasize or highlight the attendant circumstances of an action or event that already occurred. These circumstances can involve time (when), place (where), place of orgin (from where), manner (how), or purpose (for what). The sentence pattern is:

Subject + 是 shì + Attendant Circumstances + V + 的 de (+ Object).

① A：你是什么时候预订的房间？ When did you make the reservation? (when)
Nǐ shì shénme shíhou yùdìng de fángjiān?

B：我是上个月预订的房间。I made the reservation last month.
Wǒ shì shàng ge yuè yùdìng de fángjiān.

② A：你是在哪儿预订的房间？ Where did you make the reservation? (where)
Nǐ shì zài nǎr yùdìng de fángjiān?

B：我是在网上 (on internet) 预订的房间。I made the reservation online.
Wǒ shì zài wǎng shang yùdìng de fángjiān.

③ A：你是怎么预订的房间？ How did you make the reservation? (how)
Nǐ shì zěnme yùdìng de fángjiān?

B：我是用信用卡 (credit card) 预订的房间。I made the reservation with credit card.
Wǒ shì yòng xìnyòngkǎ yùdìng de fángjiān.

④ A：你是为什么事情 (things) 预订的房间？ Why did you make a reservation? (purpose)
Nǐ shì wèi shénme shìqing yùdìng de fángjiān?

B：我是为开会 (meeting) 预订的房间。I made the reservation for a meeting.
Wǒ shì wèi kāihuì yùdìng de fángjiān.

⑤ A：你是从哪儿来的？ Where are you from? (from where)
Nǐ shì cóng nǎr lái de?

B：我是从美国来的。I am from the U.S.
Wǒ shì cóng Měiguó lái de.

The negative is formed with "不是 bú shì": 我不是在餐厅吃的早饭 Wǒ bú shì zài cāntīng chī de zǎofàn (I didn't eat breakfast in the dining hall).

One quirk: When the "是 shì……的 de" construction appears in a sentence that includes a "verb+object", "的 de" may be placed either before, or after the object.

⑥ 你是在哪儿换的美元？ Where did you change US dollars?
Nǐ shì zài nǎr huàn de měiyuán?

⑦ 你是在哪儿换美元的？ Where did you change US dollars?
Nǐ shì zài nǎr huàn měiyuán de?

This internal pattern (V - "的 de" - O) is more a feature of northern speech. It is not usual in Southern Mandarin, or in Taiwan Mandarin. In addition, the internal pattern (V - "的 de" - O) does not occur with a pronoun object. Thus, with "她 tā" as object, only the following is possible: "我是在北京认识她的 Wǒ shì zài Běijīng rènshi tā de" (I met her in Beijing).

▶ G3. More on the particle "的 de"

In the previous lesson, you encountered the modifying particle "的 de" in location phrases such as "药店的旁边 yàodiàn de pángbiān", in which "的 de" indicates that the preceding phrase is modifying the following position word.

In this lesson, you see "的 de" function as a possessive marker, Tom's which is very similar to the usage of the apostrophe in English (cf. "Tom's passport", below). For example:

您的房间	nín de fángjiān	your room
他的钥匙	tā de yàoshi	his key
Tom 的护照	Tom de hùzhào	Tom's passport
老师的课本	lǎoshī de kèběn	the teacher's textbook

When the context makes it clear, the noun following "的 de" may be omitted:

① 这本护照是我的护照。 → 这本护照是我的。
Zhè běn hùzhào shì wǒ de hùzhào. → Zhè běn hùzhào shì wǒ de.

② 1420房间是他的房间。 → 1420房间是他的。
Yāo-sì-èr-líng fángjiān shì tā de fángjiān. → Yāo-sì-èr-líng fángjiān shì tā de.

At other times, the modifier is descriptive, and the "的 de" functions like the English relative clause marker, "that": "临街的房间 línjiē de fángjiān" (a room that faces the street).

Note that the word order of the structure (Modifier - "的 de" - Noun) in Chinese is quite different from that of English. English "the room facing the street" is expressed in Chinese as "the facing-the-street room". It is helpful to remember that the general rule for the modifying relation in Chinese is "modifier before modified", and this is true whether the modifier is a possessive or a descriptive phrase, as the following examples show.

③ 您的房间的钥匙 your room key
nín de fángjiān de yàoshi

④ 您的房间的号码 your room number
nín de fángjiān de hàomǎ

⑤ 我房间的空调 the air-conditioning in my room
wǒ fángjiān de kōngtiáo

⑥ 临街的房间 a room facing the street
línjiē de fángjiān

⑦ 干净的房间 a clean room
gānjìng de fángjiān

⑧ 北京大学的学生 students from Peking University
Běijīng Dàxué de xuésheng

▶ G4. "给 gěi" as a main verb

"给 gěi" may function as a main verb meaning "to give": "请给我您的护照 Qǐng gěi wǒ nín de hùzhào" (Please give me your passport). Like English "give", "给 gěi" takes two objects. The first is the indirect object (the recipient), the second is the direct (the "gift"). In Chinese (but not in Engish), the direct object need not be expressed when the context makes it clear: "给你 gěi nǐ" (I'm giving it to you – it's for you).

"给 gěi" may also function as a preposition, in which case it corresponds to English "for (the benefit of)", as in: "我尽量给您安排 Wǒ jǐnliàng gěi nín ānpái" (I will do my best to arrange it for you). As a preposition, it indicates who benefits or gains from an action or transaction. The sentence patterns for these two usages are as follows:

Subject + 给 gěi + Someone + Something. ("给 gěi" as a verb)

① 他给我两个苹果。He gives me two apples.
Tā gěi wǒ liǎng ge píngguǒ.

② 我给你我的护照。I'm giving you my passport.
Wǒ gěi nǐ wǒ de hùzhào.

Subject + 给 gěi + Someone + VO. ("给 gěi" as a preposition)

③ 你给我买两个苹果，好吗？Buy two apples for me, will you?
Nǐ gěi wǒ mǎi liǎng ge píngguǒ, hǎo ma?

④ 我朋友给我预订房间了。My friend booked a hotel room for me.
Wǒ péngyou gěi wǒ yùdìng fángjiān le.

⑤ 我还没有给你打扫房间。I have not cleaned your room yet.
Wǒ hái méiyǒu gěi nǐ dǎsǎo fángjiān.

▶ G5. Duration phrases

While time words such as "今天 jīntiān" (today) appear before the verb in Chinese, duration phrases, which denote length of time, such as "三天 sān tiān" (three days), appear after the verb, as part of the predicate. If an object is present, there are two options, with slightly different nuances of meaning. One option is to place the duration phrase between the verb and its object:

① 教了一年英语 taught English for a year
jiāole yì nián Yīngyǔ

With that option, the modifying relationship between the duration phrase and the object can be made explicit by the addition of "的 de": "教了一年的英语 jiāole yì nián de Yīngyǔ", which makes the expression parallel to English "taught a year's English".

The other option is to state the verb with its object first (but without "了 le" or any other verbal suffix), then to repeat the verb with the duration phrase – but without the object.

② 教英语教了一年 taught English for a year
jiāo Yīngyǔ jiāole yì nián

The question phrases for duration are "多久 duō jiǔ" (how long) or "多长时间 duō cháng shíjiān" (how long a time).

③ A：您打算住多久？How long are you planning to stay?
Nín dǎsuàn zhù duō jiǔ?

B：我住三天。I'm staying for three days.
Wǒ zhù sān tiān.

④ A：清洁工打扫房间需要多长时间？
Qīngjiégōng dǎsǎo fángjiān xūyào duō cháng shíjiān?
How long does it take the custodian to clean a room?

B：清洁工打扫房间需要半个小时。
Qīngjiégōng dǎsǎo fángjiān xūyào bàn ge xiǎoshí.
It takes the custodian half an hour to clean the room.

▶ G6. "好 hǎo" as a verb complement

Verbs in Chinese can be combined with verb complements, either adjectival or non-adjectival ones, to form compounds. One such complement is the adjective "好 hǎo". In combination, "好 hǎo" conveys meanings such as "ready, proper, safe".

① 这是押金收据，请收好。This is a receipt for your deposit receipt; please keep it safe.
Zhè shì yājīn shōujù, qǐng shōuhǎo.

② 您的房间打扫好了。Your room has been cleaned (and is ready).
Nín de fángjiān dǎsǎo hǎo le.

▶ G7. "……的时候 de shíhou" (when, during, while)

In Chinese, clauses of time ("when" clauses) are subordinated by the familiar "的 de" particle to the noun "时候 shíhou " (time), so that in effect "when" is expressed as "the time of".

① 你打扫洗澡间的时候，能不能多给我一条毛巾？
Nǐ dǎsǎo xǐzǎojiān de shíhou, néng bu néng duō gěi wǒ yì tiáo máojīn?
When you clean the bathroom, could you give me an extra towel?

Clauses subordinated by "……的时候 de shíhou" can correspond to English clauses with conjunctions, such as "during, while, when", all of which appear at the beginning of the clause in English rather than at the end. In English terms, the Chinese expresses "when you clean the bathroom" as "you clean bathroom time". More examples:

② 我们在中国教英文的时候也学中文。
Wǒmen zài Zhōngguó jiāo Yīngwén de shíhou yě xué Zhōngwén.
When we teach English in China, we also study Chinese.

③ 我在北京大学学习的时候认识了很多外国朋友。
Wǒ zài Běijīng Dàxué xuéxí de shíhou rènshile hěn duō wàiguó péngyou.
When I studied at Peking University, I got to know many foreign friends.

④ 你去餐厅吃饭的时候我叫人来修空调了。
Nǐ qù cāntīng chī fàn de shíhou wǒ jiào rén lái xiū kōngtiáo le.
When you went to eat at the dining hall, I had someone fix your AC.

▶ G8. Pivotal constructions

Lesson 4 introduced "verbs in series" in which a single subject governs pairs of verbs (or verbs with their objects) to represent a sequence of events, one following the other: "我去商店买东西 Wǒ qù shāngdiàn mǎi dōngxi". This lesson introduces another type of construction, called the pivotal construction. On the surface, it looks similar to verbs in series, in the sense that verbs (with their objects) are simply juxtaposed. But in the pivotal construction, the object of the first verb is simultaneously the subject of the second. In other words, one noun pivots from object to subject. The sentence pattern for the pivotal construction is:

Subject + V + Object/Subject + V(+Object).

First verbs of pivotal constructions – the pre-pivot verbs – must have meanings like "cause to, let, tell, request, and want". The example in this lesson's dialogue is:

① 我叫人来修。I'll have someone come and fix it.
Wǒ jiào rén lái xiū.

"人 rén" is the object of "叫 jiào" and the subject of "来修 lái xiū". Other examples:

请 qǐng ② 老师请我们吃饭。The teacher invited us for a meal.
Lǎoshī qǐng wǒmen chī fàn.

叫 jiào ③ 我叫人打扫洗手间。I will have someone clean the bathroom.
Wǒ jiào rén dǎsǎo xǐshǒujiān.

让 ràng ④ 行李我让服务员给你送到房间。
Xíngli wǒ ràng fúwùyuán gěi nǐ sòngdào fángjiān.
I'll have the porter take your luggage to your room.

Pivotal constructions can be negated in the regular fashion, with "没 méi" or "不 bù":

⑤ 老师没请我们吃饭。The teacher hasn't invited us over for a meal.
Lǎoshī méi qǐng wǒmen chī fàn.

⑥ 他不叫人来修，他自己修。
Tā bú jiào rén lái xiū, tā zìjǐ xiū.
He won't call anyone to come over and fix it, he will fix it himself.

Consolidation & Practice

1. Use the "是 shì……的 de" construction to answer the questions

(1) A：你是怎么预订的酒店？
Nǐ shì zěnme yùdìng de jiǔdiàn?

B：________________________________。(用朋友的名字 yòng péngyou de míngzi)

(2) A：你是在哪儿换的美元？
Nǐ shì zài nǎr huàn de měiyuán?

B：________________________________。(在银行 zài yínháng)

(3) A：那个留学生是从哪儿来的？
Nàge liúxuéshēng shì cóng nǎr lái de?

B：________________________________。(美国 Měiguó)

(4) A：你们是在哪儿吃的饭？
Nǐmen shì zài nǎr chī de fàn?

B：________________________________。(麦当劳 Màidāngláo)

(5) A：那个外教是从哪儿来的？
Nàge wàijiào shì cóng nǎr lái de?

B：________________________________。(英国 Yīngguó)

(6) A：你是和谁去的超市？
Nǐ shì hé shéi qù de chāoshì?

B：________________________________。(朋友 péngyou)

(7) A：服务员是什么时候叫醒你的？
Fúwùyuán shì shénme shíhou jiàoxǐng nǐ de?

B：________________________________。(六点 liù diǎn)

(8) A：你是在中国学的中文吗？
Nǐ shì zài Zhōngguó xué de Zhōngwén ma?

B：________________________________。(no, not in China, in America)

2. Use the appropriate question words to ask questions that elicit the answers given (谁 shéi, 谁的 shéi de, 多久 duō jiǔ, 什么时候 shénme shíhou……)

(1) A：________________________________？

B：他是英国留学生。
Tā shì Yīngguó liúxuéshēng.

(2) A：________________________________?

B：他住1221号房间。
Ta zhù yāo-èr-èr-yāo hào fángjiān.

(3) A：________________________________?

B：我点了素菜。
Wǒ diǎnle sùcài.

(4) A：________________________________?

B：老师付房费。
Lǎoshī fù fángfèi.

(5) A：________________________________?

B：张老师教汉语。
Zhāng lǎoshī jiāo Hànyǔ.

(6) A：________________________________?

B：这是张老师的护照。
Zhè shì Zhāng lǎoshī de hùzhào.

(7) A：________________________________?

B：我用老师的名字预订了宾馆。
Wǒ yòng lǎoshī de míngzi yùdìngle bīnguǎn.

(8) A：________________________________?

B：这一百美元是他的。
Zhè yìbǎi měiyuán shì tā de.

(9) A：________________________________?

B：这钥匙是我的。
Zhè yàoshi shì wǒ de.

(10) A：________________________________?

B：那个留学生来中国一年了。
Nàge liúxuéshēng lái Zhōngguó yì nián le.

(11) A：________________________________?

B：去图书馆要走十分钟。
Qù túshūguǎn yào zǒu shí fēnzhōng.

(12) A：________________________________?

B：我打算在中国住一年。
Wǒ dǎsuàn zài Zhōngguó zhù yì nián.

(13) A：________________________________?

B：我八点去学校。
Wǒ bā diǎn qù xuéxiào.

(14) A：________________________________?

B：我十二点去吃饭。
Wǒ shí'èr diǎn qù chī fàn.

(15) A：________________________________?

B：你六点叫醒我。
Nǐ liù diǎn jiàoxǐng wǒ.

(16) A：________________________________?

B：我的朋友明天来。
Wǒ de péngyou míngtiān lái.

3. Rearrange the sentences based on the English meaning, using the sentence pattern

Subject (+ Place) + V + Time Duration + 的 de + Object.

(1) 在中国 那个留学生 学了 两年 中文
zài Zhōngguó nàge liúxuéshēng xuéle liǎng nián Zhōngwén

____。
(That foreign student took two years of Chinese in China.)

(2) 一年 这个外教 英语 教了
yì nián zhège wàijiào Yīngyǔ jiāole

____。
(This foreign expert taught English for a year.)

(3) 房间 清洁工 一天 打扫了
fángjiān qīngjiégōng yì tiān dǎsǎole

____。
(The cleaner spent the whole day cleaning the room.)

(4) 半天 钥匙 找了 我
bàntiān yàoshi zhǎole wǒ

____。
(I was looking for the key for hours.)

4. Use "给 gěi" to do the following

(1) Use "给 gěi" as a verb

Subject + 给 gěi + Someone + Something.

(1) Ask the front desk (at the hotel) for your room key.
(2) Ask the custodian to give you a large towel.
(3) Ask the shop assistant for a receipt.
(4) Remind the hotel clerk that she needs to return your passport.
(5) Ask for a (hotel) room facing the street.

(2) Use "给 gěi" as a preposition

Subject + 给 gěi + Someone + VO.

(1) Ask the custodian to clean the room for you.
(2) Ask at the front desk if they would fix your AC.
(3) Ask your friend to buy you some apples.
(4) Ask your friend to buy you breakfast.
(5) Ask your friend to make a hotel reservation for you.

5. Finish the following sentences using the appropriate "V+Complement" compound: 修好 xiūhǎo, 收好 shōuhǎo, 走好 zǒuhǎo, 做好 zuòhǎo, 坐好 zuòhǎo

(1) 这是你的护照，____________________。
Zhè shì nǐ de hùzhào, ____________________.

(2) 我的床坏了，请____________________。
Wǒ de chuáng huài le, qǐng ____________________.

(3) 去药店要过马路，____________________。
Qù yàodiàn yào guò mǎlù, ____________________.

(4) 老师来了，____________________。
Lǎoshī lái le, ____________________.

(5) 我要的辣子鸡丁____________________了吗?
Wǒ yào de làzi-jīdīng ____________________ le ma?

6. Finish the sentences with "……的时候 de shíhou" (when, during, while)

(1) ____________________，清洁工要打扫房间。
(When I was taking a shower) qīngjiégōng yào dǎsǎo fángjiān.

(2) ____________________，空调坏了。
(While we were having dinner) kōngtiáo huài le.

(3) ____________________，服务员要我的护照和押金。
(When checking in at the hotel) fúwùyuán yào wǒ de hùzhào hé yājīn.

(4) ______________________________，没有临街的房间了。
(When I made the reservation for a room)　méiyǒu línjiē de fángjiān le.

(5) ______________________________，没有人民币了。
(When I went shopping)　méiyǒu rénmínbì le.

(6) ______________________________，银行没有美元了。
(When I went to exchange money)　yínháng méiyǒu měiyuán le.

7. Following the English guidelines, rearrange the words to form pivotal sentences

(1) 明天　外教　请　吃饭　我们
míngtiān　wàijiào　qǐng　chī fàn　wǒmen

____。
(The foreign expert has invited us for a meal tomorrow.)

(2) 修好了　人　服务员　叫　我的空调
xiūhǎole　rén　fúwùyuán　jiào　wǒ de kōngtiáo

____。
(The hotel attendant had someone fix my AC.)

(3) 老师　我　预订　让　酒店
lǎoshī　wǒ　yùdìng　ràng　jiǔdiàn

____。
(The teacher asked me to book the hotel room.)

(4) 请　我　预订了　朋友　酒店
qǐng　wǒ　yùdìngle　péngyou　jiǔdiàn

____。
(I asked my friend to book a hotel room.)

(5) 老师　学生　让　换钱　去银行
lǎoshī　xuésheng　ràng　huàn qián　qù yínháng

____。
(The teacher told the students to go to the bank to change money.)

Pronunciation Notes

1. The sounds represented by *Pinyin* "z, c, s" and "zh, ch, sh"

Pinyin "z, c, s" and "zh, ch, sh" represent two sets of related initial sounds. Getting used to the reading of these letters (particularly "z", "c", and "zh", which are quite counterintuitive for people used to English spelling), as well as learning how to form the sounds that they represent is a major difficulty in learning to read and write *Pinyin*. Note especially that *Pinyin* "c" is always a "ts" sound, never a "k": cf. "cānguǎn", "xīcān", "zhōngcān".

The tongue position for "z", "c", and "s" is very like that of English "s", the difference being that for "z" and "c", the tongue tip actually blocks the air momentarily by pressing against the top of the lower teeth (rather like English "dz" and "ts").

The tongue position for "zh", "ch" and "sh" (as well as for "r" – see below) is rather like that of English "r" (for many English speakers): the tongue is pulled back slightly and the tip is raised towards the roof of the mouth (in what is known as retroflex position). (An approximate representation of the sounds in English spelling would be "zhr, chr, shr.")

Adding to the complications is the sound of (letter) "i" after these two sets of initial letters. In all cases, the "i" is swallowed up by the initials, so that the vowel is hardly more than an extension of the sounds "z, c, s" and "zh, ch, sh". Examples:

Pinyin	Characters	English meaning
zī	资	capital
cì	刺	thorn; to pierce
sī	丝	silk
zhīdào	知道	to know
chī fàn	吃饭	to eat a meal
lǎoshī	老师	teacher

2. *Pinyin* initial "r"

For most English speakers, "r" is pronounced with the lips slightly extended (pursed) and rounded: "road", "raise", "real". The Chinese "r" sound, by contrast, has the lips closer together and slightly spread: "ran, ren, ruo, rong". Like the "zh, ch, sh" series, "r" is pronounced with the tongue tip rolled upwards towards or touching the alveolar ridge (the rough strip near the base of the upper teeth) and the lower jaw thrust slightly forward. Chinese "r" often has a lot of friction, so that it sounds like the voiced counterpart of "sh": cf. "shén" and "rén". Examples:

Pinyin	Characters	English meaning
rè	热	hot
rén	人	people
Rìběn	日本	Japan

Note that with initial "r" (like "zh, ch, sh"), "i" is never pronounced "ee"; it is swallowed up by the initial sound.

Pronunciation Exercises

1. Read the following words and phrases aloud, paying particular attention to “zi, ci, si” and “zhi, chi, shi, ri”

	Pinyin	Characters	English meaning
1	Yīngwénxì	英文系	English Department
2	zìzhìqū	自治区	autonomous region
3	zìxí	自习	self-study
4	mínǐ	迷你	mini (miniskirt)
5	chídào	迟到	to be late, to arrive late
6	háizi	孩子	child
7	sīchóu	丝绸	silk
8	sìshēng	四声	four tones
9	Rìběn	日本	Japan
10	cíqì	瓷器	porcelain ware
11	zhīshi	知识	knowledge
12	chǐzi	尺子	ruler
13	shīzi	狮子	lion
14	jiérì	节日	holiday

2. Read the following words aloud, paying attention to the initial “r”

	Pinyin	Characters	English meaning
1	ròucài	肉菜	meat dish
2	zīrùn	滋润	to moisten
3	ruòxiǎo	弱小	small and weak
4	róngyì	容易	easy
5	Rìběnrén	日本人	Japaness
6	rè	热	hot
7	ràng	让	to allow, to let, to yield
8	rèshuǐ	热水	hot water

	Pinyin	Characters	English meaning
9	rén	人	people
10	réngjiù	仍旧	still
11	suīrán	虽然	although
12	rènao	热闹	bustling
13	rénkǒu	人口	population
14	dǎrǎo	打扰	to disturb
15	wūrǎn	污染	to pollute; pollution

3. Here are (compound) words related to hospitals, read them aloud

	Pinyin	Characters	English meaning
1	yīyuàn	医院	hospital
2	yīwùshì	医务室	clinic
3	guàhàochù	挂号处	registration office
4	nèikē	内科	department of internal medicine
5	wàikē	外科	surgical department
6	yákē	牙科	department of dentistry
7	jízhěnshì	急诊室	emergency room
8	qǔyàochù/yàofáng	取药处/药房	pharmacy
9	huàyànshì	化验室	laboratory
10	X-guāngshì	X光室	X-ray room
11	zhùshèshì	注射室	injection room
12	zhùyuànchù	住院处	admission office
13	zhōngyī	中医	traditional Chinese medical science
14	xīyī	西医	western medicine

4. Here are some instructions from a doctor for you to read aloud

	Pinyin	Characters	English meaning
1	Qǐng bǎ zuǐ zhāngkāi.	请把嘴张开。	Please open your mouth.
2	Qǐng bǎ shétou shēn chulai.	请把舌头伸出来。	Please stick out your tongue.
3	Shēn hūxī.	深呼吸。	Take a deep breath.
4	Qǐng bǎ yīfu tuōdiao.	请把衣服脱掉。	Please take off your clothes.
5	Tǎngxia.	躺下。	Lie down.
6	Zhàn qilai.	站起来。	Stand up.
7	Qǐng bǎ xiùzi juǎn qilai.	请把袖子卷起来。	Please roll up your sleeves.
8	Zhàn jìn yìdiǎnr.	站近一点儿。	Please move/stand closer.

Listening Comprehension

1. Listen to the dialogue between a customer and an attendant; then answer the questions below

(1) Under whose name was the hotel reservation made?
(2) What kind of room did the man reserve?
(3) How long is the room reservation for?
(4) How much deposit does the hotel require?
(5) What is the man's room number?

2. Listen to the dialogue, then decide whether the statements below are true or false

	T	F
(1) The man doesn't need his bed sheets changed.		
(2) The man asks for more towels.		
(3) The man asks for someone to come and fix the air-conditioner.		
(4) The man will eat before the woman comes to clean the room.		
(5) The Western style restaurant is on the second floor.		

Communication Activities

Pair Work

Scenario I: Take roles of guest and hotel maid or room cleaner. The guest can request the room cleaned, the sheets changed, that someone come to fix the air-conditioner, etc. The maid or room cleaner answers accordingly.

Scenario II: Take roles of hotel guest and desk clerk. The guest asks the clerk if they have the reservation, and describes the room he/she wants. The clerk responds by asking under whose name the room was reserved, asking to see a passport, and asking how long they stay, then states the amount of the deposit, hands over the key, and explains where the room is. The clerk adds information about the location of the elevator and the restaurants (one Chinese, one Western).

Scenario III: Take roles of hotel guest and desk clerk. Phone the desk and explain that your air-conditioner is broken and that the room is hot – request that someone come and fix it. The clerk responds that there's no one available at the moment, but that someone will come later to fix it.

Review Exercises

I. Match the verbs in the left-hand list with the words in the right-hand list

(1) 换 huàn	A. 押金收据 yājīn shōujù
(2) 收好 shōuhǎo	B. 您的护照 nín de hùzhào
(3) 预订 yùdìng	C. 多少美元 duōshao měiyuán
(4) 打扫 dǎsǎo	D. 大床房 dàchuángfáng
(5) 修 xiū	E. 床单 chuángdān
(6) 给 gěi	F. 空调 kōngtiáo
(7) 叫 jiào	G. 清洁工 qīngjiégōng
(8) 换洗 huànxǐ	H. 酒店房间 jiǔdiàn fángjiān
(9) 需要 xūyào	I. 朋友的电话 péngyou de diànhuà
(10) 等 děng	J. 你的房间 nǐ de fángjiān

II. Examine the answers for each item below, then provide appropriate questions, using the question words/phrases "怎么 zěnme", "谁 shéi/shuí", "谁的 shéi/shuí de", "多久 duō jiǔ", and "什么时候 shénme shíhou"

1. A: ______________________________? (who)

B：房间是我朋友给我预订的。
Fángjiān shì wǒ péngyou gěi wǒ yùdìng de.

2. A：______________________? (whose)

B：我是用谢英的名字预订的房间。
Wǒ shì yòng Xiè Yīng de míngzi yùdìng de fángjiān.

3. A：______________________? (how long)

B：我只住一天。
Wǒ zhǐ zhù yì tiān.

4. A：______________________? (what time)

B：请早上七点叫醒我。
Qǐng zǎoshang qī diǎn jiàoxǐng wǒ.

5. A：______________________? (how)

B：过了马路往南走。
Guòle mǎlù wǎng nán zǒu.

6. A：______________________? (whose)

B：这是我的护照。
Zhè shì wǒ de hùzhào.

7. A：______________________? (when)

B：我是十天以前打扫的房间。
Wǒ shì shí tiān yǐqián dǎsǎo de fángjiān.

8. A：______________________? (who)

B：单人间是酒店昨天给我安排的。
Dānrénjiān shì jiǔdiàn zuótiān gěi wǒ ānpái de.

9. A：______________________? (when)

B：请等一会儿叫醒我。
Qǐng děng yíhuìr jiàoxǐng wǒ.

10. A：______________________? (how)

B：我可以用信用卡付押金。
Wǒ kěyǐ yòng xìnyòngkǎ fù yājīn.

III. Complete the following sentences with a phrase that includes "给 gěi", and in each case, indicate whether "给 gěi" is being used as a verb or a preposition

1. 我去银行换钱，可是因为没有护照，工作人员______________。(won't change it for me)
Wǒ qù yínháng huàn qián, kěshì yīnwèi méiyǒu hùzhào, gōngzuò rényuán ______________.

2. A：房间是你预订的吗？
Fángjiān shì nǐ yùdìng de ma?
B：不是，我的朋友____________________。(booked it for me)
Bú shì, wǒ de péngyou ____________________.

3. 你买了哪种水果？____________________。(Show them to me)
Nǐ mǎile nǎ zhǒng shuǐguǒ? ____________________.

4. 咖啡25元，你给了我50元，____________________。(I'll give you 25 *yuan* in change)
Kāfēi èrshíwǔ yuán, nǐ gěile wǒ wǔshí yuán, ____________________.

5. 你需要____________________。(give me your passport)
Nǐ xūyào ____________________.

6. 爸爸妈妈让我周末____________________。(call them)
Bàba māma ràng wǒ zhōumò ____________________.

IV. Answer the following questions with a duration phrase

1. A：我的房间你打算打扫多长时间？
Wǒ de fángjiān nǐ dǎsuàn dǎsǎo duō cháng shíjiān?
B：____。

2. A：李大伟等服务员等了多久？
Lǐ Dàwěi děng fúwùyuán děngle duō jiǔ?
B：____。

3. A：你昨天到麦当劳走了多久？
Nǐ zuótiān dào Màidāngláo zǒule duō jiǔ?
B：____。

4. A：钱英在洗手间洗手洗了多久？
Qián Yīng zài xǐshǒujiān xǐ shǒu xǐle duō jiǔ?
B：____。

5. A：她每个星期在超市买东西买多久？
Tā měi ge xīngqī zài chāoshì mǎi dōngxi mǎi duō jiǔ?
B：____。

6. A：那个外教教英文教了多长时间？
Nàge wàijiào jiāo Yīngwén jiāole duō cháng shíjiān?
B：____。

7. A：你每天换衣服需要换多长时间？
Nǐ měi tiān huàn yīfu xūyào huàn duō cháng shíjiān?
B：____。

8. A：那个英国人来中国多久以后，可以用中文点菜？
Nàge Yīngguórén lái Zhōngguó duō jiǔ yǐhòu, kěyǐ yòng Zhōngwén diǎn cài?

B：____。

9. A：你等他洗澡等了多久？
Nǐ děng tā xǐzǎo děngle duō jiǔ?

B：____。

10. A：这个中文名字，你用了多长时间？
Zhège Zhōngwén míngzi, nǐ yòngle duō cháng shíjiān?

B：____。

V. Answer the following questions using the "when" construction: "……的时候 de shíhou"

1. A：你什么时候说中文？
Nǐ shénme shíhou shuō Zhōngwén?

B：____。
(when I'm at the fruit market)

2. A：外教在中国都住酒店，对不对？
Wàijiào zài Zhōngguó dōu zhù jiǔdiàn, duì bu duì?

B：不对，____。
Bú duì, (only when in Hong Kong)

3. A：留学生每天都需要用护照吗？
Liúxuéshēng měi tiān dōu xūyào yòng hùzhào ma?

B：____。
(when in class, there's no need)

4. A：在中国，什么时候可以用信用卡？
Zài Zhōngguó, shénme shíhou kěyǐ yòng xìnyòngkǎ?

B：____。
(when staying in hotels)

5. A：你什么时候需要护照？
Nǐ shénme shíhou xūyào hùzhào?

B：____。
(when I go to the bank to exchange money)

6. A：请问，____？
Qǐngwèn, (when do I give you my passport)

B：请稍等一会儿。
Qǐng shāo děng yíhuìr。

7. A：清洁工为什么不打扫我的房间？
Qīngjiégōng wèi shénme bù dǎsǎo wǒ de fángjiān?

B：____。
(She came in when you were taking a shower)

8. A：服务员什么时候给房间钥匙？
Fúwùyuán shénme shíhou gěi fángjiān yàoshi?

B：____。
(when the guest signs in)

9. A：你的学生什么时候叫你的英文名字？
Nǐ de xuésheng shénme shíhou jiào nǐ de Yīngwén míngzi?

B：____。
(when I'm teaching English)

10. A：你经常去吃西餐吗？
Nǐ jīngcháng qù chī xīcān ma?

B：不，________________________________。
Bù, (only when my American friends come to see me)

VI. Complete the following sentences using the "Modifier - 的 de - Noun" structure

1. ______________________________ 近一点儿。
(the bank across the street) jìn yìdiǎnr.

2. ______________________________ 没有坏。
(the elevator on the 2nd floor) méiyǒu huài.

3. ______________________________ 是一个大床房。
(the professor's room) shì yí ge dàchuángfáng.

4. ______________________________ 只有一个。
(room key) zhǐ yǒu yí ge.

5. ______________________________ 是中餐厅。
(the cafeteria on the 3rd floor) shì zhōngcāntīng.

6. ______________________________ 每天都换。
(the towels in the bathroom) měi tiān dōu huàn.

7. ______________________________ 能说英文吗？
(the clerks in the bank) néng shuō Yīngwén ma?

8. ______________________________ 是你的吗？
(the name on the receipt) shì nǐ de ma?

9. ______________________________ 每天都打扫。
(the school library) měi tiān dōu dǎsǎo.

10. ______________________________ 尽量少一点儿。
(today's arrangements) jǐnliàng shǎo yìdiǎnr.

VII. Complete the B sentences by forming pivotal constructions with verbs "叫 jiào", "请 qǐng", "让 ràng", and "要 yào"

1. A：空调坏了，我自己不会修。
Kōngtiáo huài le, wǒ zìjǐ bú huì xiū.

B：______________________________
(call the hotel clerk to fix it)

2. A：现在能帮我打扫房间吗？
Xiànzài néng bāng wǒ dǎsǎo fángjiān ma?

B：______________________________
(I'll get a custodian to clean it now)

3. A：在中餐馆，你用中文点菜吗？
Zài zhōngcānguǎn, nǐ yòng Zhōngwén diǎn cài ma?

B：不，______________________________
Bù, (I ask a friend to help)

4. A：你教学生的时候，要他们说中文还是英文？
Nǐ jiāo xuésheng de shíhou, yào tāmen shuō Zhōngwén háishi Yīngwén?

B：______________________________
(I make them speak Chinese)

VIII. Perform the following tasks (This exercise can be written or presented orally)

1. You are checking into a hotel in China. Find out if they have your reservation. Then request a single room with a double bed – one not facing the street.
2. Find out if there are any shops near the hotel, or a cafeteria, a bank, etc.
3. Ask for someone at the hotel to come and fix the bathroom and the air conditioning.
4. Ask the custodian to come and clean your room and change the linen.
5. Find out how to make telephone calls from your room; then find out from the front desk if there's a wake-up service.
6. Remind the front desk clerk to return your deposit.
7. Ask the front desk to change your hotel room for you (because you don't like the room facing the street).
8. Ask your friend to pay for your hotel (because you don't have your credit card with you).

Culture Notes

1. Types of hotels

Words for hotel in Chinese vary according to their grade, or quality. "宾馆 bīnguǎn", "饭店 fàndiàn", and "酒店 jiǔdiàn" are usually four- or five-star hotels of the type where foreigners usually stay. The staff at such hotels generally speak some English. "旅馆 lǚguǎn" or "旅店 lǚdiàn" tend to be, at most, three-star hotels (or lower), and their staff often do not speak any English. Finally, "招待所 zhāodàisuǒ" (guest houses or hostels) and "疗养院 liáoyǎngyuàn" (health resorts), are usually state-run guest houses or government institutions that were turned into hotels after the economic reforms of the 1980s. They are usually low-cost, and only some of them allow foreigners to stay.

2. Taking care of valuables

Four- or five-star hotels generally have a small safe in the room for storing valuables. Lower-grade hotels sometimes let guests deposit valuables at the front desk.

3. Arranging an Internet connection and making long-distance telephone calls

Nowadays, most hotels have free broadband connection. Some also offer free Wi-Fi. For long-distance telephone calls, guests are often charged a service fee (on top of the charge for the call) – typically 15% at four- and five-star hotels, 10% at lower grade hotels. To make a long-distance call from your hotel room, you first pay a deposit at the front desk; then the desk clerk will activate the long-distance line in your room.

4. Room inspection at checkout

At checkout, guests have to wait at the front desk while the floor attendant checks the room to see that everything is there and the room is in order. This is routine for all guests.

Lesson Eight Making Phone Calls

第八课 打电话

Dì-bā Kè Dǎ Diànhuà

In this lesson you will learn how to do the following

- Make inquiries about domestic and international phone calls
- Ask how to make inexpensive calls from your hotel room
- Find out how to buy and use phone-cards

Grammar

- Sentence pattern "先 xiān……再 zài……" (first…then…)
- "来 lái" (to come) and "去 qù" (to go) used as directional complements
- "太 tài……了 le" (too…, excessively…)
- Conditional sentences: "如果 rúguǒ……就 jiù……" (if...[then]...)
- Adverbs "都 dōu" (all) and "也 yě" (also)
- Verb reduplication

Culture Notes

- Telephone cards
- Busy signals
- Public phones
- Cheap times for long-distance calls
- Time zones in China
- Time differences between Beijing (or China) and North America

Dialogue

A：李大伟 Lǐ Dàwěi　**B**：服务员 fúwùyuán　**C**：报亭小贩 bàotíng xiǎofàn

A：喂[1]，是前台吗？
Wèi[1], shì qiántái ma?

B：是。
Shì.

A：我是1408房间的客人。请问我怎么往外打电话？
Wǒ shì yāo-sì-líng-bā fángjiān de kèren. Qǐngwèn wǒ zěnme wǎng wài dǎ diànhuà?

B：您先拨9，再拨您要打的电话号码[G1]。
Nín xiān bō jiǔ, zài bō nín yào dǎ de diànhuà hàomǎ[G1].

A：请问，别人怎么给我的房间打电话？
Qǐngwèn, biéren zěnme gěi wǒ de fángjiān dǎ diànhuà?

B：您房间的直拨电话号码是82105173。
Nín fángjiān de zhíbō diànhuà hàomǎ shì bā-èr-yāo-líng-wǔ-yāo-qī-sān.

A：从美国打来[G2]呢？
Cóng Měiguó dǎlai[G2] ne?

B：从美国打来是011−86−10−82105173 。
Cóng Měiguó dǎlai shì líng-yāo-yāo bā-liù yāo-líng bā-èr-yāo-líng-wǔ-yāo-qī-sān.

A：打去[G2]美国的长途是多少钱一分钟？
Dǎqu[G2] Měiguó de chángtú shì duōshao qián yì fēnzhōng?

B：八块钱一分钟，加上百分之[2]十五的服务费。
Bā kuài qián yì fēnzhōng, jiāshang bǎi fēnzhī[2] shíwǔ de fúwùfèi.

A：太贵了[G3]。市话多少钱一分钟？
Tài guì le[G3]. Shìhuà duōshao qián yì fēnzhōng?

B：我们酒店市话是免费的。如果您用电话卡打国际长途，不需要付长途费和服务费，就很便宜[G4]。

Notes

1. "喂 wèi" (hey, hello) is an interjection that is used to get people's attention (or to respond to someone else's "喂 wèi"). As the opening word in a telephone conversation, it corresponds to English "hello"; elsewhere, it functions like "hey".
2. Percentages are expressed in Chinese as "百分之 bǎi fēnzhī" plus x, i.e. x parts of 100: "百分之一 bǎi fēnzhī yī" (1%); "百分之二十五 bǎi fēnzhī èrshíwǔ" (25%). Fractions are formed in the same way, with the total parts stated first, then the fraction of the total: "三分之一 sān fēnzhī yī" (one third). Note that for fractions and percentages (which are fractions based on 100), the Chinese order is the reverse of the English.

Wǒmen jiǔdiàn shìhuà shì miǎnfèi de. Rúguǒ nín yòng diànhuàkǎ dǎ guójì chángtú, bù xūyào fù chángtúfèi hé fúwùfèi, jiù hěn piányi[G4].

A: 在哪儿能买电话卡？
Zài nǎr néng mǎi diànhuàkǎ?

B: 街上的报亭和手机店都[G5]卖。有的邮局和小商店也[G5]卖。
Jiē shang de bàotíng hé shǒujīdiàn dōu[G5] mài. Yǒude yóujú hé xiǎo shāngdiàn yě[G5] mài.

A: 大门外面那个报亭有吗？
Dàmén wàimiàn nàge bàotíng yǒu ma?

B: 您去问问[G6]吧。
Nín qù wènwen[G6] ba.

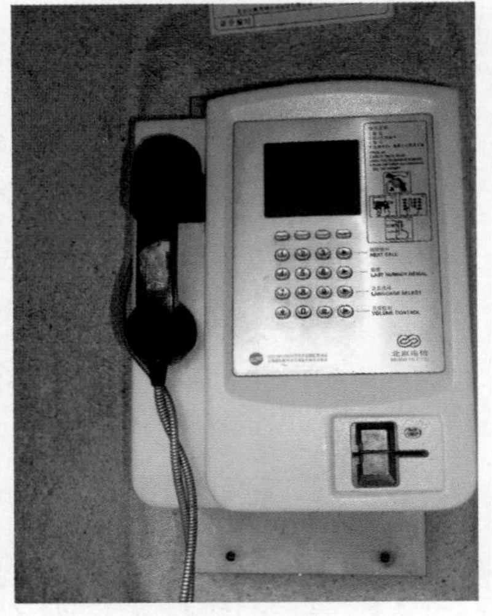

（在报亭 Zài bàotíng）

A: 请问，您有电话卡吗？
Qǐngwèn, nín yǒu diànhuàkǎ ma?

C: 有。您要哪种电话卡？
Yǒu. Nín yào nǎ zhǒng diànhuàkǎ?

A: 我要可以打美国长途的，便宜的。
Wǒ yào kěyǐ dǎ Měiguó chángtú de, piányi de.

C: 中国电信的IP卡打美国长途三毛钱一分钟，是最[3]便宜的。这个卡面值100元， 您只[4]要付45元。
Zhōngguó Diànxìn de IP kǎ dǎ Měiguó chángtú sān máo qián yì fēnzhōng, shì zuì[3] piányi de. Zhège kǎ miànzhí yìbǎi yuán, nín zhǐ[4] yào fù sìshíwǔ yuán.

A: 这个卡能打多少分钟？
Zhège kǎ néng dǎ duōshao fēnzhōng?

C: 可以打三百多分钟。
Kěyǐ dǎ sānbǎi duō fēnzhōng.

A: 好。我就要这个卡。
Hǎo. Wǒ jiù yào zhège kǎ.

---

3. "最 zuì" (most, exceedingly) is an adverb. It precedes adjectival and other kinds of verbs to form superlative expressions: "最便宜 zuì piányi" (cheapest), "最近 zuì jìn" (nearest), "最爱吃中餐 zuì ài chī zhōngcān" (like to eat Chinese food most of all).
4. "只 zhǐ" is a restrictive adverb, meaning "only" or "merely". In this case, it applies to the amount (45 *yuan*).

New Words

1	打	dǎ	V	to hit, to make (a phone call), to fight, to play (ball-games)
2	电话/電話	diànhuà	N	telephone
3	报亭/報亭	bàotíng	N	newsstand, newspaper kiosk
4	小贩/小販	xiǎofàn	N	street vender, peddler
5	喂	wèi	Intj	hey, say (hailing someone), hello
6	前台/前臺	qiántái	N	the front desk, counter (in a hotel, etc.)
7	客人	kèren	N	guest, visitor, customer
8	往外	wǎng wài	Phrase	toward the outside
	外（边/邊）	wài (bian)	PW	outside
9	先	xiān	Adv	first, earlier
10	拨/撥	bō	V	to poke, to stir, to dial (telephone)
11	再	zài	Adv	and then
12	别人	biéren	N	others, other people
13	直拨/直撥	zhíbō	V	to dial directly
14	长途/長途	chángtú	Attr	long-distance
15	加上	jiāshang	V	to add to, to increase
	加	jiā	V	to add, to plus (in arithmetic)
16	百分之	bǎi fēnzhī	BF	percent
17	服务费/服務費	fúwùfèi	N	service fee, service charge
18	贵/貴	guì	Adj	expensive
19	市话/市話	shìhuà	N	local call, in-city phone call
20	免费/免費	miǎnfèi	VO	to not have to pay anything, to be free of charge
21	如果	rúguǒ	Conj	if, in case
22	电话卡/電話卡	diànhuàkǎ	N	phone-card
23	就	jiù	Adv	then, in that case, right away
24	便宜	piányi	Adj	cheap, inexpensive

25	街上	jiē shang	Phrase	in the street, on the street
26	手机/手機	shǒujī	N	cellular phone
27	店	diàn	N	shop, store, inn ("手机店 shǒujīdiàn", *cell-phone store*)
28	卖/賣	mài	V	to sell
29	有的	yǒude	Pron	some
30	邮局/郵局	yóujú	N	post office
31	小商店	xiǎo shāngdiàn	Phrase	small shop
32	外面	wàimiàn	PW	outside
33	哪种/哪種	nǎ zhǒng	Phrase	what kind, which type
34	中国电信 / 中國電信	Zhōngguó Diànxìn	PropN	China Telecom
35	卡	kǎ	N	card
36	最	zuì	Adv	most, -est (as in "fastest"), very
37	面值	miànzhí	N	face value, denomination
38	只	zhǐ	Adv	only, merely, just

Re-enacting the Dialogue

A: David Lee **B: an attendant** **C: a newspaper vendor**

A: Hello. Is this the front desk?
B: It is.
A: I'm the guest in room 1408. May I ask you how to make an outside call?
B: Dial nine first, then dial the number you want to call.
A: How do other people make phone calls to my room, please?
B: The number to dial directly to your room is 82105173.
A: How do people phone me from the U.S.?
B: Calling from the U.S. [the number] is 011-86-10- 82105173.
A: How much is it per minute to call to the U.S.?
B: It's 8 *yuan* a minute, plus 15% service charge.
A: That's too expensive. How much are local calls per minute?
B: Local calls from the hotel are free. If you use a phone-card for your international long distance calls, you won't have to pay the long distance fee or the service fee, then it's very cheap.

A: Where can I buy a phone-card?

B: They're sold at newsstands on the street and at cell-phone stores. Some post offices and small shops sell them as well.

A: Does the newsstand outside the front door have them?

B: Please go there and ask them.

(At the newsstand)

A: Do you have phone-cards, please?

C: We do. Which kind of card do you want?

A: I'd like one that you can phone long-distance to the U.S. with – a cheap one.

C: The cheapest is the China Telecom IP card, which is 3 *mao* a minute to phone the U.S. This card has a 100 *yuan* face value, but you only pay 45.

A: How many minutes do I get with this card?

C: You can call for over 300 minutes.

A: Okay, I'll take this card.

Grammar

▶ G1. Sentence pattern "先 xiān……再 zài……" (first…then…)

Adverbs "先 xiān" and "再 zài" can be linked to emphasize a sequence of events, particularly when one event has to be held up until another has taken place (cf. English "first… and then…"). The sentence pattera is:

(Subject +) 先 xiān + V (+ Object), (Subject +) 再 zài + V (+ Object).

① 先买电话卡，再打电话。Buy a phone-card first, (and) then make phone calls.
Xiān mǎi diànhuàkǎ, zài dǎ diànhuà.

② 您先拨9，再拨您要打的电话号码。Dial nine first, then dial the number you want to call.
Nín xiān bō jiǔ, zài bō nín yào dǎ de diànhuà hàomǎ.

③ 您先给我护照，我再给您房间钥匙。
Nín xiān gěi wǒ hùzhào, wǒ zài gěi nín fángjiān yàoshi.
First let me have your passport, and then I'll give you the room key.

▶ G2. "来 lái" (to come) and "去 qù" (to go) used as directional complements

In previous lessons you have seen that "来 lái" and "去 qù" may function as main verbs, meaning "come" and "go", with objects indicating destinations, e.g.: "去学校 qù xuéxiào" (go to the school), "来中国 lái Zhōngguó" (come to China).

This lesson illustrates another function: "来 lái" and "去 qù" (both generally with neutral tone) can appear in conjunction with a previous verb as directional complements, indicating direction towards the speaker (V +来), or direction away from the speaker (V +去).

① 我朋友打电话来。My friend called me. (here)
Wǒ péngyou dǎ diànhuà lai.

② 我给朋友打电话去。I called my friend. (there)
Wǒ gěi péngyou dǎ diànhuà qu.

③ 他给我买来一个手机。He bought me a phone. (here)
Tā gěi wǒ mǎilai yí ge shǒujī.

④ 你给他带去两个苹果吧！Take two apples to him! (there)
Nǐ gěi tā dàiqu liǎng ge píngguǒ ba!

▶ G3. "太 tài…… 了 le" (too…, excessively…)

In Lesson 5 (G5) the sentence final particle "了 le" was introduced with its typical function of marking a new phase or a change of state: "现在好了 Xiànzài hǎo le" (It's fine now). In this lesson, "了 le" appears with the adverb "太 tài" to suggest excess. The pattern is:

太 tài + Adj + 了 le!

① 太便宜了！ That's so inexpensive!
Tài piányi le!

② 太好吃了！ It's really delicious!
Tài hǎochī le!

③ 太热了！ It's just too hot!
Tài rè le!

This pattern can be considered a subtype of the "change of situation" meaning, with "太 tài" (very, too) suggesting exceeding a limit or crossing a boundary – in other words, a change of situation. Negative statements do not imply the same degree of excess: "不太好 bú tài hǎo" (not too good) is a mild statement which is not compatible with final "了le".

▶ G4. Conditional sentences: "如果 rúguǒ……就 jiù……" (if... [then]...)

In Chinese, the conditional relationship ("if-then") is expressed with the conjunction "如果 rúguǒ" and the adverb "就 jiù". The sentence pattern is:

如果 rúguǒ + Subject + V(+ Object), (Subject +) 就 jiù + V (+ Object).

The second subject can be omitted if it refers to the same person as the first.

① 如果你没有手机，就需要买电话卡。
Rúguǒ nǐ méiyǒu shǒujī, jiù xūyào mǎi diànhuàkǎ.
If you don't have a cell-phone, you'll need to buy a phone-card.

② 如果你用电话卡打电话，就便宜。
Rúguǒ nǐ yòng diànhuàkǎ dǎ diànhuà, jiù piányi.
If you use a phone-card to make phone calls, it'll be inexpensive.

③ 如果你打国际长途电话，就很贵。
Rúguǒ nǐ dǎ guójì chángtú diànhuà, jiù hěn guì.
If you make an international call, it would be expensive.

▶ G5. Adverbs "都 dōu" (all) and "也 yě" (also)

"都 dōu" is an inclusive (or exclusive) adverb, with the sense of "all" (or if two, "both") or "none of" ("neither"). It always refers back to something that has been mentioned.

① 街上的报亭和手机店都卖电话卡。
Jiē shang de bàotíng hé shǒujīdiàn dōu mài diànhuàkǎ.
Newsstand on the street and cell-phone stores all sell phone-cards.

② 我们都没有手机。 None of us has a cell-phone.
Wǒmen dōu méiyǒu shǒujī.

③ 中餐和西餐我都喜欢。I like both Chinese food and Western food.
Zhōngcān hé xīcān wǒ dōu xǐhuan.

"也 yě" expresses inclusion, in the sense of "also, as well, too".

④ 有的邮局和小商店也卖。Some post offices and small shops also sell them.
Yǒude yóujú hé xiǎo shāngdiàn yě mài.

Adverbs such as "都 dōu" and "也 yě" may appear in succession, in which case, "也 yě" precedes "都 dōu" or other adverbs (such as "不 bù").

⑤ 我们也都要买电话卡。We all want to buy phone-cards too.
Wǒmen yě dōu yào mǎi diànhuàkǎ.

⑥ 我也不需要换钱。I don't need to exchange money either.
Wǒ yě bù xūyào huàn qián.

▶ G6. Verb reduplication

Verbs of activity can be repeated to indicate casualness, tentativeness or brevity. For instance, "问问 wènwen" (just ask); "打打电话 dǎda diànhuà" (casually make some calls); "走走 zǒuzou" (take a walk); "坐坐 zuòzuo" (sit for a bit). Note that the reiterated verb is toneless, as shown. Disyllabic verbs can also be reduplicated, though in this case, they retain their tones: "打扫打扫 dǎsǎo dǎsǎo" (do a bit of cleaning). Here are some other examples:

① 您去问问。Go and ask.
Nín qù wènwen.

② 在校园走走 take a stroll on the campus
zài xiàoyuán zǒuzou

③ 打扫打扫我的房间 clean up my room a bit
dǎsǎo dǎsǎo wǒ de fángjiān

Consolidation & Practice

1. Use "先 xiān……再 zài……" (first…then…) to sequence the activities listed in each item below

(1) 买电话卡，　打电话
mǎi diànhuàkǎ, dǎ diànhuà

(2) 拨001，拨地区号码和电话号码
bō líng-líng-yāo, bō dìqū hàomǎ hé diànhuà hàomǎ

(3) 换人民币，　买东西
huàn rénmínbì, mǎi dōngxi

(4) 喝汤，　吃饭
hē tāng, chī fàn

(5) 去银行，　去商店
qù yínháng, qù shāngdiàn

(6) 看红绿灯，过马路
kàn hónglǜdēng, guò mǎlù

(7) 换床单，　打扫卫生间
huàn chuángdān, dǎsǎo wèishēngjiān

Say the following in Chinese:

(1) Let me have your passport then I'll give you your key.
(2) Give me the deposit first, then I'll give you a receipt.

2. Fill in the blanks with the appropriate directional complement: "来 lái" or "去 qù"

(1) 今天早上妈妈从美国给我打（　　　）电话。
Jīntiān zǎoshang māma cóng Měiguó gěi wǒ dǎ (　　　) diànhuà.

(2) 喂，可以给我送（　　　）早饭吗？我的房间是409。
Wèi, kěyǐ gěi wǒ sòng (　　　) zǎofàn ma? Wǒ de fángjiān shì sì-líng-jiǔ.

(3) 请问，打（　　　）美国的长途电话多少钱一分钟？
Qǐngwèn, dǎ (　　　) Měiguó de chángtú diànhuà duōshao qián yì fēnzhōng?

(4) 我的中国朋友给我买（　　　）了很多水果。
Wǒ de Zhōngguó péngyou gěi wǒ mǎi (　　　) le hěn duō shuǐguǒ.

(5) 服务员给我送（　　　）了行李。
Fúwùyuán gěi wǒ sòng (　　　) le xíngli.

(6) 你没有手机吗？我的朋友给我买（　　　）两个，你拿（　　　）一个吧！
Nǐ méiyǒu shǒujī ma? Wǒ de péngyou gěi wǒ mǎi (　　　) liǎng ge, nǐ ná (　　　) yí ge ba!

3. Use the expression "太 tài + Adj + 了 le" to describe the following things/situations

这个手机 zhège shǒujī	我的房间 wǒ de fángjiān	酒店的服务员 jiǔdiàn de fúwùyuán

这个餐馆的饭 zhège cānguǎn de fàn	酒店的西餐 jiǔdiàn de xīcān	
他的行李 tā de xíngli	我房间的空调 wǒ fángjiān de kōngtiáo	这个酒店的服务 zhège jiǔdiàn de fúwù

4. Use "如果 rúguǒ……就 jiù……" to connect the phrases listed below

(1) 用电话卡，　　很便宜
yòng diànhuàkǎ, hěn piányi

(2) 空调坏了，　　叫人来修
kōngtiáo huài le, jiào rén lái xiū

(3) 你还没有吃饭，　　我们现在去餐馆
nǐ hái méiyǒu chī fàn, wǒmen xiànzài qù cānguǎn

(4) 你要换钱，　　去银行
nǐ yào huàn qián, qù yínháng

(5) 在酒店打长途电话，　　要付服务费
zài jiǔdiàn dǎ chángtú diànhuà, yào fù fúwùfèi

(6) 外国人住酒店，　　要有护照
wàiguórén zhù jiǔdiàn, yào yǒu hùzhào

(7) 这个最便宜，我买这个
zhège zuì piányi, wǒ mǎi zhège

5. Fill in the blanks with the appropriate adverb: "再 zài" (and then), "都 dōu" (all), "也 yě" (also)

(1) 打长途电话要先拨地区号码，(　　　) 拨电话号码。
Dǎ chángtú diànhuà yào xiān bō dìqū hàomǎ, (　　　) bō diànhuà hàomǎ.

(2) 我们要先换人民币，(　　　) 去住宾馆。
Wǒmen yào xiān huàn rénmínbì, (　　　) qù zhù bīnguǎn.

(3) 我这三天 (　　　) 住这儿。
Wǒ zhè sān tiān (　　　) zhù zhèr.

(4) 百分之九十的学生 (　　　) 学习英语。
Bǎi fēnzhī jiǔshí de xuésheng (　　　) xuéxí Yīngyǔ.

(5) 他买了电话卡，我 (　　　) 买了。
Tā mǎile diànhuàkǎ, wǒ (　　　) mǎile.

(6) 留学生和外教 (　　　) 学中文。
Liúxuéshēng hé wàijiào (　　　) xué Zhōngwén.

(7) 他要了素菜，我们（　　　　）（　　　　）要了素菜。
Tā yàole sùcài, wǒmen (　　　　) (　　　　) yàole sùcài.

(8) 报亭卖电话卡，邮局和小商店（　　　　）（　　　　）卖电话卡。
Bàotíng mài diànhuàkǎ, yóujú hé xiǎo shāngdiàn (　　　　) (　　　　) mài diànhuàkǎ.

6. Following the English guidelines, use a reduplicated verb to complete the following sentences

(1) 我们一起去街上____________，好吗？(take a stroll)
Wǒmen yìqǐ qù jiē shang ____________, hǎo ma?

(2) 服务员，请叫人来____________。(clear up my room a little bit)
Fúwùyuán, qǐng jiào rén lái ____________.

(3) 你去____________哪儿有洗手间。(ask briefly)
Nǐ qù ____________ nǎr yǒu xǐshǒujiān.

(4) 请您先____________，李老师马上就来。(sit here for a second)
Qǐng nín xiān ____________, Lǐ lǎoshī mǎshàng jiù lái.

(5) 你________，我去买张电话卡。(wait here for a bit)
Nǐ ________, wǒ qù mǎi zhāng diànhuàkǎ.

(6) 我的手机坏了，请您____________。(try and fix it)
Wǒ de shǒujī huài le, qǐng nín ____________.

Pronunciation Notes

Pinyin letter "e"

There are three readings of the letter "e", depending on the context.

a. Written "e" followed or preceded by "i"

Written "e" followed by "i" (ei) rhymes with English "day". You are already familiar with examples such as "gěi", "Běijīng", "méiyǒu", and "Měiguó".

Written "e" preceded by "i" (ie) rhymes with English "yeah" (the informal pronunciation of "yes"), a vowel that is pronounced with the mouth more open than "ei". For "ie", you have the examples "xièxie" and "bié de" or "biéren", as well as "yě". (In the case of "yě", because of the lack of a true initial consonant, "i" is written "y".)

b. In all other contexts (e, en, eng), written "e" is pronounced with a central "shwa" vowel, whose quality is like the unstressed vowels (underlined) in English "about", "telephone" or "camera". In Chinese, the vowel is stressed and pronounced with lips spread and lower jaw slightly thrust out – English speakers have a tendency to pronounce it with rounded lips instead.

Examples in all three contexts:

	Pinyin	Characters	English meaning
1	Éguó	俄国	Russia
	Wǒ è le.	我饿了。	I am hungry.
	hé	河	river
	chē	车	vehicle, car
	wǒ de	我的	mine, my
	Déguó	德国	Germany
	Dézhōu	德州	Texas
2	ēn	恩	kindness, grace
	gēn	根	root
	zhēn	真	real
3	dēng	灯	light
	zhēng	蒸	to steam
4	měi	美	beautiful
	hēi	黑	black
	bēizi	杯子	cup
5	Chūn Jié	春节	Spring Festival
	guāngdié	光碟	VCD

Pronunciation Exercises

1. Read the following words aloud, being careful to distinguish the different readings of *Pinyin* "e"

(1) "e" as a syllable

	Pinyin	Characters	English meaning
1	Éguó	俄国	Russia
2	ézi	蛾子	moth
3	étou	额头	forehead
4	Wǒ è le.	我饿了。	I am hungry.

(2) "e" as a rhyme

	Pinyin	Characters	English meaning
1	shé	蛇	snake
2	kuàilè	快乐	happy
3	qìchē	汽车	automobile
4	zhèngcè	政策	policy
5	Huáng Hé	黄河	the Yellow River
6	tèkuài	特快	express train
7	Kěkǒu Kělè	可口可乐	Coca-Cola
8	Déguó	德国	Germany
9	Dézhōu	德州	Texas
10	bú kèqi	不客气	you're welcome

(3) "e" in the rhymes "en" or "eng"

	Pinyin	Characters	English meaning
1	shén	神	god, deity, divinity
2	mén	门	door
3	Měnggǔ	蒙古	Mongolia
4	mèng	梦	dream
5	hěn hǎo	很好	very good
6	néng	能	can, able to

(4) "e" in the rhymes "ei" and "ie"

	Pinyin	Characters	English meaning
1	mèimei	妹妹	younger sister
2	gěi	给	to give
3	Běijīng	北京	Beijing
4	zéi	贼	thief
5	jiějie	姐姐	older sister
6	tiělù	铁路	railway
7	zhédié	折叠	to fold
8	dǎliè	打猎	to hunt

2. Read the following words aloud, being careful to pronounce *Pinyin* "e" correctly

	Pinyin	Characters	English meaning
1	jiéguǒ	结果	result
2	hē shuǐ	喝水	to drink water
3	wǔ fēn	五分	five *fen*
4	Měiguó	美国	America
5	gēge	哥哥	older brother
6	Éhài'é	俄亥俄	Ohio
7	xiǎofèi	小费	tip
8	huǒchē	火车	train
9	cèsuǒ	厕所	restroom
10	fēng	风	wind
11	shéngzi	绳子	rope

3. By group, combine initial and rhyme and read the resulting syllables aloud

Group A	Group B	Group C	Group D
b - ēi	zh - è	j - iǔ	z - ài
p - ō	ch - ǎo	q - iàn	c - ōng
m - án	sh - í	x - iāng	s - ù
f - áng	r - éng		

4. Practice reading *Pinyin* aloud with this list of color, electronic and photographic terms

	Pinyin	Characters	English meaning
1	yánsè	颜色	color
	báisè	白色	white
	hóngsè	红色	red
	lánsè	蓝色	blue
	lǜsè	绿色	green
	fěnsè	粉色	pink
	huángsè	黄色	yellow
	kāfēisè	咖啡色	brown
2	diànnǎo	电脑	computer
	diàndēngpào	电灯泡	light bulb
	chāzuò	插座	socket
	diàndēng	电灯	light
	diànchí	电池	battery
	yī hào diànchí	一号电池	D size battery (a #1)
	èr hào diànchí	二号电池	C size battery (a #2)
	wǔ hào diànchí	五号电池	AA size battery
	qī hào diànchí	七号电池	AAA size battery
	shōuyīnjī	收音机	radio
	shǒujī	手机	cell phone
	CD pán	CD 盘	CD
	lùyīndài	录音带	cassette tape
	lùyīnjī	录音机	tape recorder
	lùxiàngjī	录像机	video recorder
	guāngdié	光碟	VCD
	shùzì guāngdié	数字光碟	DVD
	ruǎnpán	软盘	floppy disk
	zhàoxiàngjī	照相机	camera

	Pinyin	Characters	English meaning
2	diànxiàn	电线	electrical wires
	chāxiāo	插销	plug
	jiēxiànbǎn	接线板	wiring board
	chāzuòbǎn	插座板	power strip
	wěnyāqì	稳压器	surge protector
	wěnyā diànyuán	稳压电源	power strip with surge protector
	diànyā zhuǎnhuànqì	电压转换器	electric voltage converter
	jīguāng chàngjī	激光唱机	CD player
	diànyā	电压	voltage
3	jiāojuǎn	胶卷	film
	hēibái jiāojuǎn	黑白胶卷	black and white film
	cǎisè jiāojuǎn	彩色胶卷	color film
	huàndēngpiàn	幻灯片	slide (a transparency)
	dǐpiàn	底片	negative
	zhàopiàn	照片	prints
	jìngtóu	镜头	lens

Listening Comprehension

1. Listen to the dialogue between a foreign guest and a hotel attendant, then answer the questions

   (1) What is the rate for calls to the United States?

   (2) What is the rate for calls to Japan?

   (3) How can you save money on phone calls?

2. Listen to the dialogue and indicate whether the statements are true of false

	T	F
(1) The man is asking about making calls to the U.S.		
(2) The man doesn't need to call out.		
(3) Local calls are free.		
(4) All calls are charged a service fee.		

3. Listen to the CD and write down in *Pinyin* the words you hear

(1) ________ (5) ________ (9) ________

(2) ________ (6) ________ (10) ________

(3) ________ (7) ________

(4) ________ (8) ________

Communication Activities

Pair Work

Scenario I: Make telephone calls along the lines suggested below:

(1) Call the front desk and find out where you can get phone-cards.

(2) Call a hotel and ask to speak to a friend of yours who lives there.

(3) Call a friend to find out which kinds of phone-cards are best and cheapest.

(4) Call a friend to ask for the phone number of another friend.

Scenario II: One of you needs to get a phone-card; the other is the salesman.

Buyer: explain that you need a card to make international long-distance calls; find out what sort of card would be best, and then ask how to use it.

Salesman: provide the answers.

Review Exercises

I. Match the items in the left-hand list with the words in the right-hand list

(1) 太 tài	A. 百分之五 bǎi fēnzhī wǔ
(2) 最 zuì	B. 吃饭 chī fàn
(3) 只 zhǐ	C. 贵了 guì le
(4) 先 xiān	D. 卖 IP卡 mài IP kǎ
(5) 加 jiā	E. 便宜 piányi
(6) 都 dōu	F. 免费 miǎnfèi

II. Recite these telephone numbers aloud, digit by digit, in Chinese

(010) 4216-4855	(027) 7205-7299
(021) 3217-6029	(0755) 9483-3076
(020) 2018-9840	(023) 6919-7023
(00852) 9736-7728	(001) 626-2564931

III. Complete the sentences with "来 lái" (to come) or "去 qù" (to go)

1. 你朋友（　　　　）和你一起吃饭吗？
Nǐ péngyou (　　　　) hé nǐ yìqǐ chī fàn ma?

2. 他（　　　　）买电话卡吗？
Tā (　　　　) mǎi diànhuàkǎ ma?

3. （　　　　）洗手间怎么走？
（　　　　）xǐshǒujiān zěnme zǒu?

4. 请问，怎么（　　　　）中国银行？
Qǐngwèn, zěnme (　　　　) Zhōngguó Yínháng?

5. 那个留学生是什么时候（　　　　）中国的？
Nàge liúxuéshēng shì shénme shíhou (　　　　) Zhōngguó de?

6. 请问，我朋友怎么（　　　　）这个宾馆？
Qǐngwèn, wǒ péngyou zěnme (　　　　) zhège bīnguǎn?

7. 你从外边打（　　　　）电话的时候，告诉前台我的房间号。
Nǐ cóng wàibian dǎ (　　　　) diànhuà de shíhou, gàosu qiántái wǒ de fángjiānhào.

8. 吃饭以后，我们（　　　　）外面走走，好吗？
Chī fàn yǐhòu, wǒmen (　　　　) wàimiàn zǒuzou, hǎo ma?

9. 别人都（　　　　）买东西了，只有我（　　　　）看你。
Biéren dōu (　　　　) mǎi dōngxi le, zhǐyǒu wǒ (　　　　) kàn nǐ.

10. 我房间的空调坏了，请叫人（　　　　）修修。
Wǒ fángjiān de kōngtiáo huài le, qǐng jiào rén (　　　　) xiūxiu.

IV. Answer the questions using the combination "先 xiān……再zài……" (first…then…)

1. A：你好！你什么时候给我换床单？
Nǐ hǎo! Nǐ shénme shíhou gěi wǒ huàn chuángdān?

B：____。
(clean the room for you; change the linen)

2. A：我什么时候可以拿钥匙？
Wǒ shénme shíhou kěyǐ ná yàoshi?

B：____。
(pay the deposit; give the key)

3. A：你怎么不进房间去？
Nǐ zěnme bú jìn fángjiān qu?

B：____。
(wait until custodian finishes cleaning; go in)

4. A：请问，药店怎么走？
Qǐngwèn, yàodiàn zěnme zǒu?

B：____。
(cross this road; pass a supermarket)

V. Complete the following sentences incorporating the "if…then…" pattern: "如果 rúguǒ…… 就 jiù……"

1. A：用酒店的电话给美国打长途，太贵了！
Yòng jiǔdiàn de diànhuà gěi Měiguó dǎ chángtú, tài guì le!

B：____。
(If you use a China Telecom IP card, then you only pay 3 *mao* a minute.)

2. A：现在学英文很贵，我没有很多钱。
Xiànzài xué Yīngwén hěn guì, wǒ méiyǒu hěn duō qián.

B：____。
(If you teach foreigners Chinese, they can teach you for free.)

3. A：我从房间打电话都要先拨9吗？
Wǒ cóng fángjiān dǎ diànhuà dōu yào xiān bō jiǔ ma?

B：____。
(If you call another room in the hotel, then you don't need to dial 9.)

4. A：你能看中文菜单吗？
Nǐ néng kàn Zhōngwén càidān ma?

B：不可以，________________________________。
Bù kěyǐ, (If you have an English menu, then please give me one.)

VI. Fill in the blanks with appropriate reduplicated verbs

1. 手机给您修好了，您________________________。(take a look)
Shǒujī gěi nín xiūhǎo le, nín ________________________.

2. 这是他们的新啤酒，你先____________________，我们再点。(taste a little bit)
Zhè shì tāmen de xīn píjiǔ, nǐ xiān ________________, wǒmen zài diǎn.

3. 对不起，我不要临街的房间，能不能给我________________？(change rooms)
Duìbuqǐ, wǒ bú yào línjiē de fángjiān, néng bu néng gěi wǒ ________________?

4. 前面有一个咖啡馆，我们去____________________吧。(sit briefly)
Qiánmiàn yǒu yí ge kāfēiguǎn, wǒmen qù ________________ ba.

VII. Perform the following tasks (This exercise can be written or presented orally)

1. You are staying at a hotel (in China) and need to find out how to phone home to the U.S. Find out if you can make a phone call to the U.S. from you room.
2. Ask what number you should dial first.
3. Find out how much it is per minute.
4. Say you feel that it's too expensive, and ask where you can buy a phone-card.
5. Give your name and phone number and ask if they can help you dial.

Culture Notes

1. Telephone cards

There are two basic types of phone-card sold in China: IC (Integrated Circuit) cards, and IP (Internet Protocol) cards. IC cards cannot be used to make calls from hotel or home phones. They require a card-reader so they can only be used with special public telephones called "磁卡电话 cíkǎ diànhuà" (magnetic-card phones). They can be used for local, domestic long-distance, and international calls. The charges are the same as for coin phones, with a service fee for long distance calls. IC cards can be purchased at post offices, department stores, and large hotels.

IP phone-cards, also called "200" phone cards, can be used to make local or long-distance calls on home or hotel telephones. They are the cheapest way of making international calls. They can be purchased at stores, post offices, and hotel business centers. Before using an IP card, you have to scratch off the strip that covers the pin number. Here is a translation of the instructions on the back of a typical "200" phone-card:

- Pick up the phone and dial 200
- Dial (1) for Chinese, (2) for Cantonese, (3) for English
- Enter your card number
- Enter your pin
- Dial (1) for long distance, (2) to check balance of minutes, (3) to change your code number
- Hang up

Other useful information on phone-cards:

- Push the "*" key to cancel or start again.
- After dialing 200, you can directly enter a number for choice of language.
- If you are calling a place that is outside the area code where you bought the card, dial 17550 before the card number.
- If you forget your pin number, call 9686 8002 08.
- For service, call 8818 2729 6868 0020.

2. Busy signals

Busy signals are sometimes due to busy trans-Pacific circuits rather than local circuits.

3. Public phones

Public phones are plentiful in China. They may be found on streets, at train stations, and in stores. They are marked by the sign: "公用电话 gōngyòng diànhuà", literally "public-use telephone". Coin or card-operated public telephones are usually in booths or niches. Those in stores or on the side of the street have attendants who charge you after the call is completed. Domestic long-distance and international calls from public phones are charged additional service fees.

4. Cheap times for long-distance calls

In China long-distance phone calls made between 11:00 p.m. and 7:00 a.m. are half the price of calls made during business hours.

5. Time Zones in China

Although geographically China covers five times zones, since 1949, there has been only a single time zone, called Beijing Time (北京时间 Běijīng Shíjiān), or internationally, China Standard Time. Beijing Time is Greenwich Mean Time + 8 hours, or Eastern Standard Time + 12 or 13 hours (depending on Daylight Savings). Informally, the far western regions of China, Tibet and Xinjiang, generally operate on GMT + 6 hours. China experimented with daylight savings time between 1986 and 1991, but it has not been instituted since.

6. Time differences between Beijing (or China) and North America

Noon in Beijing	Previous day / Daylight savings
Eastern (-12/-13)	11:00 p.m / 12:00 a.m.
Central (-13/-14)	10:00 p.m. / 11:00 p.m.
Mountain (-14/-15)	09:00 p.m. / 10:00 p.m.
Pacific (-15/-16)	08:00 p.m. / 09:00 p.m.

Lesson Nine What Time Is It Now?

第九课 现在几点

Dì-jiǔ Kè Xiànzài Jǐ Diǎn

In this lesson you will learn how to do the following

- Give an account of your daily schedule
- Make appointments to meet people
- Explain when activities or events occur

Grammar

- Time phrases and their position in the sentence
- Auxiliary verbs: "要 yào" (want to , have to , will, be going to), "会 huì" (be good at, likely, will), "想 xiǎng" (want, feel like doing something)
- Temporal clauses with "以前 yǐqián" (before) and "以后 yǐhòu" (after)
- Sentences with "就 jiù…… 了 le"
- Verbs with generic objects (VOs)
- The preposition "跟 gēn" (with)

Culture Notes

- 12-hour and 24-hour time systems
- Working hours in China
- A typical daily schedule for a secondary school in China

Dialogue

A：尚中 Shàng Zhōng　　　　**B**：夏武 Xià Wǔ

（在宿舍 Zài sùshè）

A：现在几[1]点[G1]了？
Xiànzài jǐ[1] diǎn[G1] le?

B：现在差五分八点。
Xiànzài chà wǔ fēn bā diǎn.

A：我八点半要[G2]上[2]汉语课，没有[3]时间吃早点了。
Wǒ bā diǎn bàn yào[G2] shàng[2] Hànyǔ kè, méiyǒu[3] shíjiān chī zǎodiǎn le.

B：我煮了鸡蛋，你吃一个吧。我们中午一起吃饭，好吗？
Wǒ zhǔle jīdàn, nǐ chī yí ge ba. Wǒmen zhōngwǔ yìqǐ chī fàn, hǎo ma?

A：好。你几点下课？
Hǎo. Nǐ jǐ diǎn xiàkè?

B：我上午教英语，十一点三刻下课。你呢？
Wǒ shàngwǔ jiāo Yīngyǔ, shíyī diǎn sān kè xiàkè. Nǐ ne?

A：我十二点一刻下课。我们十二点半在餐厅见，好吗？
Wǒ shí'èr diǎn yí kè xiàkè. Wǒmen shí'èr diǎn bàn zài cāntīng jiàn, hǎo ma?

B：好。中午见。
Hǎo. Zhōngwǔ jiàn.

Notes

1. The phrase "几点 jǐ diǎn", with the question word "几 jǐ" (how many), means literally "how many points (on the clock)", or in other words, "what time". "几 jǐ" differs from "多少 duōshao" (which can also mean "how many") in that it usually presupposes a response with single-digits, anything between one and nine. However, for clock time, "几点 jǐ diǎn" is used to question the hour without prejudice to later hours, such as eleven or twelve. "多少 duōshao", on the other hand, is used when there is no particular expectation of the number in the response. One important difference between the two words is that "几 jǐ" has to be followed by a measure: "几个人 jǐ ge rén" (how many people), "几块钱 jǐ kuài qián" (how many dollars – how much money). "多少 duōshao", on the other hand, may precede a noun directly: "多少钱 duōshao qián" (how much money).
2. Notice that "上 shàng" and "下 xià", in addition to occurring in compounds such as "早上 zǎoshang" (morning) and "下午 xiàwǔ" (afternoon), can also act as verbs, e.g. in verb-object combinations such as: "上课 shàngkè" (to go to class, to start class), "下课 xiàkè" (to end class, to get out of class), "上班 shàngbān" (to go to work, to start work) and "下班 xiàbān" (to get out of work, to stop work).
3. "没有时间 méiyǒu shíjiān" is literally "not have time". "有 yǒu" (to have) is the only verb in Chinese negated with "没 méi" (rather than "不 bù"): "我下午没有课。Wǒ xiàwǔ méiyǒu kè." (I don't have class in the afternoon.) However, "没有 méiyǒu", or just "没 méi", is also used to express the negative for past events that would be expressed in the positive with "了 le" . For example: "吃了 chīle" (I've eaten), but "还没吃 hái méi chī" (I haven't eaten yet).

（在餐厅 Zài cāntīng）

A： 你今天下午还有课吗？
Nǐ jīntiān xiàwǔ hái yǒu kè ma?

B： 没有。我要去一个公司上班，做翻译。
Méiyǒu. Wǒ yào qù yí ge gōngsī shàngbān, zuò fānyì.

A： 我下午也没有课，可是要去做家教。你几点下班？
Wǒ xiàwǔ yě méiyǒu kè, kěshì yào qù zuò jiājiào. Nǐ jǐ diǎn xiàbān?

B： 下午五点。
Xiàwǔ wǔ diǎn.

A： 你晚上打算做什么？
Nǐ wǎnshang dǎsuàn zuò shénme?

B： 下班以后[G3]我就累了[G4]，晚饭后看看电视，然后洗澡睡觉[G5]。
Xiàbān yǐhòu[G3] wǒ jiù lèi le[G4], wǎnfàn hòu kànkan diànshì, ránhòu xǐzǎo shuìjiào[G5].

A： 我今天晚上要跟[G6]朋友一起去饭馆吃饭。
Wǒ jīntiān wǎnshang yào gēn[G6] péngyou yìqǐ qù fànguǎn chī fàn.

B： 是不是常常[4]来找你的那个高富帅[5]？他是你的男朋友吗？
Shì bu shì chángcháng[4] lái zhǎo nǐ de nàge gāo-fù-shuài[5]? Tā shì nǐ de nánpéngyou ma?

A： 还不是。我不会回来太晚。明天早上我八点有课，要七点起床。
Hái bú shì. Wǒ bú huì huílai tài wǎn. Míngtiān zǎoshang wǒ bā diǎn yǒu kè, yào qī diǎn qǐchuáng.

B： 我明天上午没课，不想早起，八点以前请别叫醒我。
Wǒ míngtiān shàngwǔ méi kè, bù xiǎng zǎo qǐ, bā diǎn yǐqián qǐng bié jiàoxǐng wǒ.

A： 没问题。
Méi wèntí.

---

4. "常常 chángcháng" is an adverb, which appears in the normal position before the verb (and after the subject, if one is present). "有时候 yǒushíhou" (sometimes), on the other hand, is a time phrase. It acts like a moveable adverb, appearing either before the subject or after it (with a slight nuance of difference).
5. "高富帅 gāo-fù-shuài", literally "tall, rich and handsome" is a slick way of describing the ideal man. Cf. "白富美 bái-fù-měi", literally "white, rich and beautiful", a slick way of describing the ideal woman.

New Words

1	几点/幾點	jǐ diǎn	Phrase	what time
	几/幾	jǐ	IntPron	how many, a few, several, some
2	宿舍	sùshè	N	dormitory (for students, workers, etc.)
3	差	chà	V	to lack, to be short of, to differ (by)
4	分	fēn	Meas	part, minute, cent
5	半	bàn	Num	half ("半个 bàn ge"; "一个半 yí ge bàn")
6	上课/上課	shàngkè	VO	to go to class, to attend class, to teach a class, to give a lesson
7	汉语/漢語	Hànyǔ	PropN	Chinese, the Chinese spoken language
8	时间/時間	shíjiān	N	time
9	吃	chī	V	to eat
10	早点/早點	zǎodiǎn	N	light breakfast
11	煮	zhǔ	V	to boil, to cook
12	中午	zhōngwǔ	N	noon, mid-day
13	吃饭/吃飯	chī fàn	Phrase	to eat, to have a meal
14	好吗/好嗎	hǎo ma	Exp	Okay? Would it be all right? Do you mind?
15	下课/下課	xiàkè	VO	to get out of class, to dismiss class
16	上午	shàngwǔ	N	late morning
17	刻	kè	Meas	quarter of an hour ("三刻 sān kè", *45 minutes after, quarter to*)
18	见/見	jiàn	V	to see, to meet, to call on
19	今天	jīntiān	N	today, the present, now
20	下午	xiàwǔ	N	afternoon
21	还有/還有	hái yǒu	Phrase	still have, also have, there is/are still
22	课	kè	N	lesson, class
23	公司	gōngsī	N	company, corporation, firm
24	上班	shàngbān	VO	to go to work, to start work, to go on duty
25	做	zuò	V	to work, to do, to be

26	翻译/翻譯	fānyì	V/N	to translate, to interpret; translator, interpreter
27	可是	kěshì	Conj	but, however, yet
28	家教	jiājiào	N	private tutor (short for “家庭教师 jiātíng jiàoshī”)
29	下班	xiàbān	VO	to finish the day’s work, to go off duty
30	晚上	wǎnshang	N	evening, night
31	以后/以後	yǐhòu	PW	behind, after (cf. “后 hòu”)
32	累	lèi	Adj	tired
33	晚饭/晚飯	wǎnfàn	N	supper, dinner
34	看看	kànkan	Phrase	to take a look, to watch something leisurely
35	电视/電視	diànshì	N	television
36	然后/然後	ránhòu	Conj	then, after that
37	洗澡	xǐzǎo	VO	to take a bath, to bathe
38	睡觉/睡覺	shuìjiào	VO	to go to bed, to sleep
39	跟	gēn	Prep	with
40	饭馆/飯館	fànguǎn	N	restaurant
41	是不是	shì bu shì	Phrase	is the case that, right, isn’t it
42	常常	chángcháng	Adv	frequently, often
43	找	zhǎo	V	to look for, to seek
44	高	gāo	Adj	high, tall
45	富	fù	Adj	rich, wealthy, plenty, abundant
46	帅/帥	shuài	Adj	handsome
47	男朋友	nánpéngyou	N	boyfriend, male friend
48	会/會	huì	Aux	likely
49	回来/回來	huílai	V	to return, to come back
	回	huí	V	to return
50	晚	wǎn	Adj/N	late; night, evening
51	起床	qǐchuáng	VO	to get out of bed, to rise (in the morning)
52	早起	zǎo qǐ	Phrase	to get up early, to rise early

早	zǎo	Adj / Adv / Exp	early; as early as; good morning
起	qǐ	V	to rise, to stand up

Re-enacting the Dialogue

A: Shang Zhong **B: Xia Wu**

(In the dormitory)

A: What's the time, now?

B: It's now five to eight.

A: I've got to go to Chinese class at 8:30; there's no time for breakfast.

B: I've boiled some eggs – have one. We'll eat together at noon, OK?

A: Fine. When do you get out of class?

B: I teach English in the morning and will end class at 11:45. How about you?

A: I get out of class at 12:15. Let's meet at 12:30 in the cafeteria, okay?

B: Okay, see you at the lunch hour.

(In the cafeteria)

A: Do you have any more classes this afternoon?

B: No. I have to go to work at a company; I'm a translator.

A: I don't have any classes in the afternoon, either, but I have to go do a tutorial. When do you finish work?

B: At 5:00 p.m.

A: What are you planning to do this evening?

B: After I get off work, I get quite tired. After I eat dinner, I watch some TV, and then I have a shower and go to bed.

A: This evening, I'm going out to eat at a restaurant with a friend.

B: Is it with that tall, handsome, rich dude who's always looking for you? Is he your boyfriend?

A: Not yet he isn't. I won't be back too late. I have a class tomorrow at 8:00 a.m., so I have to be up by 7:00.

B: I don't have any classes tomorrow morning, so I don't want to get up too early. Please don't wake me up before 8:00.

A: No problem.

Grammar

▶ G1. Time phrases and their position in the sentence

Clock time is expressed in terms of "点 diǎn" (points on the clock), and "分 fēn" (minutes): "几点 jǐ diǎn" (what hour); "十一点二十五分 shíyī diǎn èrshíwǔ fēn" (11:25). The half hour is expressed with "半 bàn" acting as a suffix to the measure word: "十二点半 shí'èr diǎn bàn" (half past twelve). The quarter hours are expressed with "刻 kè" (literally, "a cut", referring to the marks made on a water clock): "十二点一刻 shí'èr diǎn yí kè" (quarter past twelve); "十一点三刻 shíyī diǎn sān kè" (three quarters past eleven, i.e. 11:45). Time before the hour is expressed as "差 chà" (to lack) plus number of minutes: "差五分三点 chà wǔ fēn sān diǎn", literally, "less 5 minutes to 3 o'clock", i.e. "five minutes to three".

The divisions of the day include: "早上 zǎoshang" (early morning), "上午 shàngwǔ" (late morning), "中午 zhōngwǔ" (noon, noonish), "下午 xiàwǔ" (afternoon), and "晚上 wǎnshang" (evening). The days themselves include: "昨天 zuótiān" (yesterday), "今天 jīntiān" (today), and "明天 míngtiān" (tomorrow).

(1) The placement of time expressions

Time expressions (as opposed to duration phrases, cf. Lesson 7, G5) are placed either at the beginning of a sentence, or after the subject (if one is present) and before the verb. Notice that there is no preposition (comparable to English "at") in time phrases: "十一点起床 shíyī diǎn qǐchuáng" (get up at 11:00).

a. At the beginning of a sentence

① 五点五分我去找你。I will go and look for you at 5:05.
Wǔ diǎn wǔ fēn wǒ qù zhǎo nǐ.

② 晚上你常常做什么？What do you usually do in the evening?
Wǎnshang nǐ chángcháng zuò shénme?

b. After the subject (but before the verb)

③ 我十一点睡觉。I go to bed at 11:00.
Wǒ shíyī diǎn shuìjiào.

④ 我下午有英语课。I have English class in the afternoon.
Wǒ xiàwǔ yǒu Yīngyǔ kè.

c. Time interrogatives are placed immediately before the verb

⑤ 你早上几点起床？What time do you get up in the morning?
Nǐ zǎoshang jǐ diǎn qǐchuáng?

⑥ 晚上你什么时候睡觉？When do you go to bed in the evening?
Wǎnshang nǐ shénme shíhou shuìjiào?

(2) Order within time phrases

Time expressions are ordered from larger periods to smaller; English tends to have the opposite order, with smaller units placed first.

⑦ 早上十一点半 half past eleven in the morning
zǎoshang shíyī diǎn bàn

⑧ 今天下午三点一刻 3:15 this afternoon
jīntiān xiàwǔ sān diǎn yí kè

(3) The relative order of time and place

Time phrases precede location phrases, as follows:

Subject + Time + Place + V (+ Object).

⑨ 我四点半在饭馆等你。I'll be waiting for you in the restaurant at 4:30.
Wǒ sì diǎn bàn zài fànguǎn děng nǐ.

⑩ 他每天早上七点半在宿舍吃饭。He eats in his dorm at 7:30 everyday morning.
Tā měi tiān zǎoshang qī diǎn bàn zài sùshè chī fàn.

▶ G2. Auxiliary verbs: "要 yào" (want to, have to, will, be going to), "会 huì" (be good at, likely, will), "想 xiǎng" (want, feel like doing something)

Auxiliary verbs (Aux) were first introduced in Lesson 5 (G1). They are verbs that express desire, likelihood, ability, or need, and they are followed by a main verb. The sentence pattern is:

Subject + Aux + V + Object.

Several appear in this lesson, including "要 yào" (want to, have to, will, be going to), discussed earlier. The others are: "会 huì" (be good at, likely, will), "想 xiǎng" (want, feel like doing something) and "打算 dǎsuàn" (plan to, intend to).

① 我八点半要去上汉语课。I'm going to Chinese class at 8:30.
Wǒ bā diǎn bàn yào qù shàng Hànyǔ kè.

② 我想去一个公司做翻译。I'd like to work for a company as a translator.
Wǒ xiǎng qù yí ge gōngsī zuò fānyì.

③ 我今天晚上会去饭馆吃饭。I'll go out to dinner tonight.
Wǒ jīntiān wǎnshang huì qù fànguǎn chī fàn.

④ 你晚上打算做什么？ What do you plan to do in the evening?
Nǐ wǎnshang dǎsuàn zuò shénme?

⑤ 我会跟男朋友去看电影。I'll go to a movie with my boyfriend.
Wǒ huì gēn nánpéngyou qù kàn diànyǐng.

▶ G3. Temporal clauses with "以前 yǐqián" (before) and "以后 yǐhòu" (after)

In Lesson 7 (G7), you were introduced to "……的时候 de shíhou", which unlike the English equivalent "when", appears at the foot of the clause: "打扫洗澡间的时候 dǎsǎo xǐzǎojiān de shíhou" (when you clean the bathroom). "Before" and "after" clauses follow the same pattern, with the conjunctions "以前 yǐqián", sometimes reduced to "前 qián" (before), and "以后 yǐhòu" or "后 hòu" (after), both positioned at the end of the clause.

① 下班以后我就累了。I get quite tired after work.
Xiàbān yǐhòu wǒ jiù lèi le.

② 吃晚饭后看看电视。I watch some TV after I eat dinner.
Chī wǎnfàn hòu kànkan diànshì.

③ 睡觉以前，我不喝咖啡。I don't drink coffee before I go to bed.
Shuìjiào yǐqián, wǒ bù hē kāfēi.

④ 八点以前请别叫醒我。Please don't wake me up before 8:00.
Bā diǎn yǐqián qǐng bié jiàoxǐng wǒ.

▶ G4. Sentences with "就 jiù……了 le"

Lesson 8 (G4) introduced "就 jiù" as an adverb that appeared in association with a previous conditional ("if") clause, often explicitly indicated with "如果 rúguǒ": "如果你不买电话卡，我就买 Rúguǒ nǐ bù mǎi diànhuàkǎ, wǒ jiù mǎi" (If you don't buy phone-card, then I'll buy one). In such cases, "就 jiù" can be translated as "in that case", or "then". More generally, "就 jiù" indicates a close linkage between two actions. In this lesson, the linkage is temporal:

① 她下了课就回家。She goes home as soon as she gets out of class.
Tā xiàle kè jiù huí jiā.

The sequential sense can be made more explicit with "以后 yǐhòu" (after):

② 他吃早饭以后就去上课。After breakfast, he goes to class.
Tā chī zǎofàn yǐhòu jiù qù shàngkè.

The addition of final "了 le" indicates a change of state resulting from the first action:

③ 下班以后我就累了。I get quite tired after work.
Xiàbān yǐhòu wǒ jiù lèi le.

④ 我晚上喝咖啡以后就不想睡觉了。
Wǒ wǎnshang hē kāfēi yǐhòu jiù bù xiǎng shuìjiào le.
After I drink coffee in the evening, I don't feel like going to sleep.

▶ G5. Verbs with generic objects (VOs)

Verbs in Chinese can be single syllables, like "喝 hē" (to drink) and "看 kàn" (to look). They can also be disyllabic, like "安排 ānpái" (to arrange) and "预订 yùdìng" (to book [a hotel room, etc.]). The latter function as unitary verbs: "预订了一个房间 yùdìngle yí ge fángjiān" (booked a room). However, compounds such as "洗澡 xǐzǎo" (to bathe), "睡觉 shuìjiào" (to sleep) and "吃饭 chī fàn" (to eat), which generally correspond to intransitive verbs in English (verbs with no object), behave like combinations of verb plus object, and that is usually how they are labeled: VOs.

In the case of "吃饭 chī fàn", "饭 fàn" can be given an independent meaning of "meal or cooked rice" and its status as a noun object looks unremarkable. But in the case of "洗澡 xǐzǎo" and "睡觉 shuìjiào", neither "澡 zǎo" nor "觉 jiào" can function independently and neither can be provided with a meaning. Nevertheless, for all three examples, the second syllables are detachable: "洗个澡 xǐ ge zǎo" (have a bath); "睡一会儿觉 shuì yíhuìr jiào" (have a nap); "吃了饭以后 chīle fàn yǐhòu" (after the meal).

Verbs labeled VOs, it should be noted, are directed towards an activity, not towards an object. That is why they correspond to intransitive verbs in English: "All I do is rise (qǐchuáng), bathe (xǐzǎo), eat (chī fàn) and sleep (shuìjiào)". If the verbal activity is directed towards an object, however, the pseudo objects will be replaced: "吃早点 chī zǎodiǎn" (eat breakfast), "洗衣服 xǐ yīfu" (wash clothes), etc.

▶ G6. The preposition "跟 gēn" (with)

"跟 gēn" (with) combines with a following object (noun or pronoun) to form a prepositional phrase that appears directly before the main verb. Prepositional phrases with "跟 gēn" are often followed by the adverb "一起 yìqǐ" (together). For example:

① 我今天晚上要跟朋友一起去饭馆吃饭。
Wǒ jīntiān wǎnshang yào gēn péngyou yìqǐ qù fànguǎn chī fàn.
This evening, I'm going out to eat at a restaurant with a friend.

In this function, "跟 gēn" is synonymous with "和 hé":

② 我和朋友一起去商店买东西。I'm going shopping at the store with my friends.
Wǒ hé péngyou yìqǐ qù shāngdiàn mǎi dōngxi.

Consolidation & Practice

1. Using the verb phrases and the time words listed below, interview your partner, in Chinese, about his or her daily routine, then report your findings to the class

Example: A：你几点起床？
Nǐ jǐ diǎn qǐchuáng?

B：我七点起床。
Wǒ qī diǎn qǐchuáng.

(1) 起床，洗澡，喝咖啡，吃早饭，上课，上班，学中文，
qǐchuáng, xǐzǎo, hē kāfēi, chī zǎofàn, shàngkè, shàngbān, xué Zhōngwén,
看电影，给美国打电话，去买东西，看朋友，回宿舍，
kàn diànyǐng, gěi Měiguó dǎ diànhuà, qù mǎi dōngxi, kàn péngyou, huí sùshè,
休息，看电视，去买电话卡，跟朋友一起吃饭
xiūxi, kàn diànshì, qù mǎi diànhuàkǎ, gēn péngyou yìqǐ chī fàn

(2) 点，分，一刻，上午，中午，下午，晚上，睡觉以前，
diǎn, fēn, yí kè, shàngwǔ, zhōngwǔ, xiàwǔ, wǎnshang, shuìjiào yǐqián,
起床以后，吃饭以后，下课以后，上课以前，换钱以后，
qǐchuáng yǐhòu, chī fàn yǐhòu, xiàkè yǐhòu, shàngkè yǐqián, huàn qián yǐhòu,
看电影以后
kàn diànyǐng yǐhòu

Your report:

(1)

(2)

(3)

(4)

(5)

(6)

(7)

(8)

(9)

(10)

2. Following the English cues, complete the sentences using the auxiliary verbs "想 xiǎng", "要 yào", "会 huì"

(1) 我今天晚上＿＿＿＿＿＿＿＿。(going to an internet café)
Wǒ jīntiān wǎnshang ＿＿＿＿＿＿＿＿.

(2) 我下课以后＿＿＿＿＿＿＿＿。(planning on going to the library)
Wǒ xiàkè yǐhòu ＿＿＿＿＿＿＿＿.

(3) 我明天＿＿＿＿＿＿＿＿。(probably going shopping)
Wǒ míngtiān ＿＿＿＿＿＿＿＿.

(4) 我今天晚上没有事，＿＿＿＿＿＿＿＿。(I'd like to go to a concert with some friends)
Wǒ jīntiān wǎnshang méiyǒu shì, ＿＿＿＿＿＿＿＿.

(5) 你＿＿＿＿＿＿＿＿去看电影吗？(feel like)
Nǐ ＿＿＿＿＿＿＿＿ qù kàn diànyǐng ma?

(6) 今天晚上＿＿＿＿＿＿＿＿。(I'm going to call my mom)
Jīntiān wǎnshang ＿＿＿＿＿＿＿＿.

3. Match the A clauses to B to form sentences that fit logically, and that conform to the "Subject VP 就 VP 了" pattern. Write them in the spaces provided

A	B
换了钱 huànle qián	不累了 bú lèi le
睡了觉 shuìle jiào	可以买东西了 kěyǐ mǎi dōngxi le
给她打电话 gěi tā dǎ diànhuà	屋里不热了 wū li bú rè le
用电话卡给美国打电话 yòng diànhuàkǎ gěi Měiguó dǎ diànhuà	知道她在哪里 zhīdào tā zài nǎli
空调修好以后 kōngtiáo xiūhǎo yǐhòu	便宜了 piányi le
吃两个大苹果以后 chī liǎng ge dà píngguǒ yǐhòu	不想吃饭了 bù xiǎng chī fàn le

(1)

(2)

(3)

(4)

(5)

(6)

4. In pairs or groups, suggest doing the following activities with other people, using the sentence pattern "Subject + 跟 gēn + Person + 一起 yìqǐ + V + Object"

喝咖啡，吃晚饭， 上课， 上班， 学中文， 看电影，
hē kāfēi, chī wǎnfàn, shàngkè, shàngbān, xué Zhōngwén, kàn diànyǐng

去买东西， 看朋友， 回宿舍， 看电视， 去银行换钱
qù mǎi dōngxi, kàn péngyou, huí sùshè, kàn diànshì, qù yínháng huàn qián

打扫房间， 请老师吃饭， 去图书馆， 去餐厅， 坐车
dǎsǎo fángjiān, qǐng lǎoshī chī fàn, qù túshūguǎn, qù cāntīng, zuò chē

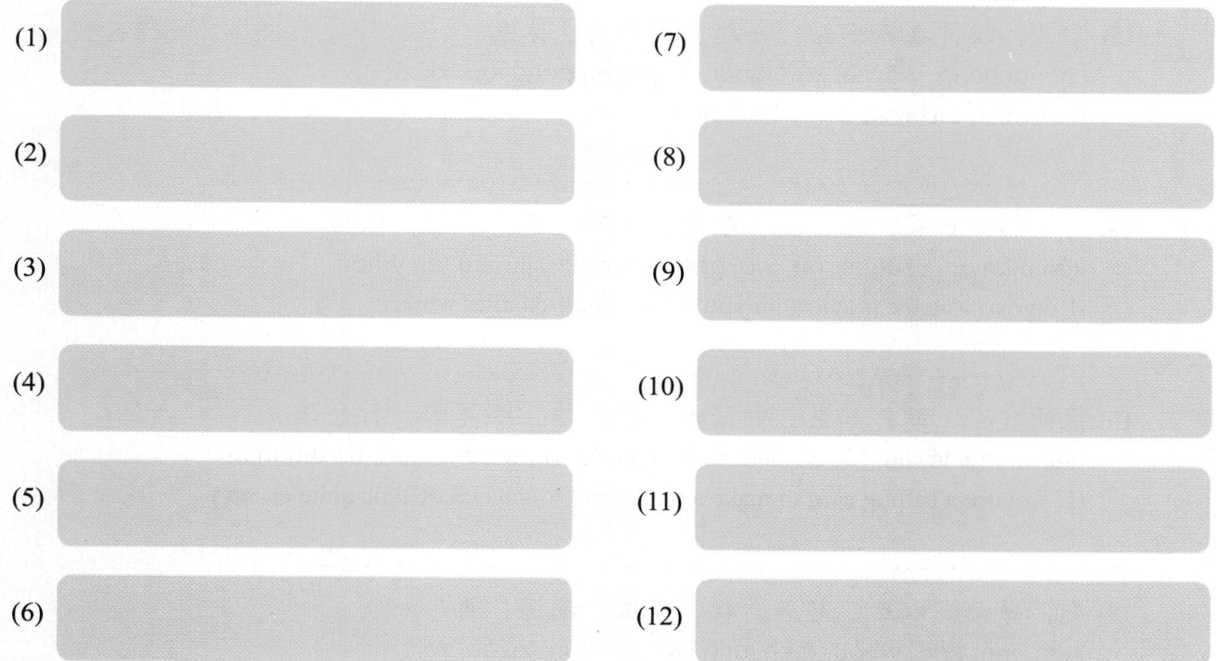

5. Rearrange the list of items to form a sentence, following the English cue

(1) 在餐厅，我，早上，每天，八点，吃饭，跟朋友
zài cāntīng, wǒ, zǎoshang, měi tiān, bā diǎn, chī fàn, gēn péngyou
(I eat breakfast with a friend every morning at 8:00 a.m.)

→ ………………………………………………………………

(2) 要，翻译，做，去，一个公司，下午，星期五，他
yào, fānyì, zuò, qù, yí ge gōngsī, xiàwǔ, xīngqīwǔ, tā
(On Friday afternoon, he's going to a company to do some translation.)

→ ………………………………………………………………

(3) 你，做，周末，什么，打算
nǐ, zuò, zhōumò, shénme, dǎsuàn
(What do you plan to do over the weekend?)

→ ………………………………………………………………

(4) 以后，下课，会，打电话，给我妈妈，我
yǐhòu, xiàkè, huì, dǎ diànhuà, gěi wǒ māma, wǒ
(I'll call my mom after the class.)

→ ………………………………………………………………

(5) 常常，我，在咖啡馆，一起，跟朋友，休息
chángcháng, wǒ, zài kāfēiguǎn, yìqǐ, gēn péngyou, xiūxi
(I often take a break with friends at the café.)

→ ………………………………………………………………

(6) 看电影，如果，去，我，跟你，下班，就，不累，以后
kàn diànyǐng, rúguǒ, qù, wǒ, gēn nǐ, xiàbān, jiù, bú lèi, yǐhòu
(I'll go to watch a movie with you if I am not tired after work.)

→ ………………………………………………………………

(7) 很便宜了，就，如果，电话卡，用，你，给美国，打电话
hěn piányi le, jiù, rúguǒ, diànhuàkǎ, yòng, nǐ, gěi Měiguó, dǎ diànhuà
(If you use a calling card to make a phone call to the U.S. it'll be quite cheap.)

→ ………………………………………………………………

(8) 先，每天，以后，起床，我，吃饭，洗澡，再
xiān, měi tiān, yǐhòu, qǐchuáng, wǒ, chī fàn, xǐzǎo, zài
(Every day, after I get up, I eat first and then take a shower.)

→ ………………………………………………………………

Pronunciation Notes

1. The sound "ü"

After the *Pinyin* initials "j", "q" and "x" (as well as "y", which is regarded as a medial in the *Pinyin* system), *Pinyin* "u" is always pronounced "ü", a sound that is produced with the tongue in the position of "ee", but the lips tightly rounded (in the position of "oo"). Thus: "ju, qu, xu; jue, que, xue; yu, yue". After "n" and "l", however, and only after those two initials, the sounds "oo" and "ü" can both occur, so "ü" has to be explicitly distinguished with written "ü": "lü, nü, lüe, nüe", etc.

The words in the right table illustrate both points:

	Pinyin	Characters	English meaning
1	júzi	橘子	orange
2	qù	去	to go
3	xià xuě	下雪	to snow
4	nǚ'ér	女儿	daughter
5	lǜchá	绿茶	green tea
6	tángcùyú	糖醋鱼	sweet-sour fish

2. The sound "oo"

After initials other than "j, q, x" (and medial "y"), *Pinyin* "u" is pronounced "oo", much as in English "cool, drool, fool": "lu, lun (l-oo-n), luo, wu", etc. English speakers have a tendency to make the syllable "wu" too short. Words like "五 wǔ" (five) and "屋子 wūzi" (room) are pronounced with a long "oo".

	Pinyin	Characters	English meaning
1	lù	路	road
2	wǔ	五	five
3	wūzi	屋子	room
4	wǔshù	武术	martial arts
5	tǔdì	土地	land, earth
6	gǔdài	古代	ancient time
7	mǔqin	母亲	mother
8	dǔchē	堵车	traffic jam
9	rúguǒ	如果	if
10	dùzi	肚子	stomach
11	dìtú	地图	map
12	cù	醋	vinegar

Pronunciation Exercises

1. Read the following words aloud. Notice that they all contain the sound "ü" (represented in *pinyin* by "u" after "j, q, x" or "y", and by "ü" after "n" or "l")

	Pinyin	Characters	English meaning
1	jūnduì	军队	army
2	quántǐ	全体	all, whole
3	xuéxiào	学校	school
4	lǚxíngshè	旅行社	travel agency
5	zǐnǚ	子女	children
6	yǔsǎn	雨伞	umbrella
7	yànxiě	验血	to have blood test
8	fǎlǜ	法律	law
9	yuèliang	月亮	moon
10	jùyuàn	剧院	theatre
11	qùnián	去年	last year
12	yùyuē	预约	to make an appointment
13	jùzi	句子	sentence
14	xià yǔ	下雨	to rain
15	xuéxí	学习	to study
16	júzhǎng	局长	bureau director
17	xūyào	需要	to need
18	xiǎoqū	小区	residential compound
19	jūmín	居民	resident
20	qúnzi	裙子	skirt, dress

2. Read the following words aloud. Notice that in this case they all contain the sound "oo" (represented by *Pinyin* "u")

	Pinyin	Characters	English meaning
1	wūyún	乌云	black cloud
2	wūguī	乌龟	turtle
3	wūlóngchá	乌龙茶	Oolong tea
4	Wúxī	无锡	*a city name*
5	wúhuāguǒ	无花果	fig
6	wúmíng	无名	unknown
7	wǔqì	武器	weapon
8	wǔlì	武力	military force
9	wǔyuè	五月	month of May
10	wǔxīng	五星	five-star
11	wǔfàn	午饭	lunch
12	kùzi	裤子	pants
13	wùhuì	误会	to misunderstand
14	wùlǐ	物理	physics
15	wùjià	物价	(commodity) price
16	gūlì	孤立	isolated
17	Tánggū	塘沽	*a place name*
18	Zhū Jiāng	珠江	*a river name*
19	zūjīn	租金	rent
20	dúlì	独立	independent
21	dúshū	读书	to study
22	tòngkǔ	痛苦	pain, suffering
23	zǔguó	祖国	motherland
24	dùzi	肚子	stomach

3. In each of the groups below, combine the initials with the rhymes to make complete syllables, then read them aloud

Group A	Group B	Group C	Group D
g - āi	y - áng	d - āi	zh - uāng
k - uài	w - āng	t - uì	ch - í
h - uǎn	w - ān	l - ún	sh - ùn
n - uǎn	g - uān	k - uáng	h - uàn

4. Read the following names of body parts, symptoms, and other medical terms aloud

	Pinyin	Characters	English meaning
1	shēntǐ	身体	body
2	bízi	鼻子	nose
3	bèi	背	back
4	ěrduo	耳朵	ear
5	dùzi	肚子	stomach
6	gēbo	胳膊	arm
7	liǎn	脸	face
8	yāo	腰	waist
9	shétou	舌头	tongue
10	shǒu	手	hand
11	tóu	头	head
12	tuǐ	腿	leg
13	yǎnjing	眼睛	eye
14	zhǐjia/zhījia	指甲	nail
15	yá	牙	teeth
16	zhèngzhuàng	症状	symptoms
17	fāshāo	发烧	to have a fever
18	fālěng	发冷	to feel chilly
19	fāyán	发炎	to have an infection
20	gǎnmào	感冒	to catch a cold
21	guòmǐn	过敏	to have an allergy

	Pinyin	Characters	English meaning
22	késou	咳嗽	to cough
23	hūxī	呼吸	to breath
24	tóuyūn	头晕	dizzy
25	tù	吐	to throw up
26	lā dùzi	拉肚子	to suffer from diarrhea
27	liú bítì	流鼻涕	to have a runny nose
28	liúxuè	流血	to bleed
29	shāoshāng	烧伤	burn
30	téng	疼	hurt
31	tángniàobìng	糖尿病	diabetes
32	shíwù zhòngdú	食物中毒	food poisoning
33	xiāohuà bùliáng	消化不良	indigestion
34	hūxī kùnnan	呼吸困难	to have trouble in breathing
35	yào	药	medicines
36	chángyòngyào	常用药	commonly used medicine
37	āsīpǐlín	阿司匹林	aspirin
38	chuāngkětiē	创可贴	band-aid
39	gǎnmàoyào	感冒药	cold medicine
40	késouyào	咳嗽药	cough medicine
41	máyào	麻药	anaesthetic
42	nèifúyào	内服药	medicine for oral use
43	wàiyòngyào	外用药	medicine for external use
44	wēndùjì	温度计	thermometer
45	wéishēngsù	维生素	vitamin
46	xīyào	西药	western medicine
47	yǎnyàoshuǐ	眼药水	eye drops
48	zhǐxièyào	止泻药	anti-diarrhea medicine
49	zhōngyào	中药	Chinese medicine
50	zhǐténgyào	止疼药	pain killer

Listening Comprehension

1. Listen to the dialogue between a foreign guest and the hotel housekeeper, then answer the questions

   (1) What time of day does this conversation take place?

   (2) What time does the woman plan to clean the room, and what time would the man like the room to be cleaned?

   (3) Why does the man want the room cleaned?

   (4) Why does the man want the room cleaned earlier than scheduled?

2. Listen to the dialogue between two students; then answer the questions

   (1) What is the relation between the two students?

   (2) Why is the first student planning to take a shower in the evening?

   (3) What is the second student going to do in the evening?

   (4) Why doesn't the second student want to be woken up?

Communication Activities

Pair Work

Scenario I: Take turns asking questions about each other's daily schedule and giving answers.

Scenario II: Daily schedules: Working in pairs, one person asks (in Chinese): "What do you do at … o'clock?" The other person answers (in Chinese, of course) according to the information in column B. Continue in this way until all the times in the list below have been covered. When that is done, take turns asking each other about your own daily schedules.

A	B
7:00 a.m.	get up and take a shower
7:30	eat breakfast
9:30	go to teach English
Noon	go to eat lunch
1:00 p.m.	rest
2:30	go to a company where you work as a translator
4:45	tutoring
6:00	get out of work
6:30	eat dinner
7:50	make a phone call to the United States
9:00	watch some TV
11:00	go to bed

Review Exercises

I. Recite the following times in Chinese

2:00 p.m.	4:10 p.m.	6:15 p.m.	9:45 a.m.
10:05 a.m.	11:00 a.m.	8:30 a.m.	7:10 a.m.
12:00 p.m.	3:50 p.m.	5:55 p.m.	1:00 p.m.

II. Fill in the blanks with a question word and provide an answer to each question

1. 你早上__________起床?
   Nǐ zǎoshang __________ qǐchuáng?
2. 下课以后你做________________?
   Xiàkè yǐhòu nǐ zuò ______________?
3. 你跟__________一起去商店?
   Nǐ gēn __________ yìqǐ qù shāngdiàn?
4. 晚上我去找你，________________?
   Wǎnshang wǒ qù zhǎo nǐ, ______________?
5. 电话卡__________钱一张?
   Diànhuàkǎ __________ qián yì zhāng?
6. 厕所在______________?
   Cèsuǒ zài ______________?
7. 你下午__________下班?
   Nǐ xiàwǔ __________ xiàbān?

III. Answer the following questions with a sentence containing “以前 yǐqián” or “以后 yǐhòu”

1. A: 你几点去上班?
   Nǐ jǐ diǎn qù shàngbān?

   B: ______________________________。(after lunch)
2. A: 你什么时候去图书馆?
   Nǐ shénme shíhou qù túshūguǎn?

   B: ______________________________。(before class)
3. A: 你每天几点睡觉?
   Nǐ měi tiān jǐ diǎn shuìjiào?

   B: ______________________________。(after 11:00 p.m.)
4. A: 你什么时候去买东西?
   Nǐ shénme shíhou qù mǎi dōngxi?

B: ______________________________________。(after work)

5. A: 你什么时候去做翻译?
Nǐ shénme shíhou qù zuò fānyì?

B: ______________________________________。(before 2:00 p.m.)

IV. Complete the following sentences with the "就 jiù……了 le" pattern

1. 今天下课以后我______________________________。(no more classes)
Jīntiān xiàkè yǐhòu wǒ ______________________________.

2. 我早上八点起床，没有吃早点______________________。(came to class)
Wǒ zǎoshang bā diǎn qǐchuáng, méiyǒu chī zǎodiǎn ______________________.

3. 女朋友今天不能跟我一起吃饭，我____________________。(ate by myself)
Nǚpéngyou jīntiān bù néng gēn wǒ yìqǐ chī fàn, wǒ ____________________.

4. 我明天早上六点去工作，晚饭以后____________________。(will go to bed)
Wǒ míngtiān zǎoshang liù diǎn qù gōngzuò, wǎnfàn yǐhòu ____________________.

5. 下课以后我有一点儿累，喝咖啡以后____________________。(became better)
Xiàkè yǐhòu wǒ yǒu yìdiǎnr lèi, hē kāfēi yǐhòu ____________________.

6. 我现在钱不多，做家教以后________________________。(will have money)
Wǒ xiànzài qián bù duō, zuò jiājiào yǐhòu ________________________.

V. Answer the following questions using "跟 gēn……一起 yìqǐ"

1. A: 你今天中午去餐厅吃饭吗?
Nǐ jīntiān zhōngwǔ qù cāntīng chī fàn ma?

B: ______________________________________。

2. A: 你自己去超市买东西吗?
Nǐ zìjǐ qù chāoshì mǎi dōngxi ma?

B: ______________________________________。

3. A: 你和哪国人上中文课?
Nǐ hé nǎ guó rén shàng Zhōngwén kè?

B: ______________________________________。

4. A: 你是和谁去香港的?
Nǐ shì hé shéi qù Xiānggǎng de?

B: ______________________________________。

5. A: 在中国，女学生为什么常常只和女学生一起买东西?
Zài Zhōngguó, nǚxuésheng wèi shénme chángcháng zhǐ hé nǚxuésheng yìqǐ mǎi dōngxi?

B: ______________________________________。

6. A: 米饭跟菜一起吃怎么样?
Mǐfàn gēn cài yìqǐ chī zěnmeyàng?

B: ____。

VI. What would you say? (Take turns asking and answering the questions)

1. Ask your friend for the current time in Beijing and New York.

2. Ask your friend if he/she wants to go and see an American movie with you this Saturday night.

3. Ask your friend where the Internet café (or some other place) is located.

4. Ask your friend about his/her plans for the weekend.

5. Ask your friend about his/her daily routine.

6. Ask each other when you generally make phone calls to the U.S.

7. Ask each other what you do on Friday nights, and where you go.

8. Ask each other whom you eat dinner with.

Culture Notes

1. 12-hour and 24-hour time systems

In China the 24-hour time system is used for official business, in media, government, commerce and in most schedules, including bus and train schedules. However, in conversation, people usually use the regular 12-hour time system, along with a time word such as "早上 zǎoshang", "上午 shàngwǔ", "下午 xiàwǔ", etc. Examples: "早上七点 zǎoshang qī diǎn" (7:00 a.m.), "下午四点 xiàwǔ sì diǎn" (4:00 p.m.), or "晚上九点 wǎnshang jiǔ diǎn" (9:00 p.m.).

2. Working hours in China

Stores and restaurants are open seven days a week. Government agencies, including banks and offices, are open Monday through Friday. Daily working hours are 8:30 a.m. to 5:30 p.m., with a one- or two-hour lunch break around noon.

3. A typical daily schedule for a secondary school in China

Morning		上午	
6:20—6:40	Morning exercises	6:20—6:40	早读
6:40—7:10	Breakfast	6:40—7:10	早餐
7:30—8:10	First period	7:30—8:10	第一节课
8:20—9:00	Second period	8:20—9:00	第二节课
9:00—9:40	Third period	9:00—9:40	第三节课
9:40—10:10	Break, exercises	9:40—10:10	课间操
10:10—10:50	Fourth period	10:10—10:50	第四节课
10:50—11:10	Eye-health exercises	10:50—11:10	眼保健操
11:10—11:50	Fifth period	11:10—11:50	第五节课

Midday		中午	
11:50—12:20	Lunch	11:50—12:20	午餐
12:20—1:50	Midday break	12:20—1:50	休息

Afternoon	
1:55	Five-minute warning bell
2:00—2:40	Sixth period
2:50—3:30	Seventh period
3:40—4:20	Eighth period
4:30—5:30	Extracurricular activities
5:30	Dinner

下午	
1:55	预备铃
2:00—2:40	第六节课
2:50—3:30	第七节课
3:40—4:20	第八节课
4:30—5:30	课外活动
5:30	晚餐

Evening	
6:45—7:45	Self-study
7:45—8:00	Break
8:00—9:30	Self-study

晚上	
6:45—7:45	自习
7:45—8:00	休息
8:00—9:30	自习

Lesson Ten My Birthday

第十课 过生日

Dì-shí Kè Guò Shēngri

In this lesson you will learn how to do the following

- Make use of units of dates: week, month and year
- Ask about birthdays and decide how to celebrate them
- Ask about age and respond to questions about age

Grammar

- Units of time
- Dates
- The verb "喜欢 xǐhuan" (to be fond of, to like to)

Culture Notes

- Chinese calendars
- The 10 Heavenly Stems and 12 Earthly Branches
- Traditional Chinese festivals

Dialogue

A：郭生 Guō Shēng　　　　**B**：周明 Zhōu Míng

（在宿舍 Zài sùshè）

A：周明，今天几[1]号？
Zhōu Míng, jīntiān jǐ[1] hào?

B：今天10月16号。
Jīntiān shíyuè shíliù hào.

A：后天[G1]是我的生日，我就要21岁了！
Hòutiān[G1] shì wǒ de shēngri, wǒ jiù yào èrshíyī suì le!

B：真的吗？你的生日是10月18号吗？
Zhēn de ma? Nǐ de shēngri shì shíyuè shíbā hào ma?

A：对，我是1992年[2]10月18日[G2]9点40分生的。
Duì, wǒ shì yī-jiǔ-jiǔ-èr nián[2] shíyuè shíbā rì[G2] jiǔ diǎn sìshí fēn shēng de.

B：我一定要给你过[3]生日。可是，后天是周四，我有三节[4]课，还有很多作业周五要交。怎么办呢？
Wǒ yídìng yào gěi nǐ guò[3] shēngri. Kěshì, hòutiān shì zhōusì , wǒ yǒu sān jié[4] kè, hái yǒu hěn duō zuòyè zhōuwǔ yào jiāo. Zěnme bàn ne?

A：我这个星期一、星期二、星期三和星期五也都有课。我正好星期四没有课，我可以自己过生日。
Wǒ zhège xīngqīyī、xīngqī'èr、xīngqīsān hé xīngqīwǔ yě dōu yǒu kè. Wǒ zhènghǎo xīngqīsì méiyǒu kè, wǒ kěyǐ zìjǐ guò shēngri.

Notes

1. In Lesson 9, "几 jǐ" was used to ask about clock time. In this lesson, it is used to ask about dates: "几号 jǐ hào" (what day [of the month]); "几月 jǐ yuè" (what month); "周几 zhōu jǐ" (what day of the week). In general, "几 jǐ" questions quantity when a relatively small number is expected in the response (cf. L9, note 1): "几分钟 jǐ fēnzhōng" (how many minutes); "几天 jǐ tiān" (how many days); "几年 jǐ nián" (how many years).
2. Years are usually spoken as a sequence of digits, followed by "年 nián" (year): "一九九二年 yī-jiǔ-jiǔ-èr nián"(1992); "二〇一四年 èr-líng-yī-sì nián" (2014).
3. "过 guò" (to pass, to cross over), in conjunction with holidays or special celebrations such as "生日 shēngri" (birthday), can be translated as "to celebrate".
4. "节 jié" (section, length, segment) is a measure word for class periods, train carriages, batteries, and other segmented things: "一节课 yì jié kè" (a class period).

B: 那我就周末再给你过生日吧。星期六我去打工。星期日我早上洗衣服，中午请你去吃饭，下午去看电影，好吗？
Nà wǒ jiù zhōumò zài gěi nǐ guò shēngri ba. Xīngqīliù wǒ qù dǎgōng. Xīngqīrì wǒ zǎoshang xǐ yīfu, zhōngwǔ qǐng nǐ qù chī fàn, xiàwǔ qù kàn diànyǐng, hǎo ma?

A: 太好了！谢谢你。你的生日是哪天？我也给你过生日。
Tài hǎo le! Xièxie nǐ. Nǐ de shēngri shì nǎ tiān? Wǒ yě gěi nǐ guò shēngri.

B: 我的生日是前天，已经过了。
Wǒ de shēngri shì qiántiān, yǐjīng guò le.

A: 你怎么没告诉我？那这个星期天我们一起过吧。
Nǐ zěnme méi gàosu wǒ? Nà zhège xīngqītiān wǒmen yìqǐ guò ba.

B: 我不喜欢[G3]过生日，一过生日我就老了一岁。
Wǒ bù xǐhuan[G3] guò shēngri, yí guò shēngri wǒ jiù lǎo le yí suì.

A: 你今年多大了[5]？
Nǐ jīnnián duō dà le?

B: 22岁了。
Èrshí'èr suì le.

A: 我们两个人都过生日，那就更应该庆祝了！这样吧，周日中午你请我吃饭，晚上我请你吃饭，吃饭以后我们一起去看一个有意思的电影，好不好？
Wǒmen liǎng ge rén dōu guò shēngri, nà jiù gèng yīnggāi qìngzhù le! Zhèyàng ba, zhōurì zhōngwǔ nǐ qǐng wǒ chī fàn, wǎnshang wǒ qǐng nǐ chī fàn, chī fàn yǐhòu wǒmen yìqǐ qù kàn yí ge yǒu yìsi de diànyǐng, hǎo bu hǎo?

B: 太好了！
Tài hǎo le!

---

5. "你多大了？Nǐ duō dà le?" (How old are you?) is the usual way of asking the age of someone the same generation as yourself. A more deferential version of the question, with "您 nín" would be used for someone older: "您多大年纪了？Nín duō dà niánjì le?" (How old are you?). For a child under the age of ten, the question is: "你几岁了？Nǐ jǐ suì le?" (How old are you?) – recall that "几 jǐ" usually presupposes a single digit number in the response.

New Words

1	过生日/過生日	guò shēngri	Phrase	to celebrate a birthday
	生日	shēngri	N	birthday
2	几号/幾號	jǐ hào	Phrase	what day of the month, what number
3	月	yuè	N	month, moon
4	后天/後天	hòutiān	N	the day after tomorrow, two days from now
5	岁/歲	suì	Meas	years (old), years of age
6	真的吗/真的嗎	zhēn de ma	Exp	(Is that) true? Really?
7	年	nián	N	year
8	日	rì	N	sun, day, daytime
9	分（钟/鐘）	fēn (zhōng)	Meas	minute (unit of time)
10	生	shēng	V	to be born
11	一定	yídìng	Adv	definite, must
12	周四/週四	zhōusì	N	Thursday
	周/週	zhōu	N	circle, week
13	节/節	jié	Meas	*for segments of time, e.g. classes*
14	作业/作業	zuòyè	N	school assignment, homework
15	周五/週五	zhōuwǔ	N	Friday
16	交	jiāo	V	to hand over, to deliver, to give
17	怎么办/怎麼辦	zěnme bàn	Exp	What is to be done?
18	星期一	xīngqīyī	N	Monday
19	星期二	xīngqī'èr	N	Tuesday
20	星期三	xīngqīsān	N	Wednesday
21	星期五	xīngqīwǔ	N	Friday
22	正好	zhènghǎo	Adv	it so happens, as it happens, just in time
23	星期四	xīngqīsì	N	Thursday
24	自己	zìjǐ	Pron	oneself, by oneself, on one's own
25	周末/週末	zhōumò	N	weekend

26	星期六	xīngqīliù	N	Saturday
27	打工	dǎgōng	VO	to work (part-time/temporarily), to do manual work
28	星期日	xīngqīrì	N	Sunday
29	洗	xǐ	V	to wash
30	衣服	yīfu	N	clothes, clothing
31	电影/電影	diànyǐng	N	movie, motion picture
32	哪天	nǎ tiān	Phrase	which day, what day
33	前天	qiántiān	N	the day before yesterday
34	已经/已經	yǐjīng	Adv	already
35	告诉/告訴	gàosu	V	to tell, to inform
36	星期天	xīngqītiān	N	Sunday
37	喜欢/喜歡	xǐhuan	V	to like, to be fond of
38	老	lǎo	Adj	old, aged
39	今年	jīnnián	N	this year
40	多大	duō dà	Phrase	how old (in questions)
41	更	gèng	Adv	more, still more, even more
42	应该/應該	yīnggāi	Aux	should, ought to, must
43	庆祝/慶祝	qìngzhù	V	to celebrate
44	这样吧/這樣吧	zhèyàng ba	Exp	(Let's) do it this way, how about this
45	有意思	yǒu yìsi	Phrase	to be interesting

Re-enacting the Dialogue

A: Guo Sheng **B: Zhou Ming**

(In the dormitory)

A: Zhou Ming, what day of the month is it today?

B: Today's the 16th of October.

A: The day after tomorrow is my birthday, I'll be 21.

B: Really? Your birthday's on October 18th?

A: Yes, I was born at 9:40 on the 18th of October, 1992.

B: I must give you a birthday party. The day after tomorrow is Thursday; I have three classes, and I have a lot of homework due on Friday. What can we do?

A: This week I have classes on Monday, Tuesday, Wednesday and Friday. It just so happens that on Thursday, my birthday, I don't have classes; I can celebrate on my own.

B: In that case, I'll organize a party for you on the weekend. On Saturday, I have to go to work. I do my washing Sunday morning. How about we have lunch at noon, then go and see a movie in the afternoon?

A: Great. Thanks. Which day is your birthday? I'll organize a party for you, as well.

B: My birthday was the day before yesterday – it's already past.

A: How come you didn't tell me? In that case, we'll celebrate our birthdays together this Sunday.

B: I don't like celebrating my birthday; every time I have a birthday, I'm a year older.

A: How old are you this year?

B: I'm 22!

A: We both have our birthdays! That means we really have to celebrate. How about this: you take me out for a meal at noon on Sunday and then I'll take you out for a meal in the evening. After we eat, we can go and see a good movie, okay?

B: Great!

Grammar

▶ G1. Units of time

(1) The week

Before the adoption of the Western calendar, Chinese measured time in years, months and days. The week, though obviously recognized as a single phase of the moon, played no special role in the rhythms of daily life. The month was sometimes divided into two periods of 15 days, or three periods of ten days, but the seven-day week did not become prominent in the organization of daily life until the modern period, when the term "星期 xīngqī" (literally "star-period") was introduced. The practice of numbering the months and days goes back to the Later Han dynasty (first centuries CE). When weeks were introduced, they too were numbered. (A blessing for students of Chinese!) Sunday is an exception: Sunday is either "星期日 xīngqīrì" (i.e. "sun-day") or "星期天 xīngqītiān" ("heaven-day"). Nowadays, the days of the week are also formed with "周 zhōu" (a cycle or circuit).

星期一 xīngqīyī	周一 zhōuyī	Monday
星期二 xīngqī'èr	周二 zhōu'èr	Tuesday
星期三 xīngqīsān	周三 zhōusān	Wednesday
星期四 xīngqīsì	周四 zhōusì	Thursday
星期五 xīngqīwǔ	周五 zhōuwǔ	Friday
星期六 xīngqīliù	周六 zhōuliù	Saturday
星期日 xīngqīrì/星期天 xīngqītiān	周日 zhōurì	Sunday

(2) The months: number + "月 yuè"

一月	yīyuè	January
二月	èryuè	February
三月	sānyuè	March
四月	sìyuè	April
五月	wǔyuè	May
六月	liùyuè	June
七月	qīyuè	July
八月	bāyuè	August
九月	jiǔyuè	September
十月	shíyuè	October
十一月	shíyīyuè	November
十二月	shí'èryuè	December

(3) The day-date: number + "号 hào"/"日 rì" ("日 rì" is more formal)

一号 yī hào　　二号 èr hào　　三号 sān hào　　三十一号 sānshíyī hào

(4) Times units past, present and future

Time words mostly function as nouns, requiring a measure word, "个 gè", if they are counted (e.g. 三个月 sān ge yuè, three months) or otherwise specified (e.g. 这个月 zhège yuè, this month). For time units that require "个 gè", "这个 zhège" (this) indicates "current", "上个 shàng ge" is "last", "下个 xià ge" is "next" and "每个 měi ge" is "every":

这个星期三	zhège xīngqīsān	this Wednesday
这个周末	zhège zhōumò	this weekend
下个周末	xià ge zhōumò	next weekend
上个星期	shàng ge xīngqī	last week
下个星期	xià ge xīngqī	next week
每个星期	měi ge xīngqī	every week
上个月	shàng ge yuè	last month
下个月	xià ge yuè	next month
每个月	měi ge yuè	every month

However, days and years are exceptional. "天 tiān" (day) and "年 nián" (year) function as measure words themselves and are, therefore, counted directly: "三天 sān tiān" (three days); "两年 liǎng nián" (two years). The compound forms for "天 tiān" and "年 nián" are as follows:

前天	qiántiān	the day before yesterday	前年	qiánnián	the year before last
昨天	zuótiān	yesterday	去年	qùnián	last year
今天	jīntiān	today	今年	jīnnián	this year
明天	míngtiān	tomorrow	明年	míngnián	next year
后天	hòutiān	the day after tomorrow	后年	hòunián	the year after next

Note that phrases like "this evening" (今天晚上 jīntiān wǎnshang) – unlike their English equivalents – do not make use of "这 zhè" (this).

▶ G2. Dates

In dates, units of time are arranged from the largest to the smallest: year-month-day. So "January 1st, 2014" is "2014 年 nián 一月 yīyuè 一号 yī hào" (or more formally, "一日 yī rì"). Note that this is the exact reverse of the European system, which writes day-month-year (1st January, 2014), and unlike the U.S. system as well, that writes month-day-year (January 1st, 2014).

① 2014年1月1号下午5点　5:00 p.m. on January 1st, 2014
èr-líng-yī-sì nián yīyuè yī hào xiàwǔ wǔ diǎn

② 去年三月五号　March 5th of last year
qùnián sānyuè wǔ hào

Expressions of time and date generally omit the verb "是 shì" (to be), unless an adverb is present (including adverb "不 bù"), in which case "是 shì" is required.

③ 今天星期几？ What day is it today?
Jīntiān xīngqī jǐ?

④ 今天星期一。Today is Monday.
Jīntiān xīngqīyī.

⑤ 明天不是星期一。Tomorrow isn't Monday.
Míngtiān bú shì xīngqīyī.

⑥ 今天几月几号？ What is today's date?
Jīntiān jǐ yuè jǐ hào?

⑦ 今天不是八月十号。Today is not August 10th.
Jīntiān bú shì bāyuè shí hào.

▶ G3. The verb "喜欢 xǐhuan" (to be fond of, to like to)

"喜欢 xǐhuan" can be followed by a noun phrase (noun, pronoun, etc.) or a verb phrase.

① 我们都喜欢那个老师。We all like that teacher.
Wǒmen dōu xǐhuan nàge lǎoshī.

② 我们很喜欢吃中国饭。We like eating Chinese food.
Wǒmen hěn xǐhuan chī Zhōngguó fàn.

③ 我不喜欢过生日。I don't like celebrating my birthday.
Wǒ bù xǐhuan guò shēngri.

Consolidation & Practice

1. Using "X 的生日是几月几号? X de shēngri shì jǐ yuè jǐ hào?", find out your partner's birthday as well as the birthday of three of his or her family members, then report your findings to the class

(1)

(2)

(3)

(4)

2. Help each other get familiar with the position of time expressions: "Subject + Time + VO" and "Time + Subject + VO"

(1) Review the list of activities given below, then find out what your partner is likely to be doing or did do on each of the dates or times listed

Examples: (1) A：你星期一做什么？
Nǐ xīngqīyī zuò shénme?
B：我星期一上中文课。
Wo xīngqīyī shàng Zhōngwén kè.

(2) A：你昨天做什么了？
Nǐ zuótiān zuò shénme le?
B：我昨天看电影了。
Wǒ zuótiān kàn diànyǐng le.

Time words and phrases:

星期一 xīngqīyī	今天晚上 jīntiān wǎnshang	明天 míngtiān	星期五 xīngqīwǔ
昨天中午 zuótiān zhōngwǔ	星期三下午 xīngqīsān xiàwǔ	前天 qiántiān	星期二 xīngqī'èr
后天 hòutiān	星期四 xīngqīsì	六号 liù hào	星期六 xīngqīliù
七月四号 qīyuè sì hào	星期日 xīngqīrì	十二月二十五号 shí'èryuè èrshíwǔ hào	周末 zhōumò

Activities:

洗衣服 xǐ yīfu	上中文课 shàng Zhōngwén kè	教英文 jiāo Yīngwén	休息 xiūxi
看电影 kàn diànyǐng	给美国打电话 gěi Měiguó dǎ diànhuà	去商店 qù shāngdiàn	去银行 qù yínháng
上班 shàngbān	做翻译 zuò fānyì	跟朋友去吃饭 gēn péngyou qù chī fàn	
打扫房间 dǎsǎo fángjiān	去中国朋友家 qù Zhōngguó péngyou jiā	买东西 mǎi dōngxi	去网吧 qù wǎngbā

(2) Ask each other what he/she is going to do at the time stated

Example: A：周末你要做什么？
Zhōumò nǐ yào zuò shénme?

B：我要洗衣服。
Wǒ yào xǐ yīfu.

星期三 xīngqīsān	上中文课 shàng Zhōngwén kè
星期二上午 xīngqī'èr shàngwǔ	教英文 jiāo Yīngwén
周日下午 zhōurì xiàwǔ	休息 xiūxi
明天 míngtiān	去商店 qù shāngdiàn
今天晚上 jīntiān wǎnshang	看电视 kàn diànshì
这个星期六 zhège xīngqīliù	看电影 kàn diànyǐng
周四上午 zhōusì shàngwǔ	去换钱 qù huàn qián
中午 zhōngwǔ	睡午觉 shuì wǔjiào
星期二上午 xīngqī'èr shàngwǔ	做翻译 zuò fānyì
星期四 xīngqīsì	上班 shàngbān

3. In pairs or groups, ask each other the dates of the days listed below

Example: A：今天几月几号，星期几?
Jīntiān jǐ yuè jǐ hào, xīngqī jǐ?

B：今天是_____月_____号，星期_____。
Jīntiān shì _____ yuè _____ hào, xīngqī _____.

昨天 zuótiān　　明天 míngtiān　　前天 qiántiān　　后天 hòutiān

感恩节 (Thanksgiving Day) Gǎn'ēn Jié

圣诞节 (Christmas Day) Shèngdàn Jié

劳动节 (Labor Day) Láodòng Jié

美国的国庆节 (American Independence Day) Měiguó de Guóqìng Jié

中国的国庆节 (China's National Day) Zhōngguó de Guóqìng Jié

4. Say the following dates out loud

7/4/1776	4/12/1988	6/17/1940	3/5/1957
5/28/1917	10/7/1947	6/1/2001	3/8/1987
11/01/2000	12/10/2010	5/25/2030	9/12/1999

5. Working in pairs or groups, use the sentence pattern "Subject + Time + 喜欢 xǐhuan + V + Object" to tell each other what you enjoy doing at each of the following times

星期五晚上 xīngqīwǔ wǎnshang　　周末 zhōumò　　睡觉以前 shuìjiào yǐqián　　下课以后 xiàkè yǐhòu　　不忙的时候 bù máng de shíhou

(1)

(2)

(3)

(4)

(5)

Pronunciation Notes

The "r" suffix

In northern Mandarin speech, and particularly in Beijing, words for many common items of daily life (mostly nouns), when used in colloquial speech, are spoken with a heavy r-influenced pronunciation. In Chinese, the r-influence is called "儿化音 érhuàyīn" or "儿化韵 érhuàyùn", literarily: "r-ized final" or "r-ized rhyme". 26 or the 38 *Pinyin* rhymes can be r-ized in this way.

Although r-influence often affects the whole syllable, *Pinyin* convention indicates it by attaching an "r" to the affected syllable – an "r" suffix. That convention allows the reader to recover the r-less pronunciation by simply removing the "r" suffix: "一点儿 yìdiǎnr" (a little, a bit) is pronounced as if "yìdiǎr" (without the "n"); removing the "r" gives "yìdiǎn", which is pronounced normally.

The character convention is to indicate the "r" suffix with a following "儿" (which is, elsewhere, pronounced "ér").The use of the character "儿" to indicate the suffix is one of very few examples where one syllable is represented with two characters: "点儿" is equivalent to *Pinyin* "diǎnr" (which, as noted above, is pronounced "diǎr"); cf. examples "哪儿 nǎr" and "花儿 huār".

In some cases, the r-version and r-less versions of a word differ in meaning. This is the case with "哪 nǎ" (which) versus "哪儿 nǎr" (where), for example. (Speakers whose dialect does not use the "r" suffix use "哪里 nǎli" instead of "哪儿 nǎr".)

Pronunciation Exercises

1. Read the following lists of words, which illustrate the "r" suffix in different contexts

(1) When "r" suffix appears directly after *Pinyin* "ɑ, e, o, u, ɑo, ou", the shift in the quality of the vowel is minimal

ɑ→ɑr	哪儿 nǎr
iɑ→iɑr	人家儿 rénjiār
uɑ→uɑr	画儿 huàr
o→or	粉末儿 fěnmòr
uo→uor	大伙儿 dàhuǒr
e→er	盒儿 hér
üe→üer	主角儿 zhǔjuér
ie→ier	字帖儿 zìtiěr
u→ur	没谱儿 méipǔr
ɑo→ɑor	小道儿 xiǎodàor
ou→our	路口儿 lùkǒur
iɑo→iɑor	豆角儿 dòujiǎor
iu→iur	打球儿 dǎqiúr

(2) The "r" suffix appearing after "i" or "ü" is pronounced with a transitional "yur" sound

i→ier	树枝儿 shùzhīr	丝儿 sīr	玩意儿 wányìr
ü→üer	唱曲儿 chàngqǔr	驴儿 lǘr	有趣儿 yǒuqùr

(3) With words spelled with final written "n", the addition of the "r" suffix results in the complete loss of the nasal sound (drop "n")

ɑn→ɑr	传单儿 chuándānr
en→er	亏本儿 kuīběnr
iɑn→iɑr	路边儿 lùbiānr
in→iɑr	手印儿 shǒuyìnr
uɑn→uɑr	好玩儿 hǎowánr
uen→uer	皱纹儿 zhòuwénr
üɑn→üɑr	手绢儿 shǒujuànr

ün→üer	花裙儿 huāqúnr

(4) With words spelled with final written "ng", the addition of the "r" suffix results in the loss of the "ng "sound, leaving only nasalization of the vowel (represented after the arrows below by "^{n}r")

ang→a^{n}r	药方儿 yàofāngr
yang→ya^{n}r	小羊儿 xiǎoyángr
uang→ua^{n}r	门窗儿 ménchuāngr
eng→e^{n}r	跳绳儿 tiàoshéngr
ong→o^{n}r	抽空儿 chōukòngr
iong→io^{n}r	小熊儿 xiǎoxióngr

(5) With the rhymes "ɑi", "ei", the addition of the "r" suffix results in the loss of the diphthong element – represented in *Pinyin* by the final "i"

ɑi→ɑr	窗台儿 chuāngtáir
ei→er	宝贝儿 bǎobèir
uɑi→uɑr	一块儿 yíkuàir
uei→uer	一对儿 yíduìr

2. In each of the groups below, combine the initials with the rhymes to make complete syllables and read them aloud

Group A	Group B	Group C	Group D
g - āi	y - áng	d - āi	zh - uāng
k - uài	w - āng	t - uì	ch - í
h - uǎn	n - uǎn	l - ún	sh - ùn

3. Three syllable compounds

Three syllable compounds are not as common as two or four syllable ones but they do occur, particularly in the noun class. The two listings of words below, one for institutions and buildings, the other for foods and dishes, are for *Pinyin* reading and pronunciation practice.

	Pinyin	Characters	English meaning
1	yóuzhèngjú	邮政局	post office
2	pàichūsuǒ	派出所	police station
3	gōng'ānjú	公安局	public security bureau
4	huǒchēzhàn	火车站	train station

	Pinyin	Characters	English meaning
5	tíngchēchǎng	停车场	parking lot
6	yóulǎnchē	游览车	tour bus
7	dānxíngdào	单行道	one-way street
8	túshūguǎn	图书馆	library
9	tǐyùchǎng	体育场	stadium
10	fúzhuāngdiàn	服装店	clothing store
11	wǔjīndiàn	五金店	hardware store
12	xiǎomàibù	小卖部	convenience store
13	měiróngyuàn	美容院	beauty salon

	Pinyin	Characters	English meaning
1	huíguōròu	回锅肉	twice cooked pork
2	suānlàtāng	酸辣汤	hot and sour soup
3	tángcùyú	糖醋鱼	sweet and sour fish
4	xiányādàn	咸鸭蛋	preserved duck eggs
5	fāngbiànmiàn	方便面	instant noodles
6	zhájiàngmiàn	炸酱面	noodles with soybean sauce
7	xiǎolóngbāo	小笼包	Shanghainese steamed dumplings
8	dòufujuǎnr	豆腐卷儿	tofu rolls
9	bàojīqiú	爆鸡球	quickfried chicken balls
10	quánjiāfú	全家福	complete home fortune (like chopsuey)
11	mùxūròu	木须肉	mooshoo (shredded pork with vegetables, etc.)
12	zházǐjī	炸仔鸡	deep fried chicken
13	kuàngquánshuǐ	矿泉水	mineral water

Listening Comprehension

1. Listen to the dialogue between two students, then answer the questions

(1) On what day of the week does the conversation take place?
(2) What class does the man have on that day, and when?
(3) Does the man have any problem with that class?
(4) At what time of day does the conversation take place?
(5) What is the man supposed to do before class?

2. Listen to the conversation between two friends, then answer the questions

(1) What does the woman have to do on the weekend?
(2) What does the man want to do?
(3) What did the man do during the week?
(4) What does the man invite the woman to do?
(5) How does the woman respond to the man's invitation?
(6) What do they end up doing?

Communication Activities

Pair Work

Scenario I: Ask each other about birthdays of family members. Write down what you hear and check with your partner to make sure you are correct.

Scenario II: Ask each other on which days of the week you have classes and how many (有几节[课] yǒu jǐ jié [kè]). Then find out which day you can have lunch together.

Scenario III: You plan to take a 2-week trip to China, so work out which month of the coming year would be best for you to travel together. Make reference to the following items.

十月	十二月	二月	五月	最好
shíyuè	shí'èryuè	èryuè	wǔyuè	zuìhǎo

要上课	要上班	不上班	没有课
yào shàngkè	yào shàngbān	bú shàngbān	méiyǒu kè

Review Exercises

I. Say the days of the week in the order given, then write them in *Pinyin* (or characters) in the blanks below

Monday ....

Tuesday ....

Wednesday ....

Thursday ....

Saturday ....

Friday ....

Sunday ....

II. Recite the following list of months in Chinese, then write them in *Pinyin* (or characters) in the blanks provided

January ....

November ....

October ....

December ....

May ....

April ....

March ....

July ....

February ....

June ....

August ....

September ....

III. Recite the following national day dates: Canada (July 1st); the United States (July 4th); the People's Republic of China (October 1st); and that of one other country whose date you are familiar with. Then write the dates in *Pinyin* (or characters) in the blanks provided

Canada .... United States ....

People's Republic of China .... Other ( ) ....

IV. Say the following phrases in Chinese, then write them in *Pinyin* (or characters)

1. Monday morning ....
2. Thursday at 3:30 p.m. ....
3. July 4th, 1776 ....
4. May 1st, 2001 ....
5. October 1st, 1949 ....
6. Sunday afternoon ....
7. the afternoon on November 24th ....
8. the morning of December 25th ....

V. Fill in the blanks below, paying attention to whether or not a measure word is needed

1. ________ 星期三是 ________ 月 ________ 号。(next)
   ________ xīngqīsān shì ________ yuè ________ hào.
2. ________ 我 ________ 岁。(this year)
   ________ wǒ ________ suì.
3. ________ 我去中国。(next month)
   ________ wǒ qù Zhōngguó.
4. 我 ________ 天有三节课。(every)
   Wǒ ________ tiān yǒu sān jié kè.
5. ________ 我朋友来看我。(last Friday)
   ________ wǒ péngyou lái kàn wǒ.

VI. Talk about your weekly schedules, as follows

1. Explain the following to your partner (in Chinese)

(1) On Friday – tomorrow – I have Chinese class in the afternoon.

(2) I teach English on Tuesday and Wednesday.

(3) My birthday is on December 15th – I'll be celebrating it in China.

(4) I do laundry every Saturday afternoon, and I watch TV Sunday evening.

(5) On Monday, I'm going to go to the Bank of China to exchange money.

(6) I am going to phone the United States tonight.

2. Write out your weekly schedule in Chinese, then exchange with your partner and talk about similarities and differences

Example:

星期一 xīngqīyī	上午 shàngwǔ	8:30—11:30	中文课 Zhōngwén kè
	中午 zhōngwǔ	12:30—1:30	休息 xiūxi
	下午 xiàwǔ	2:30—4:30	英文课 Yīngwén kè
	晚上 wǎnshang	6:30—8:00	跟朋友吃饭 gēn péngyou chī fàn

Culture Notes

1. Chinese calendars

Like the rest of the world, China uses the solar calendar (阳历 yánglì) for everyday dating. Traditionally, however, China used the lunar calendar (阴历 yīnlì), based on the moon's monthly rotation around the earth. The dates of the traditional Chinese holidays, as well as auspicious dates for weddings and other important events, are determined by the lunar calendar. Chinese solar calendars usually give lunar calendar information in small print.

The Chinese lunar calendar is actually a luni-solar calendar because it is adjusted so it stays in alignment with the solar calendar. Since the moon takes about 29.5 days to encircle the earth, the lunar months vary in their number of days, some being 29, others being 30. A lunar year is shorter than a solar year by about 11 days (254 versus 365). Without correction, the lunar months would drift right around the solar cycle, approximately 11 days per year. To prevent this, the Chinese lunar calendar adds intercalary months when needed. As a result, the Chinese New Year ranges only from late January to mid-February.

2014年日历

2014年1月

日	一	二	三	四	五	六
			1 元旦节	2 初二	3 初三	4 初四
5 小寒	6 初六	7 初七	8 腊八节	9 初九	10 初十	11 十一
12 十二	13 十三	14 十四	15 十五	16 十六	17 十七	18 十八
19 十九	20 大寒	21 廿一	22 廿二	23 小年	24 廿四	25 廿五
26 廿六	27 廿七	28 廿八	29 廿九	30 除夕	31 春节	

2014年2月

日	一	二	三	四	五	六
						1 初二
2 初三	3 初四	4 立春	5 初六	6 初七	7 初八	8 初九
9 初十	10 十一	11 十二	12 十三	13 十四	14 元宵节	15 十六
16 十七	17 十八	18 十九	19 雨水	20 廿一	21 廿二	22 廿三
23 廿四	24 廿五	25 廿六	26 廿七	27 廿八	28 廿九	

2014年3月

日	一	二	三	四	五	六
						1 2月大
2 初二	3 初三	4 初四	5 惊蛰	6 初六	7 初七	8 妇女节
9 初九	10 初十	11 十一	12 植树节	13 十三	14 十四	15 十五
16 十六	17 十七	18 十八	19 十九	20 二十	21 春分	22 廿二
23 廿三	24 廿四	25 廿五	26 廿六	27 廿七	28 廿八	29 廿九
30 三十	31 3月小					

2014年4月

日	一	二	三	四	五	六
		1 初二	2 初三	3 初四	4 初五	5 清明节
6 初七	7 初八	8 初九	9 初十	10 十一	11 十二	12 十三
13 十四	14 十五	15 十六	16 十七	17 十八	18 十九	19 二十
20 谷雨	21 廿二	22 廿三	23 廿四	24 廿五	25 廿六	26 廿七
27 廿八	28 廿九	29 4月大	30 初二			

2014年5月

日	一	二	三	四	五	六
				1 劳动节	2 初四	3 初五
4 青年节	5 立夏	6 初八	7 初九	8 初十	9 十一	10 十二
11 母亲节	12 十四	13 十五	14 十六	15 十七	16 十八	17 十九
18 二十	19 廿一	20 廿二	21 小满	22 廿四	23 廿五	24 廿六
25 廿七	26 廿八	27 廿九	28 三十	29 5月小	30 初二	31 初三

2014年6月

日	一	二	三	四	五	六
1 儿童节	2 端午节	3 初六	4 初七	5 初八	6 芒种	7 初十
8 十一	9 十二	10 十三	11 十四	12 十五	13 十六	14 十七
15 父亲节	16 十九	17 二十	18 廿一	19 廿二	20 廿三	21 夏至
22 廿五	23 廿六	24 廿七	25 廿八	26 廿九	27 6月大	28 初二
29 初三	30 初四					

2014年7月

日	一	二	三	四	五	六
		1 建党节	2 初六	3 初七	4 初八	5 初九
6 初十	7 小暑	8 十二	9 十三	10 十四	11 十五	12 十六
13 十七	14 十八	15 十九	16 二十	17 廿一	18 廿二	19 廿三
20 廿四	21 廿五	22 廿六	23 大暑	24 廿八	25 廿九	26 三十
27 7月小	28 初二	29 初三	30 初四	31 初五		

2014年8月

日	一	二	三	四	五	六
					1 建军节	2 七夕节
3 初八	4 初九	5 初十	6 十一	7 立秋	8 十三	9 十四
10 中元节	11 十六	12 十七	13 十八	14 十九	15 二十	16 廿一
17 廿二	18 廿三	19 廿四	20 廿五	21 廿六	22 廿七	23 处暑
24 廿九	25 8月大	26 初二	27 初三	28 初四	29 初五	30 初六
31 初七						

2014年9月

日	一	二	三	四	五	六
	1 初八	2 初九	3 初十	4 十一	5 十二	6 十三
7 十四	8 中秋节	9 十六	10 教师节	11 十八	12 十九	13 二十
14 廿一	15 廿二	16 廿三	17 廿四	18 廿五	19 廿六	20 廿七
21 廿八	22 廿九	23 秋分	24 9月大	25 初二	26 初三	27 初四
28 初五	29 初六	30 初七				

2014年10月

日	一	二	三	四	五	六
			1 国庆节	2 重阳节	3 国庆节	4 十一
5 十二	6 十三	7 十四	8 寒露	9 十六	10 十七	11 十八
12 十九	13 二十	14 廿一	15 廿二	16 廿三	17 廿四	18 廿五
19 廿六	20 廿七	21 廿八	22 廿九	23 霜降	24 闰9月大	25 初二
26 初三	27 初四	28 初五	29 初六	30 初七	31 初八	

2014年11月

日	一	二	三	四	五	六
						1 初九
2 初十	3 十一	4 十二	5 十三	6 十四	7 立冬	8 十六
9 十七	10 十八	11 十九	12 二十	13 廿一	14 廿二	15 廿三
16 廿四	17 廿五	18 廿六	19 廿七	20 廿八	21 廿九	22 小雪
23 初二	24 初三	25 初四	26 初五	27 初六	28 初七	29 初八
30 初九						

2014年12月

日	一	二	三	四	五	六
	1 初十	2 十一	3 十二	4 十三	5 十四	6 十五
7 大雪	8 十七	9 十八	10 十九	11 二十	12 廿一	13 廿二
14 廿三	15 廿四	16 廿五	17 廿六	18 廿七	19 廿八	20 廿九
21 三十	22 冬至	23 初二	24 初三	25 圣诞节	26 初五	27 初六
28 初七	29 初八	30 初九	31 初十			

2. The 10 Heavenly Stems and 12 Earthly Branches

Traditional Chinese dating systems have made use of two sets of signs, the ten Heavenly Stems (天干 tiāngān) and twelve Earthly Branches (地支 dìzhī). These are paired together in sequence ("甲子 jiǎzǐ", "乙丑 yǐchǒu", and so on) to provide 60 different ordered combinations which are used to enumerate (lunar calendar) years in cycles of 60. For example, the year 2004 is the "甲申年 jiǎshēnnián", 2005 is "乙酉年 yǐyǒunián". The 1911 Revolution, which ended the Qing dynasty and established the Republic, is often called the "辛亥 xīnhài" Revolution, after the traditional dating of the year 1911.

Heavenly Stems: 甲 jiǎ 乙 yǐ 丙 bǐng 丁 dīng 戊 wù 己 jǐ 庚 gēng 辛 xīn 壬 rén 癸 guǐ

Earthly Branches: 子 zǐ 丑 chǒu 寅 yín 卯 mǎo 辰 chén 巳 sì 午 wǔ 未 wèi 申 shēn 酉 yǒu 戌 xū 亥 hài

In traditional China, the Earthly Branches were also used to label the 12 double-hours of the 24 hour day. For example: "子时 zǐshí" (the hour of "子 zǐ") was 11:00 p.m. to 1:00 a.m. and "酉时 yǒushí" was 5:00 p.m. to 7:00 p.m.

3. Traditional Chinese festivals

SPRING FESTIVAL (春节 Chūn Jié): the first day of the first month of the lunar calendar, usually in January or February in the Western calendar. The Spring Festival is also called "过年 guònián" (the New Year celebration). The eve of the new year is called "除夕 chúxī". The Spring Festival is the most important and liveliest of the traditional holidays in China.

LANTERN FESTIVAL (元宵节 Yuánxiāo Jié): takes place on the fifteenth day of the Lunar New Year (in January or February). It marks the end of the Spring Festival. People hang lanterns and eat boiled stuffed dumplings made of glutinous rice flour (汤圆 tāngyuán).

QINGMING FESTIVAL (清明节 Qīngmíng Jié): takes place on April 4th or 5th (solar calendar). On Qingming, one mourns one's ancestors. Traditional activities include sweeping the ancestral graves, offering sacrificial foods and burning paper money for the dead to spend in their world.

DRAGON BOAT FESTIVAL (端午节 Duānwǔ Jié): takes place on the fifth day of the fifth month in the lunar calendar (in April or May). The Dragon Boat festiveal commemorates the death of "Qū Yuán" (475–221 BCE), the father of Chinese poetry. People eat sticky-rice dumplings steamed in lotus leaves (粽子 zòngzi). Some areas in the south have dragon boat races.

MID-AUTUMN FESTIVAL (中秋节 Zhōngqiū Jié): takes place on the fifteenth day of the eighth month in the lunar calendar (in September or October). It commemorates an unsuccessful rebellion against the Mongolian rulers of the Yuan Dynasty (1271–1368). The Mid-Autumn festival is a time of family reunion. On the eve of the festival, after eating dinner, people view the moon while eating "moon cakes" (月饼 yuèbing) and fruit.

Vocabulary 词汇表 Cíhuì Biǎo

A

ānpái	安排	V/N	to arrange, to make arrangements; arrangements	L7

B

bā	八	Num	eight	L4
ba	吧	Part	suggestive; why don't [we]… (cf. "就这样吧 jiù zhèyàng ba", *let's do it that way, then*)	L5
báicài	白菜	N	Chinese cabbage, bok choy	L5
bǎi	百	Num	hundred	L4
bǎi fēnzhī	百分之	BF	percent	L8
bàn	半	Num	half ("半个 bàn ge"; "一个半 yí ge bàn")	L9
bāngmáng	帮忙/幫忙	VO	to help out, to lend a hand, to do a favor	L7
bàotíng	报亭/報亭	N	newsstand, newspaper kiosk	L8
bēi	杯/盃	N	cup	L5
bēizi	杯子/盃子	N	cup, glass	L7
běi	北	PW	north	L6
běibian (r)	北边（儿）/ 北邊（兒）	PW	north side	L6
bian	边/邊	Suf	side	L5
biéren	别人	N	others, other people	L8
bō	拨/撥	V	to poke, to stir, to dial (telephone)	L8
bú kèqi	不客气/不客氣	Exp	you're welcome, don't mention it	L6
bú xiè	不谢/不謝	Exp	don't thank me, not at all, it's nothing	L6
bù	不	Adv	no, not	L3
bù néng	不能	Phrase	cannot, must not, unable	L7

C

càidān	菜单/菜單	N	menu	L5
cānguǎn	餐馆/餐館	N	restaurant	L5
cāntīng	餐厅/餐廳	N	dining room, dining hall	L7

cǎoméi	草莓	N	strawberry	L4
céng	层/層	Meas	floor, story (storey), layer	L7
chá	茶	N	tea	L5
chà	差	V	to lack, to be short of, to differ (by)	L9
chángtú	长途/長途	Attr	long-distance	L8
chángcháng	常常	Adv	frequently, often	L9
chāoshì	超市	N	supermarket (cf. "超级市场 chāojí shìchǎng")	L6
chǎo	炒	V	to stir-fry	L5
chī	吃	V	to eat	L9
chī fàn	吃饭/吃飯	Phrase	to eat, to have a meal	L9
chuáng	床	N	bed	L7
chuángdān	床单/床單	N	bed sheet	L7
cōngyóubǐng	葱油饼/蔥油餅	N	scallion pancake	L5
cóng	从/從	Prep	from, through	L6
cù	醋	N	vinegar	L5

D

dǎ	打	V	to hit, to make (a phone call), to fight, to play (ball-games)	L8
dǎgōng	打工	VO	to work (part-time/temporarily), to do manual work	L10
dǎsǎo	打扫/打掃	V	to clean, to sweep	L7
dǎsuàn	打算	V/N	to plan, to intend; plan, intention	L7
dà	大	Adj	big	L7
dàchuángfáng	大床房	N	single room with one large bed	L7
dàmén	大门/大門	N	front door, front gate, main gate	L6
dàtīng	大厅/大廳	N	lobby	L7
dānrénjiān	单人间/單人間	N	single room, room for one person	L7
dāngrán	当然/當然	Adv	of course, without doubt	L7
de	的	Part	signals modification (of) or possession ('s)	L6
dēng	灯/燈	N	light, lamp	L6

děng	等	V	to wait	L7
diǎn	点/點	V	to order	L5
diǎn	点/點	Meas	*used for points* (*on the clock*)	L7
diǎn cài	点菜/點菜	Phrase	to order (food, dishes)	L5
(yì) diǎnr	(一)点儿/(一)點兒	Q	a little, a bit, slightly	L5
diànhuà	电话/電話	N	telephone	L8
diànhuàkǎ	电话卡/電話卡	N	phone-card	L8
diànshì	电视/電視	N	television	L9
diàntī	电梯/電梯	N	elevator (lift), escalator	L7
diànyǐng	电影/電影	N	movie, motion picture	L10
diàn	店	N	shop, store, inn ("手机店 shǒujīdiàn", *cell-phone store*)	L8
dīng	丁	N	cube-shaped pieces	L5
dìng	订/訂	V	to reserve (a room, ticket etc.)	L7
dōngxi	东西/東西	N	things	L4
dōu	都	Adv	all	L5
dòumiáo	豆苗	N	pea sprouts	L5
duì	对/對	Adj	correct, right	L7
duìmiàn	对面/對面	PW	opposite, across from	L6
duō	多	Adj	a lot, many, more than	L4
duō	多	IntPron	to what degree, how	L6
duō dà	多大	Phrase	how old (in questions)	L10
duō jiǔ	多久	Phrase	for how long	L7
duōshao	多少	IntPron	how much, how many	L4
duō yuǎn	多远/多遠	Phrase	How far?	L6

E

èr	二	Num	two	L4

F

fānyì	翻译/翻譯	V/N	to translate, to interpret; translator, interpreter	L9

fànguǎn	饭馆/飯館	N	restaurant	L9
fáng	房	BF	room, house, building	L7
fángfèi	房费/房費	N	room rate	L7
fángjiān	房间/房間	N	room (in a hotel, house, etc.)	L7
fèi	费/費	. N	fees, cost, expenses	L7
fēn	分	Meas	part, minute, cent	L9
fēn (zhōng)	分（钟/鐘）	Meas	minute (unit of time)	L10
fúwù	服务/服務	V/N	to serve; service	L7
fúwùfèi	服务费/服務費	N	service fee, service charge	L8
fúwùyuán	服务员/服務員	N	attendant, service person	L5
fù	付	V	to pay	L7
fùjìn	附近	N	vicinity, neighborhood, region close by	L6
fù	富	Adj	rich, wealthy, plenty, abundant	L9

G

gāng	刚/剛	Adv	just, exactly, just a short while ago	L6
gāo	高	Adj	high, tall	L9
gàosu	告诉/告訴	V	to tell, to inform	L10
gè	个/個	Meas	*the most common measure word, used for various things and for people*	L4
gěi	给/給	V / Prep	to give; for (the benefit of)	L7
gēn	根	Meas	*used for long, thin objects*	L4
gēn	跟	Prep	with	L9
gèng	更	Adv	more, still more, even more	L10
gōngsī	公司	N	company, corporation, firm	L9
guì	贵/貴	Adj	expensive	L8
guò	过/過	V	to pass, to pass by, to go through, to celebrate	L6
guò shēngri	过生日/過生日	Phrase	to celebrate a birthday	L10

H

hái	还/還	Adv	also, still, even more, in addition	L4

háishi	还是/還是	Adv	still, (in alternative questions) or	L6
hái yǒu	还有/還有	Phrase	still have, also have, there is/are still	L9
Hànyǔ	汉语/漢語	PropN	Chinese, the Chinese spoken language	L9
hǎo	好	Adj	good, OK, fine	L3
hǎo ma	好吗/好嗎	Exp	Okay? Would it be all right? Do you mind?	L9
hǎoxiàng	好像	Adv	seem, be like, look like, as if	L7
hào	号/號	N	number, size (of clothing, etc.), day of the month, street or house number	L7
hàomǎ	号码/號碼	N	number (as in "telephone number")	L7
hē	喝	V	to drink	L5
hé	和	Conj	and, together with	L5
hěn	很	Adv	quite, very	L7
hóng	红	Adj	red	L6
hóngchá	红茶/紅茶	N	black tea (*literally "red-tea"*)	L5
hónglǜdēng	红绿灯/紅綠燈	N	traffic light (red-green-light)	L6
hòutiān	后天/後天	N	the day after tomorrow, two days from now	L10
hú	壶/壺	N	pot, kettle	L5
hùzhào	护照/護照	N	passport	L7
huài	坏	Adj	bad, broken	L7
huài le	坏了/壞了	Phrase	broken down, gone wrong, spoiled, bad	L7
huàn	换/換	V	to change, to exchange, to convert (currency)	L7
huí	回	V	to return	L9
huílai	回来/回來	V	to return, to come back	L9
huì	会/會	Aux	likely	L9

J

jī	鸡/雞	N	chicken	L5
jīdàn	鸡蛋/雞蛋	N	(chicken) egg	L5
jīdīng	鸡丁/雞丁	N	diced chicken	L5
jǐ	几/幾	IntPron	how many, a few, several, some	L9

jǐ diǎn	几点/幾點	Phrase	what time	L9
jǐ hào	几号/幾號	Phrase	what day of the month, what number	L10
jìsuàn	计算/計算	V	to count, to calculate	L4
jiā	加	V	to add, to plus (in arithmetic)	L8
jiāshang	加上	V	to add to, to increase	L8
jiājiào	家教	N	private tutor (short for "家庭教师 jiātíng jiàoshī")	L9
jiān	间/間	Meas	*used for rooms*	L7
jiàn	见/見	V	to see, to meet, to call on	L9
jiāo	交	V	to hand over, to deliver, to give	L10
jiāo	教	V	to teach	L3
jiǎo	角	Meas	*unit of Chinese currency, used formally for 10 cents*	L5
jiǎozi	饺子/餃子	N	stuffed dumplings	L5
jiào	叫	V	to call, to be called	L3
jiàoxǐng	叫醒	V	to awaken (by calling)	L7
jiàoxǐng fúwù	叫醒服务/叫醒服務	Phrase	wake-up call	L7
jiàoxuélóu	教学楼/教學樓	N	classroom-building	L6
jiē shang	街上	Phrase	in the street, on the street	L8
jié	节/節	Meas	*for segments of time, e.g. classes*	L10
jièlán	芥蓝/芥蘭	N	Chinese broccoli	L5
jīn	斤	Meas	*0.5 kilo* (*unit of weight* = 10 两 liǎng)	L4
jīnnián	今年	N	this year	L10
jīntiān	今天	N	today, the present, now	L9
jǐnliàng	尽量/盡量	Adv	as much as possible, do one's best to	L7
jìn	进/進	V	to enter, to go or come in	L5
jìnlai	进来/進來	V	to enter, to come in	L7
jīngguò	经过/經過	V / Prep	to undergo, to experience; via, by way of (a place)	L6
jiǔ	九	Num	nine	L4
jiǔdiàn	酒店	N	large hotel (esp. in China)	L7

jiù	就	Adv	then, in that case, right away	L8
júzi	橘子	N	orange, tangerine	L4

K

kāfēi	咖啡	N	coffee	L5
kǎ	卡	N	card	L8
kànkan	看看	Phrase	to take a look, to watch something leisurely	L9
kělè	可乐/可樂	N	cola	L4
kěshì	可是	Conj	but, however, yet	L9
kěyǐ	可以	Aux	may, can, to be fine, OK	L5
kè	刻	Meas	quarter of an hour ("三刻 sān kè", *45 minutes after, quarter to*)	L9
kèren	客人	N	guest, visitor, customer	L8
kè	课/課	N	lesson, class	L9
kōngtiáo	空调/空調	N	air conditioning, air conditioner	L7
kuài	块/塊	Meas	*unit of Chinese currency, used colloquially for yuan*	L4

L

là	辣	Adj	spicy, hot	L5
làzi	辣子	N	hot pepper, chili	L5
làzi-jīdīng	辣子鸡丁	Phrase	chili chicken	L5
lái	来/來	V	to bring, to take, to have (to cause to) to come, to arrive	L5
lǎo	老	Adj	old, aged	L10
lǎoshī	老师/老師	N	teacher	L3
le	了	Part	*post-verbal, indicating successful action, sentence final, indicating new state, new phase, up to now, etc.*	L5
lèi	累	Adj	tired	L9
lěngyǐn	冷饮/冷飲	N	cold drinks, soft drinks	L5
lí	梨	N	pear	L4
li	里/裡	PW	in, inside, the inside	L6
liǎng	两/兩	Num	two	L4

liǎng	两/兩	Meas	*a unit of weight (0.05 kilo or 1.33 ounces)*	L4
línjiē	临街/臨街	V	to face the street	L7
líng	零	Num	zero	L4
liúxuéshēng	留学生/留學生	N	student studying abroad, overseas student	L6
liù	六	Num	six	L4
lóu	楼/樓	N	building, floor ("一楼 yī lóu", *first floor*; "二楼 èr lóu", *second floor*)	L7
lù	路	N	road, path, (bus) route, line	L6
lǜ	绿/綠	Adj	green	L6
lǜchá	绿茶/綠茶	N	green tea	L5

M

mǎlù	马路/馬路	N	road, street	L6
ma	吗/嗎	Part	*turns a declarative sentence into a question*	L3
mǎi	买/買	V	to buy	L4
mǎidān	买单/買單	VO	to pay the bill (in a restaurant, etc.)	L5
mǎi dōngxi	买东西/買東西	Phrase	to go shopping	L4
Màidāngláo	麦当劳/麥當勞	PropN	McDonald's	L6
mài	卖/賣	V	to sell	L8
mántou	馒头/饅頭	N	steamed bun	L5
máo	毛	Meas	*unit of Chinese currency, used colloquially for 10 cents*	L4
máojīn	毛巾	N	towel	L7
méi wèntí	没问题/沒問題	Exp	no problem, sure, certainly	L7
méiyǒu	没有	V/Adv	to not have, there is/are not; did not, has not (= 没 méi)	L5
měi	每	Pron	every, each (cf. "每人 měi rén", *each/every person*)	L5
měi tiān	每天	Phrase	every day, daily	L7
Měiguó	美国/美國	PropN	U.S.A.	L3
Měiguórén	美国人/美國人	PropN	American (person)	L3
mǐfàn	米饭/米飯	N	cooked rice	L5

miǎnfèi	免费/免費	VO	to not have to pay anything, to be free of charge	L8
miàntiáo	面条/麵條	N	noodles	L5
miànzhí	面值	N	face value, denomination	L8
míngzi	名字	N	given name, personal name, name	L7
míngtiān	明天	N	tomorrow	L7

N

nǎr	哪儿/哪兒	IntPron	where	L6
nǎ tiān	哪天	Phrase	which day, what day	L10
nǎ zhǒng	哪种/哪種	Phrase	what kind, which type	L8
nà	那	Pron	that	L5
nàbian	那边/那邊	Pron	that side, over there	L5
nàge	那个/那個	Prop	that one	L5
nánpéngyou	男朋友	N	boyfriend, male friend	L9
nán	南	PW	south	L6
ne	呢	Part	*forms follow-up questions*	L3
néng	能	Aux	can, may, be able to	L5
nǐ	你	Pron	you	L3
nǐ hǎo	你好	Phrase	How do you do?	L3
nǐmen	你们/你們	Pron	you (plural)	L5
nián	年	N	year	L10
nín	您	N	you (polite form)	L5
nín de	您的	Phrase	(formal-polite) your, yours	L7
niúròu	牛肉	N	beef	L5

P

pángbiān (r)	旁边（儿）/旁邊（兒）	PW	next to, beside	L6
péngyou	朋友	N	friend	L7
píjiǔ	啤酒	N	beer	L5
piányi	便宜	Adj	cheap, inexpensive	L8

piàn	片	Meas	piece, slice, flakes	L4
píngguǒ	苹果/蘋果	N	apple	L4
píng	瓶	N	bottle	L4
pútao	葡萄	N	grape	L4

Q

qī	七	Num	seven	L4
qǐ	起	V	to rise, to stand up	L9
qǐchuáng	起床	VO	to get out of bed, to rise (in the morning)	L9
qiān	签/簽	V	to sign (name), to affix (one's mark)	L7
qián	前	PW	front, foward, ahead ("往前 wǎng qián", *forword*), before	L6
qiántái	前台/前臺	N	the front desk, counter (in a hotel, etc.)	L8
qiántiān	前天/前天	N	the day before yesterday	L10
qián	钱/錢	N	money, cash	L4
qīngchǎo	清炒	V	to sautéed or fry, without additional ingredients	L5
qīngjiégōng	清洁工/清潔工	N	sanitation worker, street cleaner, garbage collector	L7
qǐng	请/請	V	to invite, to treat (sb. to dinner, etc.), please	L5
qǐngwèn	请问/請問	V	Excuse me, may I ask....	L6
qìngzhù	庆祝/慶祝	V	to celebrate	L10
qù	去	V	to go	L3

R

ránhòu	然后/然後	Conj	then, after that	L9
rè	热/熱	Adj / N	hot, popular; a craze, fad, "fever"	L7
rén	人	N	person, people, humans	L3
rì	日	N	sun, day, daytime	L10
rúguǒ	如果	Conj	if, in case	L8

S

sān	三	Num	three	L4
shāngdiàn	商店	N	shop, store	L4

shàngbān	上班	VO	to go to work, to start work, to go on duty	L9
shàngkè	上课/上課	VO	to go to class, to attend class, to teach a class, to give a lesson	L9
shàngwǔ	上午	N	late morning	L9
shāo	稍	Adv	slightly, a little	L7
shǎo	少	Adj	little, a few	L4
shéi/shuí	谁/誰	IntPron	who (m)	L7
shéi/shuí de	谁的/誰的	Phrase	whose	L7
shénme	什么/甚麼	IntPron	what (in questions)	L3
shénme shíhou	什么时候/甚麼時候	Phrase	what time, when	L7
shēng	生	V	to be born	L10
shēngri	生日	N	birthday	L10
shí	十	Num	ten	L4
shíhou	时候/時候	N	time	L7
shíjiān	时间/時間	N	time	L9
shìhuà	市话/市話	N	local call, in-city phone call	L8
shì	是	V	am, are, is, were, was; yes; certainly	L3
shì bu shì	是不是	Phrase	is the case that, right, isn't it	L9
shōu	收	V	to receive, to accept	L7
shōujù	收据/收據	N	receipt	L7
shǒujī	手机/手機	N	cellular phone	L8
shūdiàn	书店/書店	N	bookstore	L6
shuài	帅/帥	Adj	handsome	L9
shuǐ	水	N	water	L4
shuìjiào	睡觉/睡覺	VO	to go to bed, to sleep	L9
sì	四	Num	four	L4
sùcài	素菜	N	vegetarian food	L5
sùshè	宿舍	N	dormitory (for students, workers, etc.)	L9
suànróng	蒜蓉	N	mashed or chopped garlic	L5
suì	岁/歲	Meas	years (old), years of age	L10

T

tā	他	Pron	he, him, other, another	L7
tā de	他的	Phrase	his (cf. "她的 tā de", *hers*)	L7
tài	太	Adv	too, extremely	L5
tāng	汤/湯	N	soup	L5
táng	糖	N	sugar, candy, sweets	L5
tángcùyú	糖醋鱼/糖醋魚	N	sweet and sour fish	L5
táo	桃	N	peach	L4
tiáo	条/條	Meas	*used for long, thin objects, such as roads, rivers, trousers, fish, etc.*	L7
tiěbǎn	铁板/鐵板	N	iron plate	L5
tóngxué	同学/同學	N	fellow student, classmate	L6
túpiàn	图片/圖片	N	picture, illustration	L5
túshūguǎn	图书馆/圖書館	N	library	L6

W

wài (bian)	外（边/邊）	PW	outside	L8
wàijiào	外教	N	foreign teacher	L6
wàimiàn	外面	PW	outside	L8
wǎn	晚	Adj/N	late; night, evening	L9
wǎnfàn	晚饭/晚飯	N	supper, dinner	L9
wǎnshang	晚上	N	evening, night	L9
wǎn	碗	N	bowl	L5
wǎng	往	Prep	towards, in the direction of	L6
wǎng wài	往外	Phrase	toward the outside	L8
wèi	喂	Intj	hey, say (hailing someone), hello	L8
wèn	问/問	V	to ask (a question)	L6
wèn lù	问路/問路	Phrase	to ask the way, to ask (for) directions	L6
wǒ	我	Pron	I, me	L3
wǒ de	我的	Phrase	my, mine	L7
wǒmen	我们/我們	Pron	we, us	L3

wū li	屋里/屋裡	Phrase	inside a house or room	L7
wǔ	五	Num	five	L4

X

xīcāntīng	西餐厅/西餐廳	N	a restaurant serving Western-style food	L7
xīguā	西瓜	N	watermelon	L4
xǐ	洗	V	to wash	L10
xǐshǒujiān	洗手间/洗手間	N	bathroom, washroom, restroom (cf. “卫生间 wèishēngjiān”)	L6
xǐzǎo	洗澡	VO	to take a bath, to bathe	L9
xǐzǎojiān	洗澡间/洗澡間	N	bathroom	L7
xǐhuan	喜欢/喜歡	V	to like, to be fond of	L10
xì	系	N	department at a university or college	L6
xiàbān	下班	VO	to finish the day’s work, to go off duty	L9
xiàkè	下课/下課	VO	to get out of class, to dismiss class	L9
xiàwǔ	下午	N	afternoon	L9
xiān	先	Adv	first, earlier	L8
xiānsheng	先生	N	sir, preceded by a surname, Mr.	L7
xiànzài	现在/現在	N	now, at present, today	L5
xiāngjiāo	香蕉	N	banana	L4
xiǎofàn	小贩/小販	N	street vender, peddler	L8
xiǎo shāngdiàn	小商店	Phrase	small shop	L8
xiàoyuán	校园/校園	N	campus, school yard, school compound	L6
xièxie	谢谢/謝謝	V	thank you, thanks	L5
xìnyòngkǎ	信用卡	N	credit card	L7
xīngqī’èr	星期二	N	Tuesday	L10
xīngqīliù	星期六	N	Saturday	L10
xīngqīrì	星期日	N	Sunday	L10
xīngqīsān	星期三	N	Wednesday	L10
xīngqīsì	星期四	N	Thursday	L10
xīngqītiān	星期天	N	Sunday	L10

xīngqīwǔ	星期五	N	Friday	L10
xīngqīyī	星期一	N	Monday	L10
xìng	姓	V/N	to be surnamed; surname	L3
xiū	修	V	to fix, to repair	L7
xūyào	需要	V/N	to need, to be needed, have to; needs	L7
xué	学/學	V	to study	L3
xuésheng	学生/學生	N	student	L3
xuéxiào	学校/學校	N	school	L3

Y

yājīn	押金	N	money deposit, earnest money	L7
yàodiàn	药店/藥店	N	drugstore, pharmacy, Chinese medicine shop	L6
yào	要	V	to want, to need (*the negative is* "不要 bú yào"*, not want to*)	L4
yào	要	Aux	would like to	L5
yàoshi	钥匙/鑰匙	N	a key (to a lock)	L7
yě	也	Adv	also, too	L3
yī	一	Num	one	L4
yīfu	衣服	N	clothes, clothing	L10
yídìng	一定	Adv	definite, must	L10
yígòng	一共	Adv	altogether	L4
yíhuìr	一会儿/一會兒	Q	a while, soon, in a while, shortly	L7
yǐjīng	已经/已經	Adv	already	L10
yǐhòu	以后/以後	PW	behind, after (cf. "后 hòu")	L9
yìqǐ	一起	Adv	together	L3
yìzhí	一直	Adv	straight, continuously	L6
yínháng	银行/銀行	N	bank (financial institution)	L6
yǐn	饮/飲	BF	drink	L5
yīnggāi	应该/應該	Aux	should, ought to, must	L10
Yīngguó	英国/英國	PropN	England, Britain, U.K.	L3

Yīngguórén	英国人/英國人	PropN	English, British	L3
Yīngwén	英文	PropN	English (language)	L3
yòng	用	V	to use	L7
yóujú	邮局/郵局	N	post office	L8
yóumàicài	油麦菜/油麥菜	N	Chinese lettuce, Chinese greens	L5
yǒu	有	V	to have, there is/are	L5
yǒude	有的	Pron	some	L8
yǒu yìsi	有意思	Phrase	to be interesting	L10
yòu	右	PW	right ("右边 yòubian", *the right side*)	L6
yú	鱼/魚	N	fish	L5
yùdìng	预订/預訂	V	to book (hotel room, ticket, etc.)	L7
yuán	元	Meas	Renminbi (cf. "美元 měiyuán", *U.S. dollar*)	L5
yuǎn	远/遠	Adj	far, distant, remote ("不远 bù yuǎn", *not far from, close to*)	L6
yuè	月	N	month, moon	L10

Z

zài	再	Adv	and then	L8
zàijiàn	再见/再見	V	good-bye, see you again	L5
zài	在	V / Prep	to be at, to exist, to be alive; at, in, on	L6
zǎo	早	Adj / Adv /Exp	early; as early as; good morning	L9
zǎodiǎn	早点/早點	N	light breakfast	L9
zǎo qǐ	早起	Phrase	to get up early, to rise early	L9
zǎoshang	早上	N	morning	L7
zěnme	怎么/怎麼	IntPron	how, in what way	L6
zěnme bàn	怎么办/怎麼辦	Exp	What is to be done?	L10
zhǎo	找	V	to look for, to seek	L9
zhè	这/這	Pron	this	L5
zhèbian	这边/這邊	Pron	this side, over here	L5
zhège	这个/這个	Pron	this one	L5

zhèr	这儿/這兒	N	here, this place	L7
zhèyàng ba	这样吧	Exp	(Let's) do it this way, how about this	L10
zhēn de ma	真的吗	Exp	(Is that) true? Really?	L10
zhènghǎo	正好	Adv	it so happens, as it happens, just in time	L10
zhíbō	直拨/直撥	V	to dial directly	L8
zhǐ	只	Adv	only, merely, just	L8
zhōngcāntīng	中餐厅/中餐廳	N	Chinese restaurant, a restaurant serving Chinese food	L7
Zhōngguó Diànxìn	中国电信/中國電信	PropN	China Telecom	L8
zhōngjiān	中间/中間	PW	in between, in the middle	L6
Zhōngwén	中文	PropN	Chinese (language)	L3
zhōngwǔ	中午	N	noon, mid-day	L9
zhōu	周/週	N	circle, week	L10
zhōumò	周末/週末	N	weekend	L10
zhōusì	周四/週四	N	Thursday	L10
zhōuwǔ	周五/週五	N	Friday	L10
zhǔshí	主食	N	principle food, staple	L5
zhǔ	煮	V	to boil, to cook	L9
zhù	住	V	to live, to lodge, to stay at	L7
zhuǎn	转/轉	V	to turn, to shift, to change, to pass on, to transfer	L6
zìjǐ	自己	Pron	oneself, by oneself, on one's own	L10
zǒu	走	V	to walk ("一直走 yìzhí zǒu", *to go straight on*), to leave	L6
zuì	最	Adv	most, -est (as in "fastest"), very	L8
zuǒ	左	PW	left ("左边 zuǒbian", *the left side*)	L6
zuòyè	作业/作業	N	school assignment, homework	L10
zuò	坐	V	to sit (cf. "请坐 qǐng zuò", *please sit down*)	L5
zuò	做	V	to work, to do, to be	L9

Listening Scripts 录音文本 Lùyīn Wénběn

第一课 拼音和标准发音

Listening Comprehension

1. (1) 中国 (2) 新加坡 (3) 韩国 (4) 瑞士 (5) 西班牙 (6) 新西兰 (7) 南非 (8) 香港 (9) 瑞典 (10) 日本 (11) 加拿大 (12) 苏格兰 (13) 沙特阿拉伯

2. (1) 西安 (2) 武汉 (3) 南京 (4) 桂林 (5) 成都 (6) 长春 (7) 乌鲁木齐 (8) 沈阳 (9) 石家庄 (10) 郑州 (11) 合肥 (12) 南昌 (13) 长沙 (14) 杭州 (15) 太原 (16) 福州 (17) 广州 (18) 昆明 (19) 贵阳 (20) 南宁 (21) 兰州 (22) 西宁 (23) 拉萨 (24) 银川 (25) 深圳 (26) 苏州 (27) 上海

3. (1) che (2) se (3) ci (4) zhi (5) zu (6) re (7) ce (8) chi (9) rui (10) shi (11) jia (12) xu (13) shui (14) ji (15) quan (16) ju (17) zi (18) xia (19) jiong (20) qie (21) sha

4. (1) dōu (2) niè (3) zǒu (4) zhào (5) lǚ (6) cì (7) zé (8) yuè (9) měi (10) rán (11) kōng (12) lín (13) gǎo (14) dōu (15) chōu (16) zuó (17) xù (18) méng (19) juān (20) wàn (21) rè

5. (1) lǎoshi (2) fēijī (3) zhǐdǎo (4) shuìjiào (5) bèijǐng (6) fēichū (7) rěhuò (8) shíjiān (9) sǎnkè (10) Dàqiū (11) zìjǐ (12) rìjì (13) qǔ xí (14) cǐzhì (15) mōsuǒ (16) yìngxiàng (17) qiángshǒu (18) cháoshèng (19) lièshì (20) zìsī (21) yǎnjìng

Review Exercises

III. (1) 湖南 (2) 长江 (3) 贵州 (4) 辽宁 (5) 湖北 (6) 广西 (7) 内蒙古 (8) 福建 (9) 江苏 (10) 西藏 (11) 越南 (12) 中国 (13) 香港 (14) 美国 (15) 加拿大 (16) 台湾 (17) 新加坡 (18) 瑞士 (19) 印度 (20) 法国

第二课 汉 字

Listening Comprehension

1. (1) 妈妈 (2) 叔叔 (3) 哥哥 (4) 金子 (5) 先生 (6) 爷爷 (7) 伯伯 (8) 孩子 (9) 银子 (10) 什么 (11) 弟弟 (12) 看了 (13) 爸爸 (14) 谢谢 (15) 我的 (16) 奶奶 (17) 你的 (18) 姐姐

第三课 你 好

Listening Comprehension

1. (1) 美国 (2) 英国 (3) 澳大利亚 (4) 法国 (5) 德国 (6) 泰国 (7) 菲律宾 (8) 希腊 (9) 巴基斯坦 (10) 肯尼亚 (11) 也门 (12) 埃及 (13) 意大利 (14) 以色列 (15) 巴西

2. 女：老师，你好。我是谢民。
   男：谢民，你好吗？
   女：我很好，你呢？
   男：我也很好。你学什么？
   女：我学中文。你也学中文吗？
   男：不，我教英文。你去学校吗？
   女：是，我去学校。你也去吗？
   男：是，我们一起去，好吗？
   女：好。

3. 钱民、谢中都不是中国人，钱民是美国学生，学中文。谢中呢？是英国老师。谢中不教钱民英文，谢中教中国人学英文。谢中去学校，钱民也一起去。

第四课 计 算

Listening Comprehension

1. (1) 十一 (2) 十七 (3) 七十一 (4) 三十六 (5) 五十九 (6) 九十九 (7) 四十四 (8) 一百零一 (9) 八百一十二 (10) 一百零三

2. 男：你去商店吗？
   女：是，我去商店。
   男：我也要买东西，我们一起去，好吗？
   女：好。你买什么？
   男：我要买三瓶水、五瓶可乐。你呢？

女：我要买两斤苹果、一个西瓜，还要买半斤草莓。
男：一斤草莓是多少钱？
女：五块。

3. 钱民去商店买六瓶水，还要买两斤桃、半个西瓜。水是一块二一瓶，桃三块八一斤，西瓜一块五一斤，半个西瓜是三斤半。一共多少钱？

第五课 在餐馆

Listening Comprehension

1. 男：你要什么？
女：我要这个菜。这个菜多少钱？
男：这个菜七块五。
女：那个菜多少钱？
男：那个菜八块钱。
女：我要一个这个菜，一个那个菜。
男：还要什么？
女：还要一碗米饭。一共多少钱？
男：两个菜都是九块，一共十八块五。
女：这是二十块钱。
男：找你一块五。
女：谢谢。
男：不谢。再见。

2. 女：请进，请这边坐。您吃点儿什么？
男：有铁板牛肉吗？
女：没有。有炒牛肉。
男：有辣子鸡丁吗？
女：有，二十五一个。
男：我要一个。
女：还要什么？
男：还要一碗鸡蛋汤。
女：要主食吗？
男：要饺子。
女：您喝什么？
男：我要一壶茶。

第六课 问 路

Listening Comprehension

1. 男：请问，图书馆在哪儿？
   女：是中文系图书馆吗？
   男：不是。我要去学校图书馆。
   女：你从这儿一直走，过了银行，往左转，有一个教学楼。大图书馆在教学楼对面。
   男：远不远？
   女：不太远。
   男：好。谢谢!
   女：不谢!

2. 女1：我要上厕所，你知道附近哪儿有洗手间吗？
   女2：附近有一个麦当劳，那里面有洗手间。
   女1：要走很远吗？
   女2：不太远。从这儿一直走，过两个红绿灯，往右转，在超市和药店旁边就是麦当劳。我也要去。
   女1：那我们一起走吧。
   女2：好。走吧。

第七课 在宾馆

Listening Comprehension

1. 男：你好。我在这个酒店预订了一个房间，是用钱英的名字订的。
   女：对不起，我们没有用钱英的名字预订的房间。
   男：他可能是用我的名字“李工”预订的。有没有用李工的名字订的房间？
   女：有。是一个单人间，大床房。您住三天，对吗？
   男：对。这是我的护照。
   女：您还需要付三天的押金。一共260美元。
   男：我可以用信用卡吗？
   女：可以。这是您的房间钥匙。您的房间号码是320。房间在3层。
   男：谢谢。

2. 女：现在可以打扫您的房间吗？
   男：可以。请你换床单，多给我一个杯子和一条毛巾。
   女：没问题。您还需要什么？
   男：我洗澡间的空调坏了，你能不能叫人来修？

女：当然可以。

男：你打扫房间的时候我去吃饭。请问，西餐厅在哪儿？

女：在一楼。

男：谢谢你。

女：不客气。

第八课 打电话

Listening Comprehension

1. 男：喂，是前台吗？

女：是。

男：请问，给美国打电话多少钱一分钟？

女：三块五。

男：给日本打电话多少钱一分钟？

女：两块钱。

男：用电话卡是不是便宜一点儿？

女：是，用电话卡便宜。

男：好。谢谢。

女：不谢。

2. 男：喂，服务员，请问我怎么往外打电话？

女：先拨0，再拨您要打的电话号码。

男：请问，怎么从美国给我的房间打电话？

女：从美国打您的房间是011-86-10-82105173。

男：别人打我的房间收不收服务费？

女：不收。

男：打市话呢？

女：市话是免费的。

男：谢谢。

3. (1) 哥哥　(3) 弟弟　(5) 德国　(7) 德州　(9) 厕所

(2) 妹妹　(4) 姐姐　(6) 日本　(8) 小费　(10) 市话

第九课 现在几点

Listening Comprehension

1. 男：喂，服务员，请问你什么时候来打扫我的房间？

女：您住哪个房间？

男：我住306。

女：早上11点以后去打扫您的房间。

男：能不能早一点儿打扫？我朋友一会儿来看我。

女：好。那我们现在就去打扫。

男：请换两个茶杯。

女：没问题。

男：谢谢。

女：不客气。

2. 女1：今天晚上你打算做什么？

女2：我跟男朋友一起去饭馆吃饭。你呢？

女1：我累了，在宿舍看看电视，然后洗澡睡觉。

女2：你怎么晚上洗澡？

女1：我明天早上八点要去学校上课，早上没有时间洗澡。

女2：我明天上午没有课，请不要叫醒我。

女1：没问题。

第十课 过生日

Listening Comprehension

1. 男：今天不是星期五吗？

女：不是。今天不是星期五，今天是星期四。

男：糟糕！今天我有中文课。我的作业还没做呢。

女：你昨天为什么没做呢？

男：昨天下课以后我去家教了。回来以后又看了一会儿电视，就没做。

女：今天你什么时候有中文课？

男：今天下午两点我有中文课。现在几点了？

女：现在九点半。还有时间，你快做吧。

2. 男：这个周末你打算做什么？

女：我要洗衣服，去超市买东西。你呢？

男：这个星期我上了八节课，星期三还去做了翻译，我想休息。

女：你打算怎么休息？

男：我想去看电影。你想跟我一起去吗？

女：我觉得看电影没有意思。我们一起去外面走走，好吗？

男：好吧。只要不做作业，我就高兴。

Bb Dd Ff

Gg Hh Jj

Kk Ll Mm

Nn Pp Qq

[similar to foeh in four]

[similar to deh in duck]

[similar to boh in boy]

[similar to jee in jeans]

[similar to huh in honey]

[similar to gu in glue]

[similar to moeh in morning]

[similar to luh in love]

[similar to ku in kangaroo]

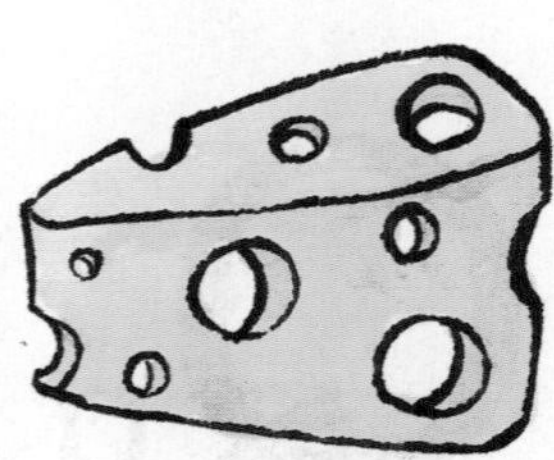

[similar to chee in cheese]

[similar to poeh in Polar (bear)]

[similar to nuh in nurse]

Rr	Tt	Xx
Cc	Chch	Ss
Shsh	Zz	Zhzh
A	-a	E

[similar to shee as in sheep]

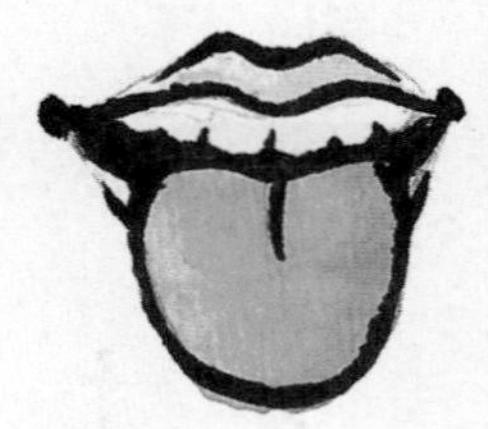

[similar to tuh in tongue]

[cross between “j” and “r” in gerbil]

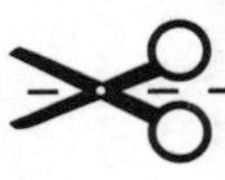

[similar to s in snake]

[similar to ch in church]

[similar to ts in cats]

[similar to dj in jar]

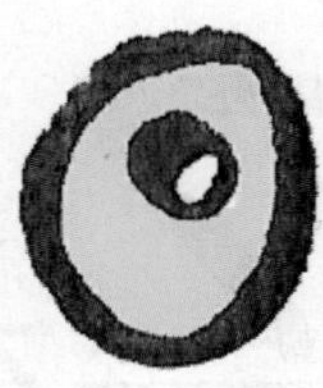

[similar to dz in zero]

[similar to sh in shirt]

[similar to uh as in usher]

[similar to ah in father]

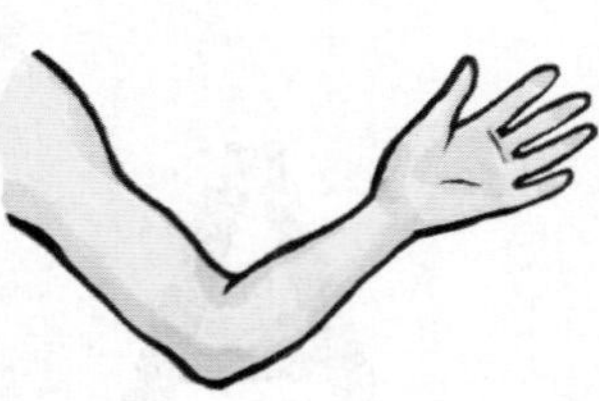

[similar to ah as in Arm]

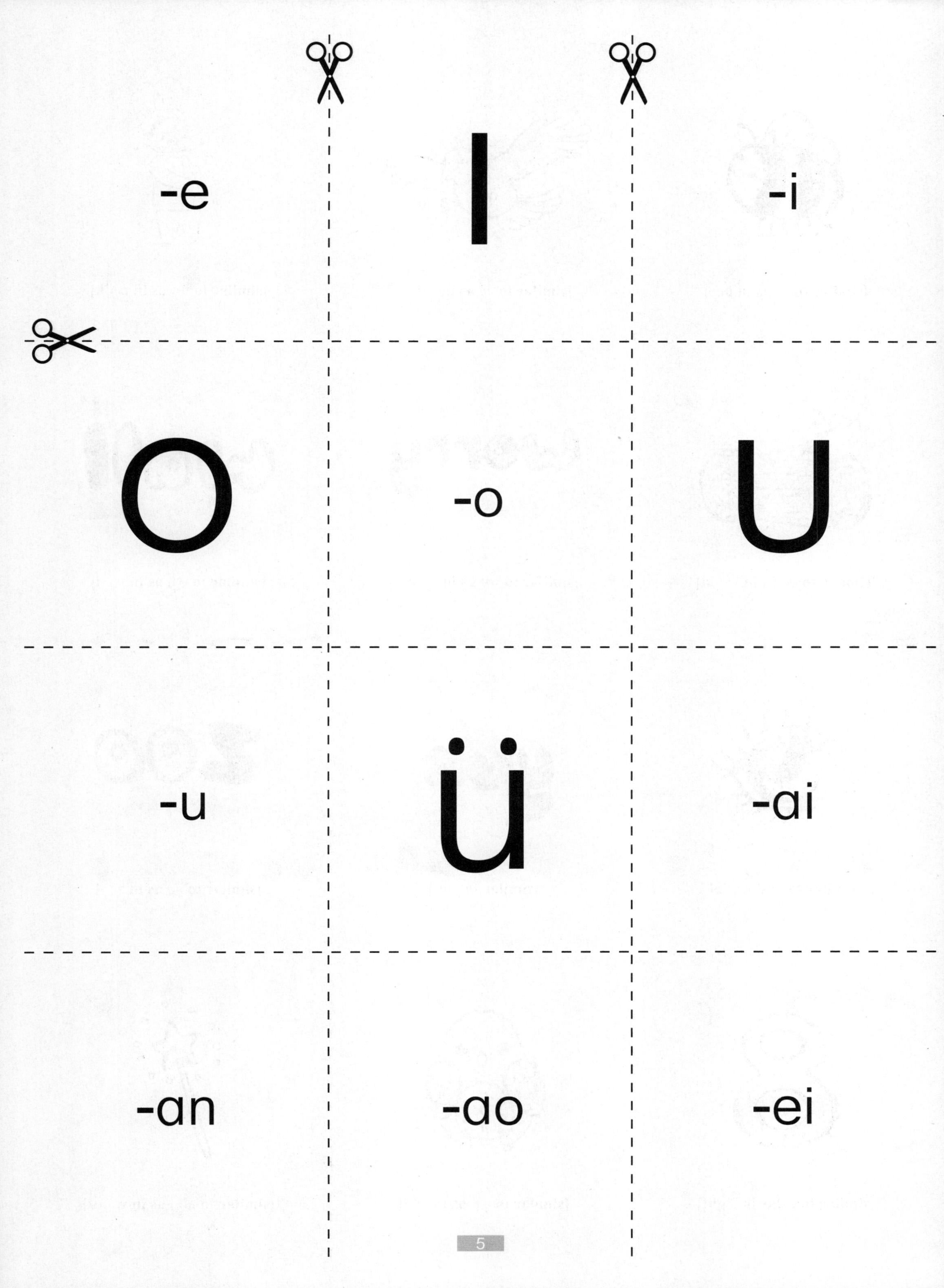
-e
I
-i
O
-o
U
-u
ü
-ai
-an
-ao
-ei

[similar to ee as in bee]

[similar to ee as in eagle]

[similar to uh as in cook]

[similar to oo as in wood]

[similar to wo as in worry]

[similar to wo as in wall]

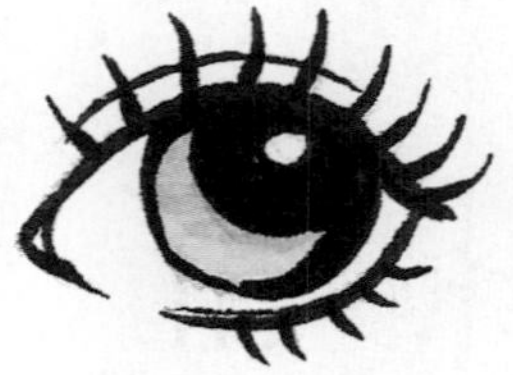

[similar to i as in eye]

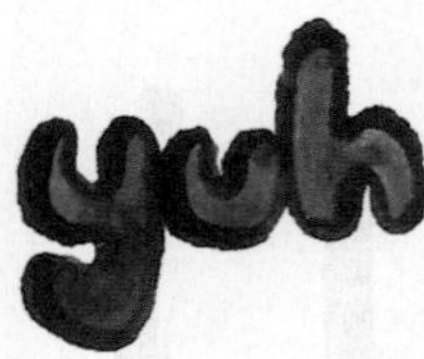

[similar to yuh]

[similar to oo as in zoo]

[similar to ay as in eight]

[similar to ow as in owl]

[similar to ahn as in wand]

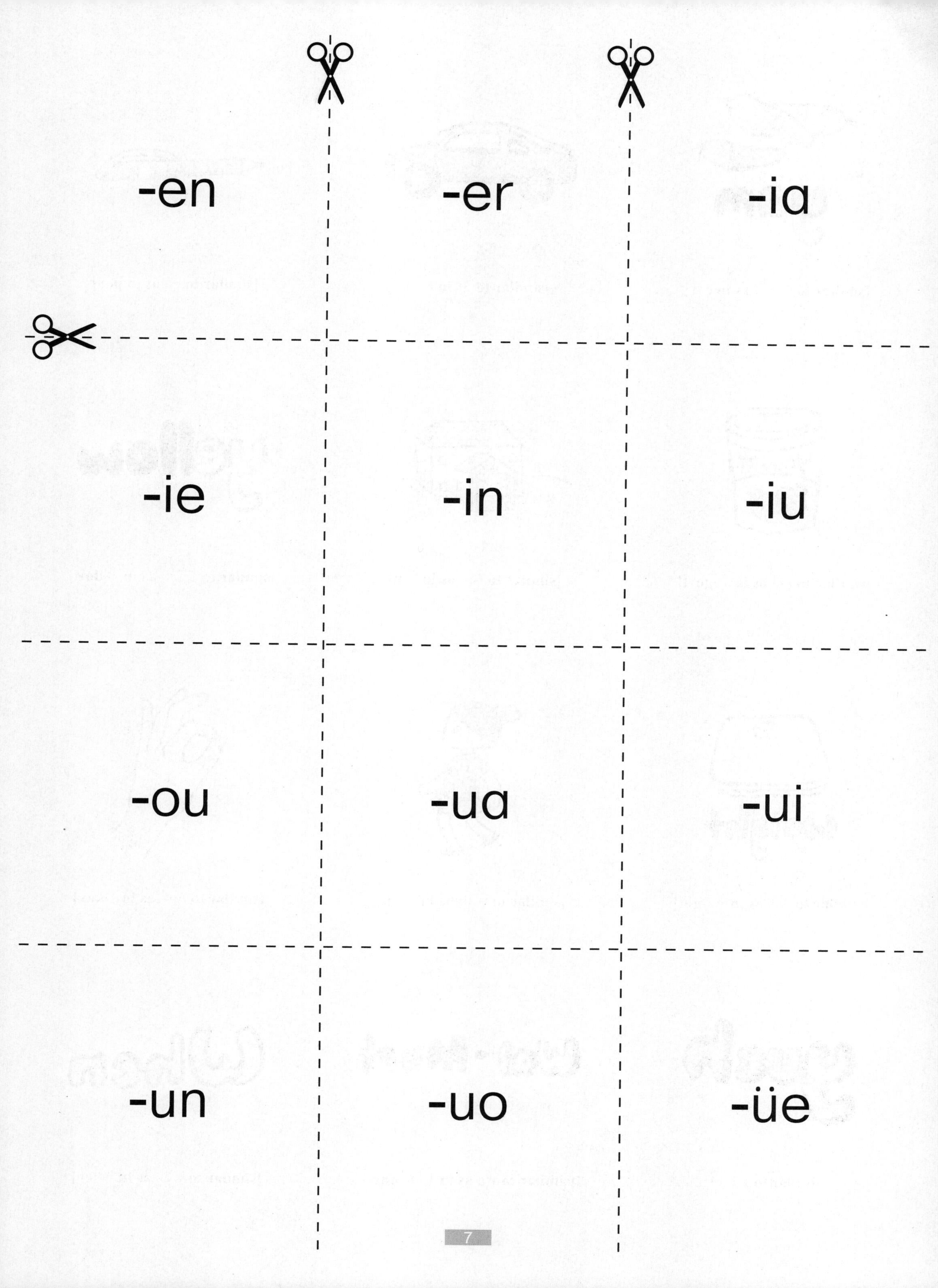

-en	-er	-ia
-ie	-in	-iu
-ou	-ua	-ui
-un	-uo	-üe

[similar to ee-ah as in car]

[similar to ar in car]

[similar to en as in pen]

[similar to e-o as in yogurt]

[similar to een as in Inn]

[similar to ee-eh as in yellow]

[similar to wei as in weight]

[similar to wah as in walk]

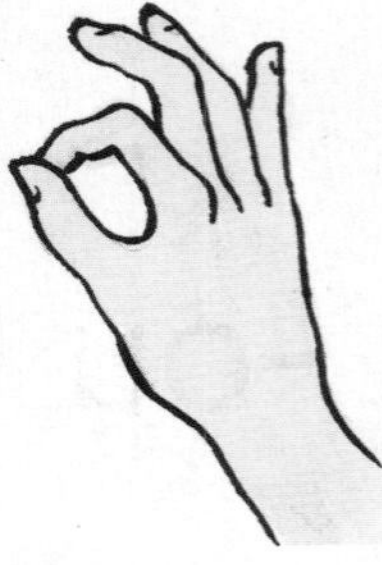

[similar to owe as in Okay]

[similar to yueh]

Wal-Mart

[similar to wo as in wal-Mart]

[similar to wen as in when]

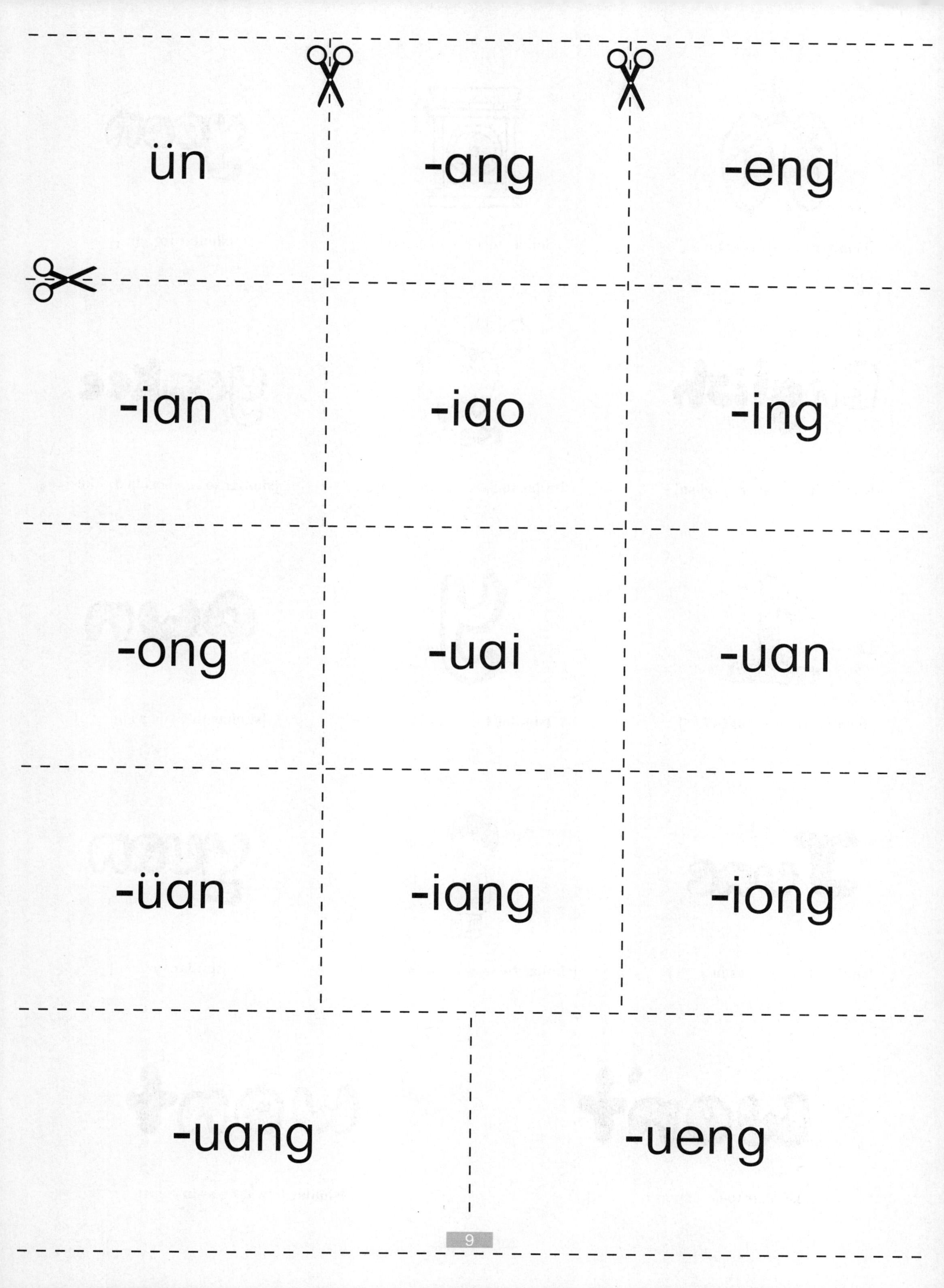
ün
-ang
-eng
-ian
-iao
-ing
-ong
-uai
-uan
-üan
-iang
-iong
-uang
-ueng

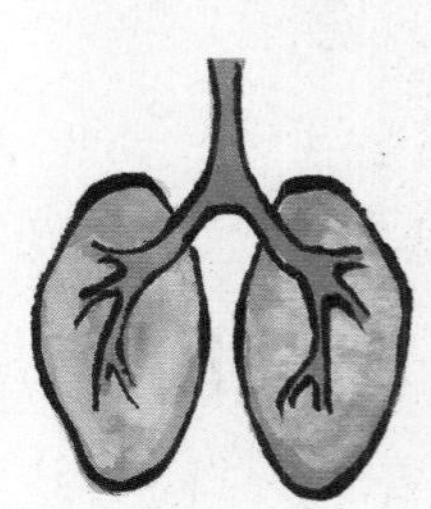

[similar to ung as in lung]

[similar to ahng in gong]

[similar to yoon]

English

[similar to ing as in English]

[similar to ee-ow as in meow]

yankee

[similar to ee-en as in Yankee]

1

[similar to wahn as in one]

y

[similar to wai as in Y]

own

[similar to owng as in own]

June

[similar to ee-ong as in June]

[similar to ee-ahng as in yown]

yuan

[similar to yuan]

[similar to oo-ung as in won't]

[similar to wahng as in want]